10/97

ROC

A FIRESIDE BOOK
Published by Simon & Schuster
New York
London
Toronto
Sydney
Tokyo
Singapore

CULT ROCKERS

WAYNE JANCIK
AND
TAD LATHROP

FIRESIDE
Rockefeller Center
1230 Avenue of the Americas
New York, NY 10020

Designed by Hyun Joo Kim

Manufactured in the United States of America

10   9   8   7   6   5   4   3   2   1

Library of Congress Cataloging-in-Publication Data
Jancik, Wayne.
Cult rockers/Wayne Jancik and Tad Lathrop.
p. cm.   "A Fireside book."
Includes discographies.
1. Rock music—Bio-bibliography—Dictionaries.
I. Lathrop, Tad.   II. Title.
ML102.R6J36 1995   781.66'09'2—dc20   [B]   95–37397   CIP   MN

ISBN 0-684-81112-X

Photo credits begin on page 343.

920
JAN
1995

CONTENTS

Contents

ACKNOWLEDGMENTS

Many people gave generously of their time and energy to make this book possible.

For their help with information gathering and interviews, thanks to Dave Alvin (the Blasters), Tom Atencio, Pam Blevins, Blowfly, Scott Booker (Hell Fire Management), Albert Bouchard (Blue Öyster Cult), Dave Brock (Hawkwind), Toni A. Brown (*Relix* magazine), Sean Byrne (Count Five), Jerry Casale (Devo), Billy Chainsaw (Mission Impossible Management), Lou Christie, Aaron Comess (Spin Doctors), Wayne Coyne (the Flaming Lips), Dick Dale, August Darnell (Kid Creole), Bo Diddley, Dr. John, Dennis Drew (10,000 Maniacs), Joe Ely, Laura Engel, Maria Ferrero (Crazed Management), David Fry (Bill Graham Presents), Robert Gordon, Florence Greenberg, Screamin' Jay Hawkins, Nancy Henderson, Joe Jackson, Wanda Jackson, Danny Kalb (the Blues Project), Bob Keane, Curt Kirkwood and Derrick Bostrom (Meat Puppets), Gary Klebe (Shoes), Bill Laswell (Material), John Lodge (Moody Blues), Nils Lofgren, Darlene Love, Phil Lynott (Thin Lizzy), Tony Maimone (Pere Ubu), Glenn Mercer (Feelies), Bill Milhizer (the Fleshtones), Country Dick Montana (Beat Farmers), Cindy Mooney (DAS Communications), Stephen Morris (Joy Division), Bill Murphy (Axiom Records), Mojo Nixon, Allen Pepper (the Bottom Line), Carl Perkins, John Popper (Blues Traveler), Lisa Prosper (Jerry Jaffe), Johnny and Joey Ramone (the Ramones), Jim and William Reid (Jesus and Mary Chain), Frank Riley (Monterey Peninsula Artists), Bobby Robinson, Mitch Ryder, Doug Sahm, Sky Saxon (the Seeds), Chad Schultz (Insight Management), Les Schwartz (Borman Entertainment), Brinsley Schwarz, Brian Setzer (Stray Cats), Steve Severin (Siouxsie and the Banshees), Andy Shernoff (the Dictators), Anson Smith, Jim Sohns (Shadows of Knight), Dick Taylor

Acknowledgments

(the Pretty Things), John Telfer (Basement Music), Dwight Twilley, and Tom Verlaine (Television).

For providing additional research material, thanks to Richard Chadwick (Opium Arts Ltd.), Chris Dodge (Alternative Tentacles Records), Hardy Fox (the Cryptic Corporation), Robert Fripp, Don Giller, Steve Kelly, André Kreft, Jon Paluska (Dionysian Productions), Robert Pruter, Anne Stebinger, Richard Sumberg, and Harry Sumrall.

A number of monthly, weekly, and daily publications were helpful sources of information. They include *The American Music Press, B-Side, BAM, Billboard, Buzz, Chicago Sun-Times, Chicago Tribune, Crawdaddy, Creem, DISCoveries, Down Beat, Goldmine, Guitar for the Practicing Musician, Guitar Player, Guitar World, Illinois Entertainer, Keyboard, Melody Maker, Musician, New Musical Express, The New York Times, Option, Pulse, Puncture, Q, Relix, Request, Rock, Rolling Stone, R.P.M., San Francisco Chronicle, Select, Spin, Trouser Press, Village Voice,* and *Vox.*

The following books provided additional background: *From the Velvets to the Voidoids* (Clinton Heylin); *The Guinness Encyclopedia of Popular Music; The Harmony Illustrated Encyclopedia of Rock; Joel Whitburn's Top Pop Singles; New Rock Record* (Terry Hounsome); *Off the Record* (Joe Smith); *The Penguin Encyclopedia of Popular Music; Rock Movers and Shakers* (Dafydd Rees and Luke Crampton); *The Rolling Stone Encyclopedia of Rock and Roll; Stambler's Encyclopedia of Pop, Rock, and Soul;* and *The Trouser Press Record Guide.*

Thanks also to Danny Peary, for his entertaining and inspiring series of books on cult movies.

At Fireside, thanks to David Dunton—whose various suggestions and recommendations were invaluable—and to Andrew Stuart, who expertly guided the book through the final editorial phase.

Appreciation is due—and is hereby extended—to the many individuals who supplied photos. They include Susan Arick (Hightone Records), Paul Barbarus (Tapestry Artists), Roberta

Bayley, Mary Coller Management, Ron Delany, Bill Durborow, Melissa Farmer (Qwest Records), Robert Fripp, Spencer Gates (Matador Records), Rich Gershon (A&M Records), Giant Records, Bolle Gregmar (Blue Öyster Cult Fan Club), John Hagleston (Rhino Records), Mark and Tim at Alligator Records, Michelle at High Noon Management, Robert Kelley (American Recordings), Greg Lapidus (Geffen), Anna LeCoche (Anthem Entertainment), Tihomic Mijatovich (Lakeside Productions), Struan Oglanby (Sister Ray Enterprises), Seb Shelton, Winston Simone, Bob Spencer, Carrie Svingen (Rykodisc), and Deborah Wilson. A special thanks to Nancy Carroll for helping with photo research and for providing ongoing encouragement and support.

INTRODUCTION

The pop-music mainstream overflows with formulaic, radio-ready entertainers—the kinds of groups and soloists whose image and music are conventional enough to appeal to the largest number of people at the moment.

This book is not about them. It's about cult rockers—those offbeat, intriguing, out-of-the-ordinary performers who have an exceptionally potent effect on a distinct cluster of fans. Their sounds invite listeners' intense involvement and close scrutiny. Their records are cherished. Their careers are carefully monitored. Other musicians emulate them. They have lasting impact.

Cult rockers don't always fit into established show-biz molds, and in some cases they actively defy convention. Where others are widely accepted without dispute, cult rockers are often the focus of contention, the subjects of heated debate. For whatever reason—their lyrics may be too obscure, their sound too sophisticated, their personality odd, their image peculiar—they may be rejected by the masses, dismissed by the mainline music industry, ignored by top-forty radio. But somehow, somewhere they find their audience—an audience of devotees who take pleasure in being among the few who "get it," who understand the message that everyone else seems to have missed or (foolishly) chosen to ignore.

Example: The Velvet Underground have long been hailed as influential by waves of punk-rockers and musical alternativists. Yet they've rarely been heard on mainline radio airwaves. They remain underground favorites. They're cult rockers.

Another: The Grateful Dead have thrived for years without the radio hits so many deem essential for survival. They've done it thanks to the support of Deadheads, their diehard fans. The Dead are cult rockers—perhaps the _kings_ of cult rockers.

Cult rockers, like the rest of us, exist on a behavioral continuum somewhere between apple-pie normal and outrageously weird. Compared to die-cut conformists, a few are what songwriter Steve Earle calls "the other kind": renegades, mavericks, loose cannons. Others are more ordinary, whose only quirky qualities are in the sounds they emit. Still others are completely mom-and-pop acceptable. (With some of the older groups, mom and pop may themselves be card-carrying cult members.)

By accident or design, a few cult rockers ultimately achieve wide recognition. But they always maintain a core group of adherents who pride themselves on having "been there at the beginning" and who will probably stick with the artist till the end.

Whether superstars or fringe-dwellers, culture heroes or social pariahs, cult rockers are the kinds of performers who inspire listeners to follow them, nomadlike, from concert to concert all across the country. Who leave trails of followers compulsively collecting bootleg recordings. Who spawn cyberspace networks of fans. Who incite audience slam-dancing, crowd-surfing, and stage-diving. Who occasionally plant the seed of wholesale chaos at their concert appearances.

Cult rockers can be found working in just about any rock and roll substyle, from punk, thrash, and speed metal to rockabilly, technopop, industrial, and grunge. They may be experimental (Robert Fripp), quirky (Devo), confrontational (Lydia Lunch), anonymous (the Residents), folksy (John Hiatt), gloomy (Joy Division), hip (Lounge Lizards), offensive (the Fugs), sophisticated (Joe Jackson), progressive (Mahavishnu Orchestra), iconoclastic (the Sex Pistols), spacey (Cocteau Twins), debauched (Johnny Thunders), or just plain bad—so bad, they're good.

But within their chosen musical genres and modes, cult rockers tend to exhibit certain characteristics—something in their sounds, lyrics, or personalities—that make them unique, controversial, and cult-appealing. Hailed by some, decried by others, these cult rockers manage to carve their own special niches in the rock pantheon and establish themselves—for better or for worse—as being unlike anything that came before.

Whatever their individual quirks, cult rockers usually offer listeners an alternative to the "straight," assembly-line system of music and entertainment. And when discovered, these groups are not just listened to. They are identified with, copied, treated by fans as a means of self-definition, used as a tool for bolstering a fan's own sense of personal idiosyncrasy and specialness. The bands and fans become entwined and inseparable. As the manager of one cult rocker put it, "The band is necessary in its audience's life."

Cult Rockers is both a celebration and a kind of roll call of these one-of-a-kind musical personalities. Our purpose has been to highlight their idiosyncrasies and draw attention to the cult-approved sounds they purvey, hopefully inspiring readers to dig further, seek out recordings, and make some sonic discoveries of their own.

There are many, many cult rockers floating around the music universe—far more than can comfortably fit into a single volume. In *Cult Rockers* we've provided a sampling rather than a would-be definitive list.

To whittle down a lengthy roster, we set a few restrictions. As the title says, the book is limited to rock. Visitors from the nearby musical planets of R&B, country, funk, and blues were simply barred from entry unless they had significant rock credentials. (Nonsinging) instrumentalists who lack noticeable solo careers were also refused admittance.

With a couple of exceptions, superstars were excluded. Why? Because the great majority of people like them; there's simply no cult. The exceptions are the odd cases where mass acceptance has taken place, yet a core group of loyalists continue to revere the rocker with something approaching religious fervor.

Other than that, the 150 rockers in these pages are ones that have been especially cult-appealing—and that we find particularly interesting. They represent most rock and roll genres, and they reach back as far as the 1930s.

In each *Cult Rockers* entry we've provided biographical details and a determination of where in the broad picture the cult rocker fits (or doesn't fit)—often in the artist's own words. Also, to help music hunters choose recordings we've included their most significant albums (in italics) and song titles (in quotes). Not listed are live albums, compilations, soundtracks, and EPs—unless they occupy a particularly important place in the artist's canon.

The cult rockers in the book are arranged alphabetically. We chose not to separate them into categories, although the following loose groupings are a place to start for the classification-inclined:

Cult Legends: History-laden veterans, like Gene Vincent, Eddie Cochran, and Ry Cooder, who never quite entered the mainstream.

Cult Megastars: Mass-market icons, like Brian Wilson, the Doors, and Steely Dan, who've retained a core cult of devotees.

Cult Innovators: The ones musicians point to as groundbreaking, including the Velvet Underground, Iggy Pop, the MC5, and the Sex Pistols.

Cult Extremists: The shock-rockers, from Iggy Pop to Suicide to the Dead Boys.

Cult Obscurities: Those little known outside cult confines, like Esquerita, Sky Saxon, and Mojo Nixon.

Cult Individualists: Those who like to stay home and tinker—people like Andy Partridge, Bill Nelson, and Todd Rundgren.

Cult Politicos: The socially conscious, from Robert Wyatt, the Dead Kennedys, and Eugene Chadbourne to the Clash and Fugazi.

Cult Casualties: The prematurely departed, from Roy

Buchanan, Tim Buckley, and Ian Curtis to Lowell George, Jim Morrison, and Gram Parsons.

For some, the term *cult* strictly connotes "weirdness." This book could have placed greater emphasis on rock and roll oddities. We might, for example, have included the Shaggs, the three Wiggins sisters from Fremont, New Hampshire, whose sound once heard is not easily forgotten (they're "unaffected by outside influences," understate the liner notes to their *Philosophy of the World* artifact); or the Plasmatics, remembered for chainsawing a car in half onstage; or Ozzy Osbourne, immortalized in part for biting the head off a dead bat during a performance.

But cult-ness isn't limited to weirdness. More than anything, cult status is a simple indicator that regardless of the music played, style embraced, image conveyed, quirk expressed, mold broken, path taken, or level of popularity reached, the cult rocker matters to someone—and is thus doing something *right*. And that, ultimately, is what joins the diverse denizens of the vast cultural underzone you're about to enter.

Welcome to the strange, wild, and wacky world of cult rockers.

AMERICAN MUSIC CLUB

Bohemian rhapsodeers with an expressive, sad-café sound, Mark Eitzel and American Music Club were underground favorites in San Francisco and England before fame spread in the early 1990s. A cult-connected few felt championed by the damaged-but-operational Eitzel, whose skid-row troubadour act was reminiscent of Tom Waits, Nick Drake, and Joy Division's Ian Curtis. With rising acclaim—Eitzel's been touted as a "poet of tenderloin passion and despair" (*The New Yorker*) and "one of the greatest living songwriters" (*Melody Maker*)—the fortunes of these chronic down-and-outers have taken an upwardly mobile turn.

"I guess I always have been a loser," Eitzel said in a *Melody Maker* interview. "I know what it's like to be on the butt end of social circumstances." Eitzel's songs are hard-luck stories, raw confessionals, soul-baring emotional exposés. In a flat, resigned monotone rising to a cathartic wail, he sings of hopes unraveling, of hanging by a thread, of accepting life's steady dole of disintegration, desolation, and rejection. "I know people who are genuinely incapable of handling the world," he said. "When I play a show I basically sing for those people who are having a really bad time."

Distinctive settings, from feedback-laced sound walls to eerily textured electronic landscapes, come from guitarist Vudi, pedal-steel player Bruce Kaphan, bassist Dan Pearson, and drummer Tim Mooney. Interludes of shimmering dissonance, underpinnings of old music-hall piano, and climaxes of operatic majesty have all been heard amid the prevailing air of "beautiful sadness."

A longtime denizen of San Francisco's seedy side, Eitzel (b. 1959, Walnut Creek, California) first emoted in a Columbus, Ohio, punk band, the Naked Skinnies. They moved to the Bay Area in 1981. Vudi saw them on the night they got banned from SF's anything-goes punk mecca, Mabuhay Gardens, for clearing the house. Impressed, he approached Eitzel. American Music Club soon coalesced. They then spent the better part of the next decade honing a sound around Eitzel's difficult, off-kilter musings.

Early performances saw the future folk hero breaking glasses over his head, drinking heavily, pouring beer on audiences, and crawling around on the floor. "I've done moves that would make Iggy Pop blush," he told Karen Schoemer in *Rolling Stone*. "Iggy is a walking, talking explosion. I was kind of a balloon deflating."

KEY RECORDINGS: *The Restless Stranger* (1986), *Engine* (1987), *California* (1988), *United Kingdom* (1990), *Everclear* (1991), *Mercury* (1993), *San Francisco* (1994); "Firefly" (1988), "Rise" (1991), "Gratitude Walks" (1993), "I've Been a Mess" (1993), "Johnny Mathis' Feet" (1993).

SYD BARRETT

"He's one of the three best songwriters in the world," said Pink Floyd's Roger Waters to *Creem*'s Nick Kent. And Syd Barrett—alive and reportedly not well, playing no instruments, writing no music, tending to his garden and coin collection in solitude—has not recorded a note in twenty years.

"He was a great artist that just stopped," friend and designer Storm Thorgerson told Kent. "He shut himself off."

Floyd freaks still await the second coming of the man who gave the voice, the shape, and the very name to Pink Floyd—England's first response to America's raga-rocking Byrds and psychedelia.

Barrett (b. Roger Keith Barrett, January 6, 1946, Cambridge, England) was raised in a large house on a nice street in Cherry Hill. His father was a classical music buff who encouraged his bright son to play music, giving him his first guitar.

Barrett (vocals, guitar) met future Floyd member Dave

Gilmour (vocals, guitar) growing up in Cambridge, and they both went on to attend Cambridge Technical College, where the former studied painting, the latter architecture. In 1962, Barrett joined the Mottoes, playing Shadows instrumentals and classic Chuck Berry. Barrett and Gilmour moved to London, the former to attend Camberwell Art College, the latter the Regent Street Polytechnic. Also at the Regent Street institution were Roger Waters (guitar, bass), Rick Wright (keyboards, guitar), and Nick Mason (drums), all like Gilmour architecture students and all set to start a band, Sigma 6, later called the Abdabs. Barrett was soon a member, with interests in mysticism, ESP, LSD, feedback, echo, delays, slide projections, and the supernatural that would come to shape the unit's future.

Barrett suggested a name change to Pink Floyd, in a gesture to honor Georgia bluesmen Pink Anderson and Floyd "Dipper Boy" Council. At first as Pink Floyd Sound they covered Stones tunes and played "Louie Louie" and "Roadrunner." Instrumental breaks began to take on importance as Barrett led the fledgling group into waves and walls of sound, canvases for his inner inclination to spray deviant splashes of audio colors.

After stops at the UFO club, late in '66, Floyd's surreal lyrics and strange doodlings and doings were taking on mythical status. Early in '67 they secluded themselves in Chelsea Sound Techniques, where they recorded "Arnold Layne," "See Emily Play," and *Piper at the Gates of Dawn*, their highly successful debut releases. Of the thirteen songs recorded in those sessions, ten were written by Barrett and two were cowritten.

Gates of Dawn is the work on which Barrett's mythical reputation is nearly entirely based. Barrett, who had dropped a lot of acid, was by album's release exhibiting bizarre behavior. The young visionary would stare off into open space, become uncommunicative, play a lone note over and over . . . and not show up for concerts.

On April 6, 1968, it was announced that Barrett was no longer with Floyd. The news surely spelled the end. Pink Floyd without Syd Barrett seemed unthinkable.

Gilmour replaced Barrett in Floyd and the group carried on, rapidly evolving their own distinctive variant on Barrett's initial sound.

Barrett found it hard to accept and continued to show up at Floyd concerts, planting himself firmly in front of the stage, staring at his band, the band that had dismissed him.

Syd Barrett released two solo albums, in 1970, assisted by members of Pink Floyd, who dedicated to him their "Shine On You Crazy Diamond." Due to continued fanatical fan cravings, outtakes from the two albums were issued in 1988 as *Opel*.

KEY RECORDINGS: Syd Barrett—*The Madcap Laughs* (1970), *Barrett* (1970), *Opel* (1988); **with Pink Floyd**—*The Piper at the Gates of Dawn* (1967); "Arnold Layne" (1967), "See Emily Play" (1967).

BIG STAR/ALEX CHILTON

At age sixteen he had national success with a group he now considers "a farce." By the early seventies Alex Chilton was fronting the now legendary Big Star, creators of what some pundits call three of the finest pop-rock albums of all time, material Chilton dismisses as "mediocre." The years since have been filled with mild-selling eccentric releases that have endeared him even more deeply to his growing numbers of hardcore fans.

Chilton (b. December 28, 1950, Memphis, Tennessee) was only sixteen and failing in school when in 1966 he was asked to replace the lead singer in the locally known Ronny and the

DeVilles, later renamed the Box Tops. "I knew of them, but personally, I didn't care for them," Chilton told Clarence A. Moore of *DISCoveries*. "They had made a few records; I didn't like them either." Chilton joined the band for what he told *Goldmine*'s Cub Koda were "purely mercenary reasons. They were a big local band that made money." Within weeks, their manager got them a chance to record "The Letter." "We didn't like it a hell of a lot," he told Koda.

Dismissing the whole experience, Chilton told *Select*'s David Cavanagh: "They were horrible slimy love songs with outside writers and big production outfits."

When the hits stopped in 1970, Chilton took off for twelve lost months in Greenwich Village. The following year, he was back in Memphis and, while attempting to record a solo album, formed Big Star with Chris Bell (guitar, vocals), Andy Hummell (bass), and Jody Stephens (drums). *#1 Record*, issued in 1972, showed the band to be heavily influenced by folk rock and the British Invasion sound of the mid-sixties. After three Big Star performances, the tensions between Bell and Chilton reached a point where Bell left the group. Bell would later release one single, "I Am the Cosmos," and move to England, where he died in a car crash in '78.

Carrying on as a trio, Big Star released *Radio City*, which included "September Gurls"—later a hit for the Bangles. With poor distribution and critical praise, the disc sank from sight. Hummell quit, leaving Chilton and Stephens to record their third, last, and darkest effort in the fall of '74. Their label was unimpressed with their strange, alcohol-influenced tunes, and the work remained unissued until 1978.

"If you take enough bad drugs and drink enough, you're gonna be writing some pretty strange music," Cavanagh was told. "I had some idea that the way forward for music was to get real crazy."

The Big Star albums are now viewed as three of the finest pop-rock albums ever. Chilton doesn't see it that way. "In the case of the Big Star, production is the whole thing," Chilton told Koda. "All the songs are mediocre."

Hounded by drug and alcohol problems, Chilton hit bottom. "My whole life was falling apart," he told Hill. Needing a change in environment, he moved to New Orleans, where he worked first as a dishwasher, later as a gardener and tree tender.

With life steadying, Chilton started recording his string of eccentric solo efforts. He produced the Cramps' *Gravest Hits* and *Songs the Lord Taught Us* and has appeared and recorded with Tav Falco's Panther Burns.

"I've thought of getting out of the whole thing permanently, but it's a little late," Hill was told. "I guess I could go to law school. But I don't plan on doing that right away."

With original member Jody Stephens, Chilton reformed Big Star in 1994 for a brief tour and a live recording.

KEY RECORDINGS: Big Star—#1 *Record* (1972), *Radio City* (1974), *3rd* (1978); "When My Baby's Beside Me" (1972), "Don't Lie to Me" (1972); **Alex Chilton**—*Like Flies on Sherbert* (1980), *Bach's Bottom* (1981), *Feudalist Tarts* (EP, 1985), *No Sex* (EP, 1986), *High Priest* (1987).

BLACK FLAG

"Black Flag is very uncool," explained tattoo-riddled Flag vocalist Henry Rollins to critic Mike Gitter. "If we all kept our hair short and kept making album after album that sounded like our early material, we'd have a lot more people following us blindly."

Though missed or dismissed by much of their homeland, they were embraced abroad as America's first and premier hardcore band. Black Flag unearthed and explored the flaky zone where punk and metal live in addled harmony.

Based in Hermosa, California, Greg Ginn (a.k.a. Dale Nixon,

guitar, bass) and Chuck Dukowski (bass) formed Black Flag in 1976. The band's lineup ever changed as they worked on their mutated musical form at L.A.'s Troubadour and Madame Wong's. It was the Ginn vision to evolve and experiment and to produce a compelling conjugation between seemingly diverse sounds, as if all had been thrust into a Veg-O-Matic.

By 1978, Ginn—as a means of maintaining control over their music—formed SST Records. Their debut discs, the four-cut *Nervous Breakdown* and five-cut *Jealous Again*, exploded with a primitive punk roar. By 1981 and *Damaged*, Black Flag's first full LP, Henry "The Illustrated Man" Rollins was lead vocalist. Soon membership included Kira (née Kira Roessler, bass) and Bill Stevenson (drums), the latter later replaced by Anthony Martinez.

Flag's unwavering experimentations with roof-shaking punk, hypermetal, and jazz confused a lot of early diehard fans. Ginn diverted energies to Gone, an instrumental band. Rollins ventured into poetry readings with X's Exene.

In 1986, a decade after formation, Ginn announced that Black Flag was no more. Their deviated dose of punk rock was no longer viable, he said. "As far as a cultural revolution, punk rock was co-opted into new wave after about a year," he told author Irwin Stambler. "Right now the music is really conservative . . . People want something safe and defined."

KEY RECORDINGS: *Damaged* (1981), *Everything Went Black* (1983), *Slip It In* (1984), *Live '84* (1984), *In My Head* (1985), *The Process of Weeding Out* (EP, 1985); "Six Pack" (1981), "Family Man" (1984).

BLOWFLY

"You don't ever hear me on the radio," says Clarence Reid's alter ego, Blowfly, a skinny runt in a latex fly-suit complete with tin-foil antennae. "I'm banned in Alabama. Man, I must be doin' something right. People that know about Blowfly think I'm dead, in jail or the nuthouse."

Reid has nearly single-handedly carried on the true-blue banner of black-and-blue comedy, the ribald and blatantly provocative tradition that dates back prior to Redd Foxx, Rusty Warren, and Doug and His Hot Nuts.

"I'm out to say it like it is, that's all," explains Blowfly. "When Frank Sinatra sings 'When someone loves you,' hell, what he's meaning is: 'When somebody fucks you, bitch.' I'm a realist."

Clarence Henry Reid (b. February 14, 1945, Cochran, Georgia) moved to Miami as a child, forming the Delmiros while still in high school. With a tune called "Ra Ra, the Big Beat Sounds," Reid's group approached Henry Stone at Dade Records. The disc was issued and quickly overlooked. After a few more group efforts, Reid started recording his legacy of underappreciated soul singles for Selma, Deep City, Reedsville, Dial, Tay-Ster, Alston, Gladys . . . Except for "Nobody But You Babe," a 1966 charting, Reid is practically a total mainstream unknown, despite his songwriting credits and production work for Wilson Pickett, Joe Tex, Betty Wright, and K.C. and the Sunshine Band.

As Blowfly, Reid entered the studios for the first time in 1963. "Oddballs" was not immediately issued; neither was his 1965 cut "Rap Dirty." "Nobody knew what to do with my stuff," he says. "They told me my stuff was shit. Then in the seventies the Sugarhill Gang started the rap scene with 'Rapper's Delight,' and my stuff didn't smell as bad."

The idea behind a bigmouthed, filthy bugger like Blowfly dates back to Reid's grammar school days. "It started when I was about nine," Reid explains. He'd come up with his own randy, raunchy lyrics to popular tunes of the time, like "What a Difference a Lay Makes" to Dinah Washington's "What a Difference a Day Makes." "I'd just pound out this mean stuff on the piano, and my grandmother would say, 'Ooooh, you're the nastiest thing I've ever met. You're no better than a blowfly.'"

With tasteless cuts like "Shittin' on the Dock of the Bay" and "My Baby Keeps Farting in My Face," *The Weird World of Blowfly* was cast out in limited edition by Weird World Records in the late 1960s. Reid, who continues to travel the land in his Blowmobile, and variously attired in a complete, species-wide line of ornamented fly-skins, claims nearly forty albums bearing the Blowfly banner have been issued.

"I never drink. I don't smoke. I don't do drugs," Reid wants to emphasize. "I'm just naturally screwed up in the head, ya understand. I read the Old Testament for inspiration and beat off."

KEY RECORDINGS: *The Weird World of Blowfly* (1967), *On TV* (1968), *At the Movies* (1970), *On Tour* (1971), *Disco Party* (1976), *Whenever Oldies But Goodies* (1978), *Rap Dirty* (1979), *Fresh Juice* (1982), *Electronic Banana* (1983), *Temple of Doom* (1984), *Blowfly for President* (1986), *The Twisted World of Blowfly* (1990).

BLUE ÖYSTER CULT

There was a calculated, sinister feel to their lyrics, album covers, and ominous sounds. For a decade, Blue Öyster Cult—nicknamed BOC—was America's primary exponent of heavy-metal noise.

They were formed in the late sixties in New York as Soft White Underbelly, recording an unreleased album for Elektra.

Through these early years their lineup fluctuated around Alan Bouchard (drums), brother Joe Bouchard (bass), Allen

Lanier (guitar, keyboards), Buck Dharma (né Donald Roeser, lead guitar), and college mate and *Crawdaddy* critic Sandy Pearlman. Various lead singers passed through: Phil King, Les Bonstein, and rock critic and author of *Aesthetics of Rock*, R. Meltzer. Eric Bloom held the slot for the first through the last Blue Öyster Cult release.

"Blue Öyster was a brew that was cooked primarily by Murray Krugman, an ex-folkie," explained Alan Bouchard of the final group jelling. "He told us Columbia was looking for a group like Black Sabbath, dark and evil. It was Murray's idea that we take on this menacing biker image. Sandy [Pearlman] was a voracious reader with ideas that we should be more mystical. It didn't always fit, but Blue Öyster became this mix."

Breakthrough came with their third album, *Secret Treaties,* in 1974, and the 1975 live set, *On Your Feet or on Your Knees.* Patti Smith, then Lanier's girlfriend, provided two songs and a guest appearance on *Agents of Fortune.* The latter garnered the group their only top-twenty hit, the Byrds-like flight "(Don't Fear) The Reaper."

" 'Reaper' was a folk song, the most un–Blue Öyster thing we had done," says Bouchard. "It felt profound and touched something. We each spend most of our lives trying not to fear the end, and 'Reaper' addressed that deep fear."

Onstage an eerie image of tension and bleakness was encouraged. The BOC banner, a variant on the Nazi swastika, incited critics to label them neofascists. "Sandy might have believed in some of our image," says Bouchard. "The rest of us didn't know enough to believe in all that voodoo and whatnot."

The following LP, 1977's *Spectres*, failed to maintain the commercial momentum. Blue Öyster Cult plowed on into the mid-eighties, with diminishing tours and fewer album sales. Bouchard left in 1982 for various session and production work. His Brain Surgeons debut CD was issued in '94.

Asked about the band's continued cult status, Bouchard said, "There was this book I lost some years ago that best describes our fans' fascination with us; translated it meant 'the pleasure from fear.' If you know that you can return to a normal world, there's a pleasure that comes from playing with the darkness. It's part escapism, part survival by confrontation. To stare at evil somehow makes it safer."

KEY RECORDINGS: *Blue Öyster Cult* (1972), *Tyranny and Mutation* (1973), *Secret Treaties* (1974), *On Your Feet or on Your Knees* (1975), *Agents of Fortune* (1976), *Spectres* (1977); "(Don't Fear) The Reaper" (1976), "This Ain't the Summer of Love" (1977), "Burnin' for You" (1981).

BONZO DOG (DOO DAH) BAND

They attempted to do to music what Marcel Duchamp had done for art, Tristan Tzara to poetry. stand it on its head. Bonzo Dog Doo Dah's musical sketches were absurd. If a comparison is needed, think Spike Jones.

Originally called the Bonzo Dog Dada Band, the troupe was the construct of art students and avid Dadaphiles Rodney Slater (sax) and Roger Ruskin Spear (sax, kazoo, robots, miscellaneous contraptions). Early groupings often included as many as thirty members, most fellow students. In 1965, when the act hit the pubs, their name was changed to Bonzo Dog Doo Dah Band, and their numbers were down to near a half-dozen.

Members of the classic Bonzo period included Slater, Spear, "Legs" Larry Smith (percussion), Viv Stanshall (ringmaster, vocals, trumpet), Vernon Dudley Bohay-Nowell (bass), Sam Spoons (percussion), and Neil Innes (keyboards, guitar, bass, vocals).

With gadgets, mechanical men, and loonies running amok, their stage style was a planned hodgepodge of musical parodies, sight gags, comic skits, nihilistic satire, and anticonformist jive. A dash of Bonzo humor can be noted in their appearance in the Beatles' *Magical Mystery Tour*. *Gorilla*, their long-play debut, included parodies of Elvis, Tony Bennett, and Prohibition-era jazz; scrambled radio interviews; and fake advertisements.

The Bonzos did set the British charts on fire with "I'm the Urban Spaceman," a top-five hit produced by one Apollo C. Vermouth (né J. Paul McCartney). *The Doughnut in Granny's Greenhouse* won a rave review in *Rolling Stone* and included such Bonzos as "Can Blue Men Sing the Whites?" and "Trouser Press."

They toured the States with the Who and Sly and the Family Stone, and played the Fillmore East with the Kinks, but normal Americans didn't get it.

Tadpoles was a return to their original sound as directed by Spear, who was displeased with the new developments. A bout of seriousness settled in, and following the release later that year of *Keynsham*, the band split up.

Members scattered but refused to go straight; that is, aside from Slater, who abandoned music for civil service. Bohay-Nowell and Spoons joined Bob Kerr's Whoopee Band. Spear appeared with his gadgets as the Giant Kinetic Wardrobe. In drag, "Legs" Larry toured the seventies with Eric Clapton and Elton John. Stanshall assembled such crazed units as Gerry Atric and the Aging Orchestra, Viv and His Gargantuan Chorus, and the Human Beans.

Innes created music for Monty Python, and with Eric Idle adapted the Beatles' story into the tall tale of the Pre-Fab Four, the Rutles.

In 1972, an attempt was made by Innes and Stanshall to re-form the madness. *Let's Make Up and Be Friendly*, utilizing members of Scaffold and Liverpool Scene, resulted in Grimms, a short-lived variation.

KEY RECORDINGS: *Gorilla* (1967), *Keynsham* (1969), *Beast of the Bonzos* (1971), *Let's Make Up and Be Friendly* (1972); "My Brother Makes the Noise for the Talkies" (1966).

ROY BUCHANAN

In 1971 Roy Buchanan was the subject of an hour-long public-television documentary aptly titled "The Best Unknown Guitarist in the World." Those in the know just called him "the finest guitarist alive." Until his mysterious death in a Virginia jail cell in 1988, the reclusive Buchanan was among the elite, a musician's musician, known for impeccable, explosive, warp-speed Telecaster runs.

Born September 23, 1939, in Ozark, Arkansas, the son of a

Pentecostal preacher, Buchanan was involved in Holy Roller revival events at the age of five. Four years later he was a guitarist
heading a trio, a house band, in a backwoods bar. At fourteen
Buchanan, rebelling against his strict upbringing, ran away to
rough roadhouse gigs with rockabilly legends Bob Luman and
second cousins Dale Hawkins and Ronnie Hawkins and the
Hawks (later the Band). Robbie Robertson, who met him then,
referred to Buchanan as the "finest rock guitarist I ever heard."

He recorded numerous sides with Dale Hawkins, excluding
his classic "Suzie Q," later a Creedence Clearwater Revival hit.
"Dale's best things never got recorded," Buchanan told
Goldmine's Bill Millar in 1985. "He always had dreams of the
top ten. He strived for it. I play what I want."

But that wasn't always the case. For years, Buchanan worked
as a session man, providing the guitar kicks for others' hits, like
Freddie "Boom Boom" Cannon. "I hated that," Millar was told.

"It was too commercial for me. I played on his 'Teen Queen of the Week,' terrible thing. I don't remember the others 'cause I sure wouldn't have listened to 'em again."

Disgusted, Buchanan left the glitzy studios for the Crossroads, a rowdy joint on Route 1, in Maryland, just twenty minutes outside of Washington, D.C. And there he remained for years, playing late-night gigs with the Snakestretchers. Word of mouth reached John Lennon and Eric Clapton; the Rolling Stones offered him the spot in their band vacated by Brian Jones. Buchanan turned the Stones down. "I didn't want to travel," he told *Guitar Player*'s Robert Berman. "To sit down and learn all those songs, that would have taken a lot of work."

Two years later, in 1971, came the PBS documentary and the resultant contract with Polydor. Five albums were issued, followed by three for Atlantic, before Buchanan, disgusted, walked away, promising never to record again. "They kept trying to make me into some kind of pop star," he told *Guitar World*'s Bill Milkowski.

The album material ranges from scorching blues to country rockers and occasional spirituals, and despite a string of mediocre vocalists and shoddy production, there's the pervasive presence of Buchanan and his ultraprecise distortions, harmonic squeals, lightning runs.

Finally, in 1985, Alligator Records offered Buchanan the opportunity to record whatever and however he wanted. The results were three of his finest efforts. Throughout there was passion, a seething rage. How did he remain calm while tearing through such cathartic solos? Milkowski asked him. "Because I'm screaming inside," he answered.

To the day he met his allegedly self-imposed end in a makeshift hangman's noose, he was a terrible self-advertisement for his extraordinary guitar skills. "I never thought that much about my playing," Buchanan told Millar. "I was adequate." Ever-growing numbers disagree. If you must, he continued, "the best stuff I've ever done is on bootleg albums."

KEY RECORDINGS: *Roy Buchanan* (1972), *Second Album* (1973), *When a Guitar Plays the Blues* (1985); "Green Onions" (1977).

TIM BUCKLEY

"There's no name yet for the places he and his voice go," wrote Lillian Roxon, author of *Rock Encyclopedia.*

He was one of the great might-have-beens—Tim Buckley, singer-songwriter with a phenomenal range, a model of diction and phrasing, an experimenter whose journey was to take him way too far for mass America and way too far for his own salvation.

Buckley (b. February 14, 1947, Washington, D.C.) spent his early years in Amsterdam, New York, listening to country music on the radio. In his teens, his family moved to Southern California. It was then that he attempted to learn to play guitar and struck up a lifelong relationship with Larry Beckett, a poet and soon collaborator on most everything Buckley would record.

When first observed by Elektra Record's Jac Holzman in 1966, Buckley was nineteen years old and working the L.A. clubs with bassist Jim Fielder (later of Buffalo Springfield and Blood, Sweat and Tears), playing a unique brand of folk music mixed with touches of rock and jazz.

His self-titled debut album was folk-rock oriented and attracted positive reviews but little sales. *Goodbye and Hello*, produced by the Lovin' Spoonful's Jerry Yester, was an immediate hit, placing Buckley in the spotlight and on the LP charts—for a brief moment.

"He was naturally brilliant," explained Lee Underwood, guitarist on all nine of Buckley's albums, to *Seconds'* Steve Fritz. "He had no musical knowledge whatsoever when I met him, no knowledge of chords, theory, harmony."

Critical acclaim remained with Buckley throughout his truncated career; commercial attention faded rapidly. "Tim *was* an artist. He was a highly creative individual and didn't look back," said Underwood. "He was always looking for new ideas."

With *Happy Sad, Blue Afternoon, Lorca,* and the inaccessible jazz of *Starsailor*, Buckley was moving to his own syncopated drummer, his interest turning toward odd time signatures, dissonance, free-form jazz, avant-garde classical forms, and making sounds in Swahili.

"He ended up being completely unacceptable in the pop world," said Underwood.

A few weeks before his death, Buckley talked to *Goldmine's* Michael Davis of his view on the difficulties he was having with maintaining a mass audience for his work: "'Goodbye and Hello' was not played on any radio station at all. 'No Man Can Find the War' was not played. 'Pleasant Street' and 'Morning Glory' were, but all the political things were carefully screened by whoever, the CIA, FBI, program directors, or whoever it is that keeps the information flow from going to the people. I thought they were terrific songs, but they were not allowed to reach mass proportions. And I daresay, today they wouldn't be either."

With *Greetings from L.A., Sefronia,* and *Look at the Fool*, Buckley attempted to produce a commercial form of white funk dance music. The response was near-nil sales.

"These [ideas I have] are not things that are going to be done by anybody else," Buckley told Davis.

Tim Buckley died June 29, 1975, apparently after mistaking a lethal dose of heroin and morphine for cocaine.

KEY RECORDINGS: *Tim Buckley* (1966), *Goodbye and Hello* (1967), *Happy Sad* (1968), *Blue Afternoon* (1969), *Lorca* (1970), *Starsailor* (1970), *Greetings from L.A.* (1974), *Dream Letter: Live in London, 1968* (1990); "Aren't You the Girl" (1966), "Once I Was" (1967), "Morning Glory" (1967).

JIMMY BUFFETT

When Jimmy Buffett plays, Parrotheads listen.

Beach-loving balladeer Buffett, dubbed in *People* magazine "the poet laureate of Florida hedonism," has also been called a pop-music enigma. The mystery? His high tide of hits—"Margaritaville" and "Cheeseburger in Paradise" among them—receded in the seventies. His sound—country-rock lite with Caribbean and Gulf Coast flavoring—has fallen out of mainline favor. Yet, year after year, Buffett continues to fill theaters across the United States.

In song, he lays back and lolls about, downing beers in a bar, watching the sun bake, and celebrating the lure and lore of the sea.

But in business, he's been noted for action. In 1994 he ranked, along with the Grateful Dead, among the top summer draws. And his good-times-in-the-sunshine ethic—boiled down to a few handy catchphrases and nautical/tropical symbols—has spawned a mini-industry of restaurants, apparel, and books.

It all has a simple, one-word explanation: Parrotheads.

They began amassing several years into the Buffett career. The colorful cult started small—first a smattering of Hawaiian shirts amid a monochromatic concert crowd. Then fans multiplied, color exploded, and odd, tropic-related doodads began appearing.

Now, Buffett concerts are Parrothead "experiences." Swarms show up in grass skirts, shark-fin caps, full-face parrot masks, and pirate togs. They sport blow-up birds, pink crustacean pins, and palm-tree shirt attachments. It's not unusual, a Parrothead claimed, to see a neighbor in foam-rubber Gumby garb. Odd vehicles have been spotted, including a three-masted Oldsmobile with a hood ornament of plastic cheeseburgers in a treasure chest.

Onstage, Buffett is flanked by the Coral Reefer Band and, on occasion, Carmen Miranda clones and an inflated "love boat." Neither a Mick Jagger monkey man nor a charismatic Bruce Springsteen, the self-effacing Buffett is more the amiable host of a one-day spring break. Attending 'Heads spend as much time eyeing each other and swilling margaritas as they do following Buffett's minimal moves.

A favored Parrothead practice—"finning"—came out of a 1979 Buffett song. "'Fins' was an in thing with the band, just a term for checking out chicks," Buffett explained to *Rolling Stone*'s Chet Flippo. "My audiences picked up on it and started 'finning.'" The act involves wagging steepled hands over the head. "Fins up," he said. "Or fins *down*. Finettes. Fin soup. Fin pie. Fins everywhere."

It wasn't always feathers and fins for the pre-Parrot Buffett. As a fledgling warbler (born on Christmas Day, 1946, in Pascagoula, Mississippi), he once peddled his wares to the powers in Nashville and got nary a squawk of recognition.

He issued a 1970 Barnaby Records debut album that flopped

like a fish in a bucket. Then, depressed, he ventured to Key West on a drive with buddy Jerry Jeff Walker. He began a love affair with the place that infused his lyrics and music. It was then that his "shrimp-boat rock" began to find ears.

Buffett's unthreatening vocals, wrapped around a repertoire mixing humorous song-tales with sentimental ballads, proved mighty popular by the mid-seventies. He and the Coral Reefers surged into the mainstream with 1977's *Changes in Latitudes* LP and bubbled along on the surface for a spell. Then, caught in a swirl of changing tastes, they dipped back into the undercurrents of hardcore-fan appeal.

It took the sudden, unexpected surge of Parrothead madness to throw the steadily sinking process into reverse.

To this day, a beaming Buffett, sometimes with shark fin attached to back, leads his concert crowds in sing-alongs and mass acts of finning. Some call it the ultimate experience. "God," announces a participant, "it's great being a Parrothead."

KEY RECORDINGS: *A White Sport Coat & a Pink Crustacean* (1973), *Living & Dying in 3/4 Time* (1974), *A1A* (1975), *Havana Daydreamin'* (1976), *Changes in Latitudes, Changes in Attitudes* (1977), *Son of a Son of a Sailor* (1978), *You Had to Be There!* (live, 1978), *Volcano* (1979), *Coconut Telegraph* (1982), *Somewhere over China* (1982), *One Particular Harbor* (1983), *Riddles in the Sand* (1984), *Last Mango in Paris* (1985), *Floridays* (1986), *Hot Water* (1988), *Off to See the Lizard* (1989), *Fruitcakes* (1994); "Come Monday" (1974), "Margaritaville" (1977).

KATE BUSH

With less ambition, Kate Bush might have ended up just another mainstream—although idiosyncratic and decidedly able—pop singer–songwriter and keyboard player. Instead, she navigated a route less traveled, ultimately gaining renown as a

unique, not-always-accessible creator in the realm of progressive "art" rock—something of a female counterpart to such broad-visioned artists as David Bowie and Peter Gabriel.

Her smooth, quivering, sometimes pixieish voice and unpredictable, theatrically inclined songs have earned her chart hits, awards, and a large following on her home shores in England. Stateside Kate-ites are fewer in number though equally devoted, linking up via computer networks to debate the relative merits of her albums, track down bootleg tapes and photos, and share tales of close Bush encounters. The more fanatical followers (one described a CD listening session as a religious experience) attend Kate-related conventions, or feed on information in the fanzine *Homeground*.

The Bush artistic vision—embracing musical experimentation, theatrical performance, video production, and texts rife with references obscure and literary—invites listeners' close scrutiny and intense involvement. Her music developed from piano-based, folk-and-Beatles–influenced showcases for her young, striking voice to multitextured digital audioscapes in which her singing becomes another instrument—a source of variable sounds, interlocking with surrounding colors, rhythms, and melodies. Musical pieces vary in length and scope: some are minidramas with lush, acoustic-style backing; others thickly layered electronic extravaganzas; one an ambitious evocation of the Tennyson poem "The Holy Grail," lasting for an entire album side ("The Ninth Wave," from 1985's *Hounds of Love*). They are each unique, "like short stories where each song is conjuring up a different mood," she once said. None of them sounds quite like the work of anyone else.

The daughter of a British doctor, Bush (b. July 30, 1958) exhibited musical talent at an early age. "She was about ten years old at the time," her brother Paddy said in *Musician*. "When Kate began working on the piano, she'd go and lock herself away and wind up spending five or six hours, seven days a week—just playing the piano."

When she was sixteen she came to the attention of Pink Floyd's David Gilmour. He financed a three-song demo and helped secure a contract with EMI Records, who groomed her for the stage and studio with voice tutoring and lessons in dance and mime before launching her career in 1978.

For the first two albums, Bush came off as a fantasy-drenched, somewhat precious-sounding vocal acrobat with an unstoppable flow of musical ideas—a potential long-term hit machine for EMI. But with her third disc, *Never for Ever*, she began taking over production of her own recordings and in later years worked with a closely knit group of musicians—including bassist-boyfriend Del Palmer—on increasingly experimental music created in her home studio. In the United States, at least, that's meant relegation to a quirk-artist niche in the musical mass market.

Instead of live concerts, Bush has focused on imaginative,

self-produced videos. Devotees, meanwhile, have been on alert for the ever-elusive tour—one that would be her first since an elaborately staged and choreographed series of dates in 1979.

"You just end up feeling quite exposed," she said in a *Pulse* interview. "It's this vulnerability. After I've done the salesman bit, I like to be quiet and retreat, because that's where I write from. I'm a sort of quiet little person."

KEY RECORDINGS: *The Kick Inside* (1978), *Lionheart* (1978), *Never for Ever* (1980), *The Dreaming* (1982), *Hounds of Love* (1985), *The Whole Story* (compilation, 1986), *The Sensual World* (1989), *This Woman's Work* (boxed set, 1990), *The Red Shoes* (1993); "Wuthering Heights" (1978), "Wow" (1978), "Babooshka" (1980), "Running Up That Hill" (1985), "Rubber Band Girl" (1993).

BUTTHOLE SURFERS

At one time viewed (from a safe distance) as just a bunch of Texas-chainsaw wackos with an unprintable name, the Butthole Surfers have hung ten long enough to qualify as underground icons—the fringe scene's resident maestros of murky slop-rock at its most squalid.

Their music has been called "stomach turning," "depraved," "shocking"—all taken as compliments in the Surf camp. Loyal Butt-o-folk, in fact, have long sworn by the sonic sludge produced in the Surfers' Driftwood, Texas, ranch-commune and elsewhere. That it makes most so-called grunge-rock seem sugar-sweet by comparison has been a major source of Surf-side pride.

The band first appeared on a 1983 self-titled EP (released on colored vinyl as *Brown Reason to Live*), having sprouted from lyric-and-music grafting experiments begun two years earlier by Gibby Haynes and Paul Leary while students at San Antonio's

Trinity University. In years since, on disc and stage, Haynes (vocals), Leary (guitar), Jeff Pinkus (bass), and King Koffey (drums) have fixated unwaveringly on graphic portrayals of bodily functions, lower life-forms (worms and such), primordial ooze, and assorted other grotesqueries.

The Haynes vocal signature is a death-choked scream, mixed with a needling insectoid whine or drunken guttural heave. Guitarist Paul Leary—a noise specialist—devolves from fuzz-blues clichés into layers of feedback squeals and deep-bowel grumblings. Little of the result—whether a thrash-metal tirade, jangly drone, or basic audio convulsion—fails to trigger extreme reactions.

Their performances are no less cathartic. The Surfers have been seen caterwauling to film clips of highway accidents and nauseating surgical procedures, while nude dancers cavort on-stage amid flashing lights and smoke.

In spite of the Buttholes' continuing refusal to water (or hose) themselves down, there have been tentative forays into the mainstream. The album *Independent Worm Saloon,* produced in 1993 by Led Zeppelin's John Paul Jones, comes close to resembling conventional guitar-powered rock, with one tune— "You Don't Know Me"—a surprisingly catchy piece of neo-sixties psychedelia.

They've also been heard, initially incognito, on MTV as station I.D. music. "It's pretty fun to turn on MTV every hour on the hour and know that they can't say our name," Jeff Pinkus told *Spin's* Dean Kuipers in 1990, "but they play us more than any other band."

KEY RECORDINGS: *Butthole Surfers* (EP, 1983), *Live PCPPEP* (1984), *Psychic . . . Powerless . . . Another Man's Sac* (1985), *Cream Corn from the Socket of Davis* (EP, 1985), *Rembrandt Pussyhorse* (1986), *Locust Abortion Technician* (1987), *Hairway to Steven* (1988), *Piouhgd* (1991), *Independent Worm Sa-*

loon (1993); "The Shah Sleeps in Lee Harvey's Grave" (1983), "Moving to Florida" (1985), "Some Dispute over T-Shirt Sales" (1993).

BUZZCOCKS

They created a series of classic three-minute eruptions—"Love You More," "Promises," "Everybody's Happy Nowadays," and "Ever Fallen in Love"—and none of it got much notice. American radio totally missed it. The Buzzcocks were born of the British punk explosion and blasted hyperpaced music, but unlike their brethren they were deviant in their use of pungent lyrics, tight harmonies, and pop melodies.

It was late in 1975 when Pete Shelley (b. Pete McNeish) met a curious-looking character, a philosophy student named Howard Devoto (b. Howard Trafford). The latter was then in charge of the pub-rock listings in a local mag. Both were freaked out over the Sex Pistols and were responsible for the band-that-changed-the-world's first appearance in Manchester.

Mere months later Devoto (vocals), Shelley (guitar, vocals), Steve Diggle (bass, guitar), and John Maher (drummer) were a punk band. Within weeks the Buzzcocks were on a basement label (New Hormones) with a four-cut EP, *Spiral Scratch*. Then Devoto was gone, off to form Magazine. With the addition of Steve Garvey (bass) and with Shelley in charge, the Buzzcocks assumed a high-profile presence opening for the Pistols, the Clash, and the Damned.

The Buzzcocks worked fast. It took little more than a year to record their legacy, three albums, the first issued early in '78, months later the second. When it came time for album three, no one knew it would be the last—for a full fifteen years.

"There was a lot of acid around in 1979," said Shelley to *Select*'s Dave Cavanagh. "And I have to admit I was taking quite a

lot of it." *A Different Kind of Tension* was strange by Buzzcock standards. There was "Radio Nine," a forty-second excursion, and the hysterical seven-minute "I Believe," a spacey mix of Scientology and mind control.

The Buzzcocks quickly toured the States, twice; but it was over. Shelley and other members were now mixing acid with heroin and cocaine. "[That tour] did my head in," said Shelley. "It was like being locked in a 'Kojak' set."

Said Shelley: "Punk for me was: 'There are no rules.' It was fun. Just a good laugh, really. There was no future in it. No money at all. It was the most uncommercial music you could imagine."

Shelley continued as a solo act with three releases in the eighties, most notably the title tune from *Homosapien*, a surprising dance-hall hit. Diggle and Maher formed Flag of Convenience; FOC later was fronted by Diggle. After Fine Young Cannibals revived the 'Cocks' hit "Ever Fallen in Love," Shelley and Diggle re-formed the act.

KEY RECORDINGS: *Another Music in a Different Kitchen* (import, 1978), *Love Bites* (import, 1978), *A Different Kind of Tension* (1979), *Singles Going Steady* (compilation, 1979), *Trade Test Transmission* (1993); "Ever Fallen in Love" (1978), "You Say You Don't Love Me" (1979).

J. J. CALE

J. J. Cale is shy, introverted, difficult to motivate, folks say. Half decades pass between recordings. He shuns publicity. Doesn't like to be photographed. Seldom grants interviews. When he does, utterances are brief. He's "the ultimate enigma in the music business," wrote a *Guitar World* critic.

Cale is a countrified blues stylist, a unique one. He's master of the laid-back—turtle-paced—a soulful, smoky-voiced guitar philosopher who lays behind the beat; takes his time with crisp, clean licks; and lives the adage "less is more."

Born Jean Jacques Cale, in Oklahoma City, Oklahoma, in the late thirties, Cale grew up playing in western swing and country bands. With rock and roll's emergence, Cale joined Gene Cross and the Rockets, a shack-shakin' rockabilly outfit. After a short stay in Nashville watering holes singing country, Cale moved to Los Angeles, where friends and fellow Tulsa musicians Leon Russell and Carl Radle were based. It was Radle (later of Derek and the Dominos) who took some of Cale's homemade tapes into Shelter Records. One of the cuts, "After Midnight," Eric Clapton saw fit to record.

Cale's career took off after Clapton had a top-twenty success with "After Midnight." *Naturally*, Cale's 1971 debut, earned him his lone top-forty intrusion, the Cajun-country, lazy rocker "Crazy Mama." A decade later, Clapton would return to Cale's portfolio, securing another hit with Cale's "Cocaine." A series of take-it-real-easy albums have been issued, each eagerly sought out by Cale appreciators.

"It always surprises me," said Cale to *Rolling Stone*'s John Grissim in a halting whisper, "that anybody'd come to see my deal. I'm not into show business. I just play and sing my tunes. People comin' up to me is a drag. I stay low. I'm too famous already."

KEY RECORDINGS: *Naturally* (1971), *Really* (1972), *Special Edition* (1984), *Travel-Log* (1990); "Crazy Mama" (1971), "After Midnight" (1972), "Goin' Down" (1973), "Cajun Moon" (1974).

CAN

Can has aptly been called the "most innovative and influential band" in modern Germany. Their late-sixties rise to limited though global notoriety came at the closing of the psychedelic era and the birthing of a jazz-rock fusion. Can was one of the first rock groups to use electronic "treatments" of instruments. Drug partakers called it "space music," others "art rock"; mainstream ears never noticed.

But batches of later progressives—from Pere Ubu and the Fall to Public Image Ltd. and Sonic Youth—found inspiration in the Can concept.

The idea was born of Irmin Schmidt. It was 1968, Cologne, West Germany, and Schmidt wanted to form an avant-garde jazz group. He found American flutist David Johnson, drummer Jaki "Lovetime" Liebezeit, and music teacher Holger Czukay and his guitar-playing student Michael Karoli. Months later, soul screamer Malcolm Mooney joined.

Czukay and Schmidt were classically trained, both having studied under famed German composer Karlheinz Stockhausen. Bassist and later telephone and radio "player" Czukay had an ear for rock music. Right from the get-go the resultant music was inspired, though decidedly disturbed, by current standards. *Monster Movie,* their debut album, contained all the

Can

47

components of a classic Can product—repetitive, trancelike rhythms, over-hung atmospheric noise, and sudden pops of distorted electronics.

Anything but canned is Can. Live shows, much as their recordings, are spontaneous events, replete with smoke and improvisations. At Can concerts, fans often call out for their favorite Can cuts. "Often, they'll be shouting, 'Yoo Doo Right,' 'Yoo Doo Right,'" explained Czukay to *Goldmine,* "and we had already played it—as a piece of a thing that they hadn't recognized."

In 1979, after numerous albums, a few European hit singles, songs on several movie soundtracks—Jerzy Skolimowski's *Deep End* and Sam Fuller's *Dead Pigeon on Beethoven Street*—and an input of new blood in the form of ex-Traffic men Reebop Kwaku Baah (percussion) and Rosko Gee (bass), and Japanese street singer Kenji "Damo" Suzuki, Can was shelved for solo projects. The group re-formed in 1986.

KEY RECORDINGS: *Monster Movie* (U.K. only, 1969), *Tago Mago* (1971), *Ege Bamyasi* (1972), *Future Days* (1973), *Soon over Babaluma* (1974), *Incandescence 1969–1977* (compilation, 1981), *Rite Time* (1989); "Silent Night" (1975), "I Want More" (1976).

CAPTAIN BEEFHEART

He lives in the Mojave Desert in a trailer with Jan, his wife of twenty years, and little money. Although he still toys with a bass clarinet, Captain Beefheart/Don Van Vliet hasn't ventured into a recording studio since 1982's *Ice Cream for Crow*.

"I'm surprised anybody still remembers me," Van Vliet told Jim Greer of *Spin* magazine.

With a four-and-a-half-octave range, punning stream-of-consciousness rap, and his unschooled and seemingly chaotic union of Delta blues, free-form jazz, twentieth-century classical music, and rock and roll, Van Vliet reinvented harmony, melody, rhythm—pop music itself.

Van Vliet (b. Glendale, California, January 15, 1941) was a child prodigy and never attended grammar school. "I tried to jump into the La Brea Tar Pits when I was three," Van Vliet told Lester Bangs in *Musician*. "I was so intrigued by those bubbles going bmp, bmp."

During his early years, he showed an unusual ability to create sculptures. At twelve he was featured on a television show with Portuguese artist Augustonio Rodriquez. In 1954 an Italian art scholarship was offered him. "They wanted to keep me away from all the 'queer' artists," said Van Vliet. "Periscopes in the tub, right?" His family moved instead to Lancaster, California, in the Mojave Desert, near where Japanese-Americans were interned during World War II. There he attended school with Frank Zappa.

About this time he got interested in the blues, picked up a harmonica, and learned to play the saxophone. "I joined a group called the Blackouts," Van Vliet explained to author Irwin Stambler. "They ended up firing me because I was a little freakish for them. They were playing rhythm-and-blues, and I was starting to experiment a little."

In 1959 he briefly attended Antelope Valley College. With Zappa he discussed forming a group, the Soots. Neither that nor the envisioned movie—*Captain Beefheart Meets the Grunt People*—happened. In 1964, however, Van Vliet did cop his moniker from the projected flick when he returned to Lancaster and formed the first Magic Band. Their blues-rock sound caught the attention of A&M Records. Two singles, "Diddy Wah Diddy" and "Manchild," were issued; "Zig Zag Wanderer" and other compositions were turned down as too depressing.

Kama Sutra took a chance and issued the rejected though rerecorded tracks—featuring then-nineteen-year-old Ry Cooder—as *Safe as Milk* in 1967. Sales were slow. Blue Thumb issued *Strictly Personal*. Sales continued their snail pace.

Disgusted, Van Vliet retired to a hideaway in the San Fernando Valley. Zappa, offering complete artistic control, got him to join his Straight label. Twenty-eight songs, written in eight-and-a-half hours and recorded in two days, comprise what many consider Van Vliet's magnum opus—*Trout Mask Replica*—featuring Zoot Horn Rollo, Rockette Morton, the Mascara Snake, and Antennae Jimmy Semens. That album and 1970's *Lick My Decals Off, Baby* brought Beefheart enough critical acclaim for a national tour.

Van Vliet and various assemblies of Magic Bands persisted, recording further slow-selling alien adventures in sound. Nothing clicked with the mainstream.

"I don't know anything about music," Van Vliet told Lester Bangs. "I don't think I do music. I think I do spells."

KEY RECORDINGS: *Safe as Milk* (1967), *Strictly Personal* (1968), *Trout Mask Replica* (1969), *Lick My Decals Off, Baby* (1970), *The Spotlight Kid* (1972), *Clear Spot* (1972), *Doc at the Radar Station* (1980), *Ice Cream for Crow* (1982); "Diddy Wah Diddy" (1965), "Yellow Brick Road" (1967), "I Want to Booglerize You" (1972), "Hard Working Man" (1978).

EUGENE CHADBOURNE/SHOCKABILLY

He shifted from one cult to another. Early on, singer-guitarist-madman Eugene Chadbourne was known only to habitués of New York's free-jazz and noise joints. Later, via the band Shockabilly and then on his own, he joined the thin ranks of oddball eclectics somehow classified as alternative rock, accruing new Chad-herents in that realm.

It started unobtrusively enough. Born on January 4, 1954, Colorado-bred Chadbourne first plucked guitar in response to the Beatles and then fuzzed it up à la Hendrix. But mainstream jazz—and soon more abstract stuff—intervened. By the mid-seventies he was amid the free-improvisation circles of downtown Manhattan, adding quirky fretwork to the collective cacophony.

Irked by the free scene's stylistic restrictions, Chadbourne switched to the mix that's since become signature. "I wanted a band to do C&W improvisation," he told *Musician's* Jim Mac-Nie. "It would be 'new music' composing, but not on such a stuffy scale."

He hit the hoedown highway, pickin' and giggin' first with a gaggle dubbed the Chadbournes, and later—starting in 1982—with bassist Mark Kramer and drummer David Licht under the name Shockabilly. The Shock shtick was to trash the tunes of tastemakers—the Beatles and the Doors, among others—while creating sufficient quantities of their own, all-original weirdness. It ended in 1985.

Since going solo, the Chad's been freely emitting collections of sounds that know no bounds. He's been heard making noise with an electric toilet plunger, rake, and power drill. Or augmenting his many voices—Bugs Bunny among them—with duck sounds or close-to-the-mike soda slurping.

Tunes on tape, a mix of covers and originals, draw from a kitchen sink of satire, political protest, and sonic unrest. One—"Live X 2" (1988)—finds him in a kind of Pee Wee's hillbilly Playhouse, uttering oddness over cartoonlike guitar chicken-picking, far-out fiddle, and jazz sax in the "wrong" key. In many others he pillories the public objects of his disdain, from the Iran-contra crazies of "Ollie's Playhouse" (1987) to the far-righters of *The President*.

His recordings are many. The sound quality has often been rough. But true believers have accepted it as all part of the essential sonic spew. "The only thing I'll admit to," said he to MacNie, "is that if I hear something that's the worst, I will try to use part of it somewhere. I like awful things."

KEY RECORDINGS: Shockabilly—*Earth vs. Shockabilly* (1983), *Vietnam* (1984), *Heaven* (1985); **Eugene Chad-**

bourne—*The President: He Is Insane* (1985), *Country Music of Southeastern Australia* (1986), *Country Protest* (1986), *Corpses of Foreign Wars* (1987), *LSD C&W* (1987), *Kill Eugene* (1987), *The Eddie Chatterbox Double Love Trio Album* (1988), *Country Music in the World of Islam* (1990).

CHEAP TRICK

They've been mixing guitar crunch with pop melody for well over two decades, yet the albums Cheap Trick produced in the late seventies are what cemented their cult reputation. For long-time fans and later emulators, those treasured discs performed an important service: They made it possible to indulge in heavy-metal power pop without feeling like a sense-dulled headbanger—or a sullied Satanist.

Guitarist-songwriter Rick Nielsen—the son of professional opera singers and a native of Rockford, Illinois—cut an album under the band name Fuse before assembling the final Cheap Trick membership of singer Robin Zander, bassist Tom Petersson, and drummer Bun E. Carlos (born Brad Carlson) by 1973. They worked the Midwest club circuit until signing with Epic in 1976 and issuing the first of three notable studio discs, all demonstrating a flair for Beatles-ish melody, hard-rock power, and flash-fingered guitar riffs. The live album *At Budokan* then went platinum, songs became hits, and Trick rose to the top—but only for a wink.

What put them there—other than showmanship and sound—was the seeming savviness with which they simultaneously embraced mainstream arena rock and irreverently undercut its grandiosity—ensuring their appeal to both traditional audiences *and* punk-era rebels. For Cheap Trick, iconoclasm was an inside job.

They had Zander and Petersson serving as the band's official teen heartthrobs while Nielsen and drummer Carlos were the "zanies," Nielsen's garb of baseball cap, bow ties, and crazily patterned sweaters opening the door for future heavy-metal dorks, dinks, and nerds. The split in members reflected a split in the music—catchy pop tunes matched with buzzing guitar distortion—that heavily influenced the later Hüsker Dü, Nirvana, and a smattering of other antiheroic grunge rockers.

In the years following the band's heady heyday, the Nielsen hat became noticeably emptier of tricks. There was a decade-long stretch of unintended invisibility, interrupted in 1988 by a radio burst called "The Flame." But insider interest in the original Trick bag continues to rise and fall in waves, and the old discs still spin on occasion. "Everybody's collection has at least one or two Cheap Trick records," Zander told *Musician*'s Ira Robbins during the band's late-eighties lull. "That's not so bad."

KEY RECORDINGS: *Cheap Trick* (1977), *In Color* (1977), *Heaven Tonight* (1978), *At Budokan* (1979), *Dream Police* (1979), *All Shook Up* (1980), *One on One* (1982), *Next Position Please* (1983), *Standing on the Edge* (1985), *The Doctor* (1986), *Lap of Luxury* (1988), *Busted* (1990), *Woke Up with a Monster* (1994); "Surrender" (1978), "I Want You to Want Me" (1979).

THE CLASH

The scene was placid. The world was in a disco snooze. It was 1977—a time, said some, of platform shoes, wide lapels, and not much else.

That's when the Clash kicked in. They went off like an alarm. Their song "White Riot" was a rebel yell. It was an urban wake-up call, the act a one-band rock uprising. They were punk-rock guerrillas, and they were staging an assault. The besieged were the authorities, the establishment, and the old-line rockers. The weapon was sound—raw, rudimentary, and played with toughness. With it, the Clash—Joe Strummer, Mick Jones, Paul Si-

Roberta Bayley

monon, and Topper Headon—secured a permanent beachhead for future rock alternativists and assured their own long-standing cult status.

The Clash were charismatic. Populist. And relevant. In the economic depression of mid-seventies England, their message had galvanizing force. It channeled anger for scads of unemployed Clashophiles. They were into blasting oppression, breaking out, fighting back. *Combat Rock* was a Clash album title; "Hate and War" a song, "Death or Glory" another. In "Guns of Brixton," they blared, "When they kick at your front door, how you gonna come? With your hands on your head or on the trigger of your gun?" In another: "I've been beat up, I've been thrown out, but I'm not down, I'm not down."

The Clash cult was fiercely devoted. In England, they made the band superstars. In the U.S., the college crowd embraced them, initially, as a secret discovery. The hip media later raved: *The Trouser Press Record Guide* called their first album "1977's finest LP bar none." *Rolling Stone* hailed their *London Calling* opus as the best record of the eighties. Many came to call the Clash "the only band that matters."

Years before they "mattered," Strummer (b. Joe Mellors, 1952) was but a self-described "no-hoper," working odd jobs and strumming tunes on the street while living in a squat—an abandoned tenement—in West London. Paul Simonon (b. 1955), the son of a sometimes unemployed social-security worker, had been similarly sheltered, as was guitarist Mick Jones (b. 1955). Before the Clash, they were delving separately into musicdom, Strummer with an R&B-bubbling outfit dubbed the 101ers—for which he sang and wrote songs—and Jones with a gigless gaggle called London SS (with future Damned members Rat Scabies and Brian James).

They came together in 1976, creating the Clash with initial drummer Terry Chimes and temporary guitarist Keith Levene (later of Public Image Ltd.). At first, they opened shows for the Sex Pistols, played in the trendsetting 100 Club Punk Festival, and rode with the Pistols in the much-ballyhooed Anarchy in the U.K. tour.

But once punk-launched, the soon four-strong Clash set their own course with a few opening salvos of sound. A debut single ("White Riot") was followed closely by an album, *The Clash*, filled with brash blarings of bile that set the stage for similarly defiant songs to come. Then, just after its release, the band brought in a new drummer, Nicholas "Topper" Headon (b. 1955), completing what would long be considered the Clash's "classic" lineup.

Onstage they had a Who-like intensity, via Strummer's pugnacious stance and heavy-accent declamations, Mick Jones's power guitar, the body-throbbing Simonon and Headon bass-and-drums team, and sounds drawn from roots rock, blues, reggae, and dance grooves. They would separate themselves further from punk's noisy limits as the style mix in their music continued to expand.

As dramatic offstage as on, the Clash's actions—carried out on a wave of rising acclaim—often were accompanied by conflict with authorities or had the flair of grand gesture. After their double-album masterwork, *London Calling*, the next—*San-*

dinista!—spread its sound over a three-disc sprawl, against the label's wishes, and prompted charges of self-indulgence. In 1983 they agreed to play at computer pioneer Steve Wozniak's US Festival for a hefty sum, and then used the occasion to publicly pressure him to donate profits to charity. And late in their career they undertook a strange "busking" tour—famous guys traveling through northern England playing in the streets for hat money.

Ironically, they were looking at grand-scale mainstream acceptance when the band began its extended decline. Headon departed just before the album *Combat Rock* and its single, "Rock the Casbah," both proved popular on establishment hit radio. Then Strummer and Jones clashed, resulting in the guitarist's ouster in 1983. "I did him wrong. I stabbed him in the back," Strummer later admitted in a *New Musical Express* interview. "My ego was definitely telling me, 'Go on, get rid of [him].'"

A revamped Clash—two new guitarists and a drummer bolstering Strummer and Simonon—met with little success. It folded in late 1985, while a resilient Jones began making headway with his new outfit, Big Audio Dynamite.

"To be honest," said Strummer in *Sounds* years after the breakup, "I wish we were still together today. It was a good band, but the trouble was we fell to ego."

KEY RECORDINGS: *The Clash* (1977), *Give 'Em Enough Rope* (1978), *London Calling* (1979), *Sandinista!* (1980), *Combat Rock* (1982), *Cut the Crap* (1985); "Train in Vain" (1979), "Rock the Casbah" (1982).

GEORGE CLINTON

He was the Starchild, Mr. Wiggles the Worm, Dr. Funkenstein, the Maggot Overlord, the Head Funkentelecktual-in-Charge of

P-Funk Labs. George Clinton didn't invent funk, but through his P-Funk complex of bands he became far and away the most significant funky dude to record in the idiom.

Clinton's funked-up circus put together the largest and most bizarre stage act in black pop history and therein forged a fanatical following—that despite his long lost and minimal mainstream appeal, refuses to de-funk and disperse. Clinton and his cohorts of pop corn brought to life a vision of futuristic idiocy, complete with mindblowing sci-fi gear and gadgets, insider jargon and neologisms, and a life-size stage-filling spacecraft.

Clinton (b. Kannapolis, North Carolina, July 22, 1940, vocals) formed his first group, the Parliaments, a doo-wop ensemble modeled after heroes Frankie Lymon and the Teenagers, in 1956. Hull issued a single, "Poor Willie." It failed, as did a second single for New. In 1959 Clinton moved to Detroit, operated a barber shop, and recorded several never-to-be-released tracks for Motown. Clinton persevered, playing the clubs and issuing more failures.

In 1967, Clinton's Parliaments finally broke into the charts with "(I Wanna) Testify." Although the next four discs failed, psychedelia was hot and the drugs and the seemingly absurd profundity of it all influenced his style for life. By 1969 Clinton was in a legal bind that kept him from using the Parliaments name. In a quick move, Clinton—not one ever to be stopped—signed the group to Westbound as Funkadelic. Months later the Parliaments name was returned to him, which he then signed over to ex-Motown producers Holland-Dozier-Holland's Invictus label.

By the time Invictus closed in '74, the Parliaments were set to be major chart-climbers for Casablanca. Fusing R&B, hard rock, and wild, drug-dipped, freak-out jams complete with lyrics that appreciated funk as the end-all answer to mankind's existential angst, Clinton's growing P-Funk empire had a steady-heady stream of hits: *Mothership Connection*, "Give Up the Funk (Tear the Roof Off the Sucker)," *Clones of Dr. Funkenstein*, *Funkentelechy vs. the Placebo Syndrome*, "Flash Light," *One Nation Under a Groove*. The funk floodgates were spread wide, and various subunits—"Bootsy" Collins's Rubber Band, Parlet, Eddie Hazel, the Horny Horns, Fuzzy Haskins, Bernie Worrell and the Brides of Dr. Funkenstein—connected. Years later, Rick James and Prince would emulate the strategic consolidate-and-diversify approach.

By the early eighties Clinton was again legally unable to use either the Parliament or Funkadelic logos. The empire was crumbling. At this point the funk master began issuing discs under his name for Capitol. *Computer Games, Atomic Dog, You Shouldn't-Nuf Bit Fish*, and *Some of My Best Friends Are Jokes* were less well received—though loyalists never let Clinton just disappear in his aging mothership.

Late in the eighties, Clinton was signed to Prince's Paisley Park label. Contemporary funk nuggets have been issued, but Clinton remains a stranger in a strange land.

KEY RECORDINGS: with Parliament—*Mothership Connection* (1975), *Funkentelechy vs. the Placebo Syndrome* (1977); "(I Wanna) Testify" (1967), "Flash Light" (1977), "Aqua Boogie (A Psychoalphadiscobetabioaquadoloop)" (1978); **with Funkadelic**—*Funkadelic* (1970), *Free Your Mind . . . and Your Ass Will Follow* (1970), *Maggot Brain* (1971), *One Nation Under a Groove* (1978), *Uncle Jam Wants You* (1979); "One Nation Under a Groove" (1978), "(Not Just) Knee Deep" (1978); **solo**—*Hey Man, Smell My Finger* (1993); "Atomic Dog" (1983), "Do Fries Go with That Shake?" (1986).

EDDIE COCHRAN

He was the "James Dean of rock 'n' roll," the most accomplished of rockabilly rebels, a first-rate guitarist and session musician who played most of the instruments on his recordings. Long before rock musicians fantasized about wanting control over their product, Eddie Cochran was involved in studio production, arranging, and multitrack techniques. His co-penned potent classics—"C'mon Everybody," "Somethin' Else," and "Summertime Blues"—captured teen life in the fifties with a perfection approached only by Chuck Berry.

Cochran (b. October 3, 1938) was born and raised in Albert Lea, Minnesota, the youngest of five. His parents were country fans; they gave Eddie his first guitar at twelve. By the time of the family's move to Bell Gardens, California, in 1953, Cochran was an excellent guitarist. In 1955, Eddie set up a duo with Hank Cochran (no relation), billed as the Cochran Brothers. Eddie met hustling songwriter and soon manager Jerry Capehart and recorded some demos; the resultant single, "Tired and Sleepy," was a poor seller.

Cochran next signed with the newly formed Liberty label and quickly made a cameo appearance in what many claim is the finest rock and roll film ever made, *The Girl Can't Help It..*

He performed "Twenty Flight Rock," though the label chose to issue "Sittin' in the Balcony." It charted, and with some of the next few releases—"Jeannie, Jeannie, Jeannie," "Summertime Blues," "C'mon Everybody," "Somethin' Else"—Eddie Cochran established himself as one of the finest rock-and-rollers, an irreplaceable.

Late in 1958 and through '59, Cochran began spending more and more time in the studio, not only working on his own tracks but producing other acts. On a version of Ray Charles's "Hallelujah I Love Her So," he worked with a plush orchestra without losing a rock feeling. His "Milk Cow Blues" was years ahead of its time in its tough rock-and-blues mixture. Cochran was on the cutting edge, as had been his good friend Buddy Holly.

"He had a premonition that he was going to die. Buddy's death changed him—a lot," says Sharon Sheeley, famed songwriter and Cochran's fiancée. "He became more withdrawn and told his record company that he'd continue to do his 'C'mon Everybody' stuff, but that he wanted to produce other acts and to do more things with the blues. He was gonna quit touring. That '59 European tour was his last, he told me.

"He died on a Sunday, Easter Sunday, the day before our marriage. All the arrangements were made. Everything was set. Eddie was through touring. It was over. He was through . . .

"We were in a taxi, on our way home, en route to the Heathrow Airport. And it happened.

"The accident . . . there's a period of time that's under a mental block. I've been under hypnosis, looking for it. I can't remember the actual impact. I barely remember the repeated dreams of me and Eddie spinning 'round and 'round on like a Tilt-A-Whirl. I had to have known, 'cause we spun wildly before the car hit that concrete lamppost. I remember that, just as it happened, Eddie and I were going over the wedding and who was going to be there. Gene [Vincent] was very drunk and had passed out. Eddie was in the middle in the backseat, which you would think was the safest place to be in a car. Eddie had two bodies—one on each side—protecting him. But he pulled me over his lap and took the blow. That broke my heart. It came out at the inquest. I hadn't known that. Gene said he woke up just before the crash and the last thing he remembered was Eddie pulling me over his lap and covering me with his body.

"I broke my neck in three places, my back in four, crushed my pelvis, split my head. I had a ten-percent chance to live, they later told me. Eddie was given a fifty-fifty chance. I went to the hospital for months, and Eddie lived eight hours. He never regained consciousness. I never got over it."

At the time of his death Eddie Cochran was—and through much of Europe he still is—more revered than Elvis Presley. His recordings are never out of print. Memorials are annual. Eddie Cochran is never to be forgotten, until the last soul who met his music is gone.

KEY RECORDINGS: *Singin' to My Baby* (1958), *Eddie Cochran* (1960), *Never to Be Forgotten* (1962); "Jeannie, Jeannie, Jeannie" (1958), "Summertime Blues" (1958), "C'mon Everybody" (1958), "Somethin' Else" (1959), "Cut Across Shorty" b/w "Three Steps to Heaven" (1960).

COCTEAU TWINS

Hypnotic, electronically processed washes of atmospheric audio plus the swooping, glassy-smooth voice of Elizabeth Fraser (don't try to decifer the lyrics)—it's the signature sound of the Cocteau Twins.

Although chronically absent from mainline U.S. airwaves, the Grangemouth, Scotland–spawned Twins have produced some of the most evocative, mesmerizing music of the post-psychedelic era.

Liz Fraser and Robin Guthrie—the act's nucleus since its

early-eighties conception—have kept to themselves and avoided publicity. Mostly what's known is that they prefer making records to performing live, and undertake the latter only as the urge infrequently strikes.

In their London studio, composer-producer Guthrie weaves colorful tracks of keyboards, guitars, and drum machines into dense, hallucinatory sonic tapestries. Vocalist Fraser supplies the lyrics and concocts the invariably abstruse song titles: "Fifty-Fifty Clown," "Iceblink Luck," "Frou-Frou Foxes in Midsummer Fires."

Verbal approximations have poured in profusion from the pens of impassioned pundits. The sound's been linked with "the crying of gulls" and "crashing waves"; tagged as "music that gushes life's hues . . . the vermilion of sex . . . the erotic tangerine of sunsets."

Its allure has drawn potency from Fraser's voice, which threads through the music in distinctive textures—from fluttery and light to rich and full—and sometimes in several contrapuntal tracks. In England, where the Twins have been most successful, she's considered one of the leading singers in pop.

The act released eight albums from 1982 to 1993, along with a number of EPs, all on the small 4AD label. *Treasure* (1984) has been cited as their best by Twins loyalists. The 1990 release *Heaven or Las Vegas* is possibly the most accessible; those who fault some of the earlier output—hearing it as formless, meandering, and a mite precious—say this one lives up to, and even enhances, the band's reputation.

KEY RECORDINGS: *Garlands* (1982), *Head over Heels* (1983), *Treasure* (1984), *Victorialand* (1986), *The Moon and the Melodies* (with Harold Budd, 1986), *Blue Bell Knoll* (1988), *Heaven or Las Vegas* (1990), *Four-Calendar Café* (1993); "Sugar Hiccup" (1983), "Song to the Siren" (Tim Buckley song, with This Mortal Coil, 1983), "Aloysius" (1984), "Otterley" (1984), "Iceblink Luck" (1990).

COMMANDER CODY AND HIS
LOST PLANET AIRMEN

They would cry out truckdriver tunes and corny, tongue-in-cheek country ballads—you know, songs about mama, drinkin', cheatin', and trains. Cody and His Lost Planet Airmen also did ditties that country folk weren't of a mind to hear—like their gettin'-high anthem, "Lost in the Ozone," and their mighty marijuana metaphor, "Seeds and Stems." Cody and band were the first and best of the hippie redneck rockers.

Commander Cody (a.k.a. George Frayne IV, b. July 19, 1944, Boise, Idaho, keyboards, vocals) was raised in New York's Brooklyn and Long Island areas. While attending the University of Michigan in Ann Arbor, he did sideline gigs in bands with names like Lorenzo Lightfoot and the Fantastic Surfing Beavers.

"I was a serious artist, a sculptor," said Cody to *Sound Trax*'s Martin Porter, "and rock 'n' roll was really quite demeaning at the time [mid-sixties] when I thought up my name [a moniker attributed to a leather-clad 1940s radio-series hero]. At the time I thought it was a good idea to keep myself in two separate identities."

It was in 1966 while seeking out a six-pack of Stroh's in an Ann Arbor bar that Cody came across what would trigger the Commander Cody trademark style: a pile of Buck Owens records on sale. "It was rock 'n' roll, and it even had a 'yahoo' in there somewhere," Cody recalled. "That's what northern hippies always like about country music—that 'yahoo,' that knee-slappin'."

The first version of Commander Cody and His Lost Planet Airmen (the band name based on an extracted line from "The Rime of the Ancient Mariner") was formed in Detroit in 1966. For a while, Cody worked on his master's degree and reportedly taught fine arts at a college in Wisconsin. Two years later, a regrouped and seemingly ever-changing organization fronted by

Cody and Bill Kirchen (guitar, vocals) was firmly planted in San Francisco. Their most cherished lineup was of this period and included "Buffalo" Bruce Barlow (bass), Steve "the West Virginia Creeper" Davis (pedal steel), Lance Dickerson (drums), Billy C. Farlow (harmonica, vocals), Andy Stein (fiddle, saxophone), and John Tichy (guitar, vocals).

In a flash, Cody's ozone oozers gained a substantial reputation, playing their distinctive mix of Texas swing, boogie-woogie, and rockabilly. They were getting known as the first hippie country band—the real thing, genuine synthesizers of flagrant flower-power and country-roots music.

"The band was a bunch of drunken hippies out to have a good time," said Cody. "But back then anybody who was taking the San Francisco scene seriously was trying to figure out, 'How can we classify these guys?' And I was unclassifiable. And they [the record companies] couldn't figure out how to sell it."

Albums only sold modestly. And Cody and His Airmen only landed on the pop charts once, with "Hot Rod Lincoln," a remake of Charlie Ryan's hick hit. The band crashed in 1976.

"We ran outta gas," he explained. "We survived longer than we ever should have, mostly because we were such a close-knit group of people that loved each other and really had a feeling that we were happening."

KEY RECORDINGS: *Lost in the Ozone* (1971), *Trucker's Favorites* (1972), *Live from Deep in the Heart of Texas* (1974) ; "Hot Rod Lincoln" (1971), "Beat Me Daddy Eight to the Bar" (1972), "Smoke, Smoke, Smoke (That Cigarette)" (1973), "Don't Let Go" (1975).

RY COODER

He's recorded numerous albums of varied musical Americana and composed many a moody and flavorful film score. Yet Ry Cooder is most revered for his state-of-the-art electric slide guitar playing.

Blues-rock cultists first noticed it on the 1970 soundtrack of the film *Performance*, where they heard gritty, intense, precise guitar fueling the Mick Jagger track "Memo from Turner" and Randy Newman's "Gone Dead Train." The Cooder slide's power and heavy-gauge density—a techno-leap beyond bottleneck's normally tinny tones—gained him a gaggle of those newly in-the-know.

His journey since then has been roundabout, often far from the beaten pop-music path, sometimes ultralow-profile. Dodging the guitar-hero grandstand, Cooder instead immersed himself in the sounds of American roots music, occasionally crossing the country to meet and learn from the little-known players he admires. Over the years he's acknowledged the influence of Hawaiian steel guitarist Gabby Pahinui, Bahamian fretman Joseph Spence, and a clutch of others. "If you hear the sound they make, you know right away it's the Sound," he told *Rolling Stone's* Tony Scherman. "It's always . . . r-r-right there, in everything they play. Those are the great masters, the people that, you know, are cool to know about. Sometimes I think I'm headed in that direction, sometimes not."

Cooder's own devotees, either clustered or separately cloistered, respect his idiosyncratic search for the perfect sound yet await rare live samples of what they feel he does best—play emotion-laden, exquisite slide solos.

Cooder's albums, which he began recording in 1970, have downplayed his guitar—although it's been evident—and emphasized the flavors of regional music he has absorbed, like Tex-Mex, gospel (via the vocals of Bobby King), Cajun music, and New Orleans jazz. Amid the eclecticism, the records have followed a recurring format, alternating between full-band, R&B-laced rockers; rootsy renditions of rock standards ("All Shook Up," "Stand by Me," "It's All Over Now"); and sparsely arranged tunes centered on Cooder's country-blues picking, folksy vocals, and wry, humorous lyrics.

The records—especially 1978's *Jazz*—have been tagged in some money-counting quarters as replications of a quaint but outmoded past, placing Cooder in the role of an earnest, modern-day Alan Lomax. "Sometimes it's seemed that's all people ever drew from my records: 'Here's this guy preserving yet *another* obscure corner of our wonderful heritage,'" he said. "Too much of that, and you get relegated as a quirk artist."

Deterred, he turned to the high-pressure but high-paying zone of movie music. Nineteen eighty's *The Long Riders* was his entry pass to Hollywood. He remains there to this day, adding to a track record of noted scores for such movies as *The Border, Streets of Fire, Brewster's Millions, Crossroads,* and *Paris, Texas.*

Cooder's vast bank of musical knowledge first opened its doors during his childhood, and he made early deposits. He was born Ryland Peter Cooder on March 15, 1947, and grew up in Santa Monica. At age four-and-a-half, he had a crucial mishap. "I blinded myself in one eye with a kitchen knife," he told *Guitar Player*'s Jas Obrecht. "I was prying loose this part from [a toy car]. The knife slipped and went right up into me, just sliced my eye right in half. Couldn't do anything about it. Took it right out. So I was despondent, quite withdrawn at that point." Unable to participate in the usual sports-oriented childhood activities, he took up the guitar and listened to folk, blues, and classical music as a pleasure mechanism.

At fifteen, Cooder was playing professionally, and soon after that was recording with the likes of Paul Revere and the Raiders, the Byrds, the Everly Brothers, Captain Beefheart, and the Rolling Stones, who at one time considered him as a possible replacement for Brian Jones. For nearly two years in the mid-sixties he played with now-legendary roots musician Taj Mahal in the Rising Sons, described in *Rolling Stone* as "the club band to beat in Los Angeles." They waxed but one album. Produced by Terry Melcher for Columbia, it remained in the can until 1993, when it emerged as a valued sixties artifact.

The slide guitar sound that first forged his fame returned to the foreground in 1992 when Ry joined the cult supergroup Little Village with John Hiatt, Nick Lowe, and Jim Keltner—the exact lineup responsible for Hiatt's outstanding 1987 album *Bring the Family.* On live dates, fans savored copious helpings of Cooder solos; peaks were reached on Hiatt's yearning ballad "Lipstick Sunset" when Cooder, with a single liquid note sustained high over a swelling crescendo, proved as able as ever to make time stand stock-still.

KEY RECORDINGS: *Performance* (soundtrack, 1970), Randy Newman's *12 Songs* (1970), *Ry Cooder* (1970), *Into the Purple Valley* (1972), *Boomer's Story* (1972), *Paradise and Lunch* (1974), *Chicken Skin Music* (1976), *Jazz* (1978), *Bop Till You Drop* (1979), *Borderline* (1980), *The Slide Area* (1982), *Get Rhythm* (1987), *Little Village* (with Little Village, 1992), *A Meeting by the River* (with Vishwa Mohan Bhatt, 1993); "Memo from Turner" (1970), "Gone Dead Train" (1970), "I Think It's Going to Work Out Fine" (1979), "Lipstick Sunset" (with John Hiatt, 1987).

JULIAN COPE/THE TEARDROP EXPLODES

"We wanted to be the biggest cult heroes in the world, to be millionaires, to be brilliant, and to be total bastards," said Julian Cope to Ira Robbins in *Spin* magazine of his time spent with the Teardrop Explodes.

Cope has been called "the last remaining Great English Eccentric of Rock," "the spiritual son of Syd Barrett and Kevin Ayers," an urban spaceman, a lifer in Copedom; a full-out

kook, a loon. And Cope agrees. "The great part of it is that when you're off your rocker, you're aware of it," Cope told *Reflex*'s Nick Griffiths.

Cope envisions himself as a selfless voyeur for societal edification. As such, he freely admits to downing piles of LSD and assorted other altering agents—all, mind you, for artistic reasons. "I've never advocated drug taking," he told Robbins, "but for myself, it's all right. Artists have to feel more brittle and tense; they have to be more fucked up. People often enjoy things by proxy— it's a necessity of the world. If everybody goes around out of their minds, nothing gets done. I get paid to be Julian Cope."

Formed in the late seventies in Liverpool were the Crucial Three, the short-lived but, Cope hoped, "most legendary group in the world." Aside from Cope, the unit consisted of Ian McCulloch and Peter Wylie. McCulloch, within a year, formed Echo and the Bunnymen; Wylie fronted Wah! Heat (later, Wah!, later still, Mighty Wah!). Meanwhile, Cope led the Teardrop Explodes, for a brief moment one of the coolest hook-laden pop bands in England.

Before it blew up in 1983, Teardrop created two albums and seven U.K.-charting singles. Halfway through recording the third album, Cope—who admitted to *Details*'s Tom Hibbert to being at the time twenty-three and "completely insane"—decided to descend into the all-consuming mess within. "Teardrop was run by weirdos for weirdos, and because I was the public voice and the public head, people think I was the most extraordinary weirdo of all," said Cope to Griffiths. "I shit you not, I was probably second or third."

In November 1983, Cope resumed societal contact with the solo single "Sunshine Playroom." *World Shut Your Mouth*—his bleakest record, his greatest triumph, his debut solo album—was then issued. Months later, *Fried*—adorned with the perversely celebrated "turtle cover," Cope huddled naked on all fours under a turtle shell in a large green pond, with the caption: "Namdam am I, I'm a madman"—continued the descent.

"If I'd tried to do an album that was really together," Cope told Robbins of his *Fried* period, "I'd still be in a semi-fucked-up situation."

For three years, he didn't record or tour. "I was Mr. Paranoid," he told Robbins. "I never opened the door." Then in '87, *Saint Julian* was unleashed and proudly announced Cope's resurrection. *My Nation Underground* continued his recovery from Copedom.

Cope-heads adore him; mainstreamers, those few attuned, continue to see him as a drug-addled fuzzball, a flake. Said Cope to Robbins in '87: "I really don't want people saying, 'There goes Julian Cope—he's really off his box.' I've spent the last few years being really together."

In 1993 Cope was dropped by Island Records. "They thought my music was annoying," he told Hibbert. "But I want my music to be annoying. And of course, they thought I was completely insane." The following year, Cope found a home at American Recordings, which issued his *Autogeddon*.

KEY RECORDINGS: The Teardrop Explodes—*Kilimanjaro* (1980), *Wilder* (1981); **Julian Cope**—*World Shut Your Mouth* (1984), *Fried* (1984), *Saint Julian* (1987), *My Nation Underground* (1988), *Peggy Suicide* (1991), *JehovanKill* (1992), *Autogeddon* (1994); "World Shut Your Mouth" (1986).

ELVIS COSTELLO

He's rock's revered man for all seasons, a full-blown pop icon, widely lauded for craftsmanship, vision, and musical range. There've been classic tracks—"Alison," "Radio Radio"—along with ventures into varied styles, collaborations with stars, and delvings into art song (*The Juliet Letters*) performed with a classical string quartet.

Yet Elvis Costello, when first seen as British new wave's prototypical cranky young man, was a show-biz oddity (to the top-forty crowd)—a "quirk artist"—pegged for consumption by those whose tastes veered toward the decidedly strange.

With suit jacket, knock-knees, and mole-man specs, his early image was of a punk Poindexter. Stage moves were wiry, spasmodic. Lyrics were acidic, sung by a Woody Allenish weirdo whose throat emitted a pugnacious elastic twang. He glorified wimpiness and gave it an angry spin in a one-man maneuver to de-glam rock and knock out its posturing machoids.

It was the return of the nerd, after years of being pummeled by metalheads and sand-kicked by surf rockers. The meek were back. And they were mad. Costello—a known abrasive, rumored to harbor a black book of enemies, and who once triggered a brawl by calling Ray Charles "an ignorant, blind nigger"—was tagged by pundits as "the Avenging Dork," "the Worm as Star," a "conflicted bully-boy," and "a mean-spirited, spiteful little creep."

But after Elvis, it was hip to be a creep.

A mess of contradictions—starting with a made-up moniker

Roberta Bayley

that conjured both the King of Rock and Roll and an old-time TV jester—Costello combined self-inflation and self-parody, vintage rock and verbal vitriol, precociousness and prickliness. He projected high-tension neurosis and insecurity spiked with enough defiant confidence to title his debut—with accuracy—*My Aim Is True.*

Costello outlasted most of his fellow punk-rockers. And he eventually shed his crackpot image, new-wave clothing, and nearly all remaining rock skin, revealing a kind of latter-day Cole Porter sophisticate. Yet his edgy restlessness and intensity remain a signature, their expression through music a key to Costello's decades-long, left-field success—and to Elvis-oids' adherence. "If [people] want a nice, easy ride and cheerful music," he told Mark Rowland in *Musician,* "there's plenty of other records in the racks."

Costello was born Declan Patrick McManus in London on August 25, 1955. "My grandfather was a first-generation immigrant from Ireland . . . a trumpet player, a bandsman," Costello said. "My mother used to sell records from the fifties through the sixties, and my dad was a trumpet player who was very much into the modern jazz and bop eras, before he became a dance-band singer . . . I got loads of records off my dad because he had to learn the songs of the day, and so there were records going on in the house all the time." Declan-acceptable were the Beatles, Motown, rhythm-and-blues. Out: "classic" rock and roll—Chuck Berry, Buddy Holly—and acid-rockers the Grateful Dead, the Jefferson Airplane, and their decibel-oozing ilk.

First stabs at songwriting were attempted in high school. In Liverpool after graduation—while working as a computer operator—he played in "a sort of folk group," mixing rock and roll tunes with a smattering of originals. (Down the road a piece—at the legendary Cavern Club—he encountered and admired pub-rockers Brinsley Schwarz, whose bassist, Nick Lowe, would later produce many a Costello disc.)

London called in 1974—this was the prepunk period—and it provided club work, along with more computer jobs. Again, McManus had a group. "We'd try to play rock 'n' roll," he told *Rolling Stone*'s Greil Marcus, "R&B numbers, some country songs—a real pub-rock mixture."

With a guitar-and-vocal demo (of songs, he admitted, that "had pretensions to a sophistication they didn't have") he attracted Jake Riviera of the small but soon punk-influential Stiff Records. Riviera liked the high-strung lad, suggested the name Elvis Costello (using Declan's mom's maiden name), and soon had him issuing a string of singles, starting with a low-commercial-impact blast at fascism, "Less Than Zero."

Amid the eruption of punk rock—its brash outrageousness duly noted by Costello—he cranked out *My Aim Is True* with now-Stiff-staffer Nick Lowe producing and the West Coast band Clover (minus member and future star Huey Lewis) in support. The 1977 disc broke him to the underground audience, becoming one of the best-selling so-called new-wave albums—and bringing Costello to the major Columbia label. With melodious, artfully structured songs; hints of Kinks, Van Morrison, and Bruce Springsteen; and querulous tales of life's bitter intrigues, *My Aim* was an off-kilter alternative to the extreme opposites of vacuous corporate pop and impenetrable punk raunch.

Costello's longtime and much-loved backup band the Attractions—Steve Nieve on keyboards, Bruce Thomas on bass, and Pete Thomas, drums—first joined him on the follow-up album *This Year's Model*. They remained for many more, including 1979's densely produced *Armed Forces* (with its definitive version of Lowe's blazing "(What's So Funny 'Bout) Peace, Love and Understanding"), the soul-injected *Get Happy!!*, and 1981's *Trust*. A later, lengthy (1986–1994) band-frontman separation ended—to fan acclaim—with the Attractions and Elvis reuniting on 1994's *Brutal Youth*.

Cross-style wanderings increased. Nineteen eighty-one's *Almost Blue* cast Costello—incongruously—as a country crooner. The following year's *Imperial Bedroom* had him trying on a number of different musical suits, from cabaret-café sounds to cocktail moods. And the highly prized *King of America*, produced in 1986 by T-Bone Burnett, brought non-Attraction musicians into the mix, including some of Elvis Presley's band. Costello then reconvened the Attractions for "an all-out, raving" record, *Blood & Chocolate*.

For 1989's *Spike*, Costello enlisted Paul McCartney (with whom he'd recently served as a surrogate John Lennon, cowriting songs for Paul's *Flowers in the Dirt*) along with Roger McGuinn, the Dirty Dozen Brass Band, Allen Toussaint, Chryssie Hynde, T-Bone Burnett, and others to produce a raft of varied arrangements and styles, all bound together by tunefulness and lyrical acuity. *Spike* nailed Costello's transition from a mostly-rock composer to an uncategorizable purveyor of pure sound, ever evolving into no-one-can-predict-what but that cultists continue to await anxiously.

All hasn't been entirely well. In record sales, Costello's remained a fringe performer compared to scores of more conventional acts. "I got the impression they thought I was a con man," he said about his former Columbia bosses. "Like I had a ready-made blueprint to sell millions, and just wouldn't make that record . . . But they never told me what that record was.

"We get so much more asked of us, the few people who are doing something that isn't so mainstream."

KEY RECORDINGS: *My Aim Is True* (1977), *This Year's Model* (1978), *Armed Forces* (1979), *Get Happy!!* (1980), *Trust* (1981), *Almost Blue* (1981), *Imperial Bedroom* (1982), *Punch the Clock* (1983), *King of America* (1986), *Blood & Chocolate* (1986), *Spike* (1989), *Mighty Like a Rose* (1991), *The Juliet Letters* (with the Brodsky Quartet, 1993) *Brutal Youth* (1994); "Alison" (1977), "Accidents Will Happen" (1979), "Oliver's Army" (1979), "Man Out of Time" (1982), "Everyday I Write the Book" (1983), "This Town" (1989).

THE COUNT FIVE

They only recorded one album and six singles; were nationally noted only for the frenzied rave-up and freak-out "Psychotic Reaction." That was near thirty years ago, but the Count Five are still spoken of reverently and adored by legions worldwide. "Psychotic Reaction" is a sixties-weekend radio staple, and it's repeatedly used by moviemakers as a time and tone setter, as in *Drugstore Cowboy* and *Less Than Zero*.

Rolling Stone in the nineties referred to the Count Five as the premier "psychedelic garage band." "A garage band, well, that we were," says Sean Byrne, the group's primary songwriter and vocalist on "Psychotic Reaction." "Psychedelic, I don't know where they get that. There's no drug connection in that song, or any of mine. That was the furthest thing from my mind. I was taking a health class—*health,* you understand—when the guy sitting next to me gave me the idea for the song. We were clean college students, we didn't do drugs—none of us. Everybody just assumed that we did, but if drugs were brought out, we'd leave. 'Psychotic Reaction' is just about a love that's gone bad. Okay?"

Five teens from San Jose, California—Kenn Ellner (vocals, harmonica), John "Sean" Byrne (vocals, rhythm guitar), Craig "Butch" Atkinson (drums), Roy Chaney (bass), and John "Mouse" Michalski (lead guitar)—donned Dracula capes and formed the group in the aftershock of the British Invasion.

"We literally worked out in the garage, until we got good enough for the clubs," Byrne adds. "Six record companies turned us down; Capitol twice. 'There's something missing,' they said." Eventually, Irwin Zuckner and his Double Shot label signed the group and waxed the single as their first release. The reaction was immediate—though short-lived.

The San Jose *News* reported and Byrne confirmed that the band was offered a million dollars to tour but turned it down to continue their educations.

"We were young. What did we know?" says Byrne. "We didn't get any support, or direction. The success caught us off guard. The album was rushed.

"It got hard when none of our other singles got noticed. We got regular jobs, got married, had kids."

Due to unrelenting interest, the Count Five—all original members—in 1986 re-formed for their high school's twentieth anniversary reunion. An album, *Psychotic Reunion: Count Five Live!,* was cut soon after and issued in 1993. Plans for future recordings and touring are in the works.

KEY RECORDINGS: *Psychotic Reaction* (1966); "Psychotic Reaction" (1966).

THE CRAMPS

"Camp is the lie that tells the truth," Lux Interior, main Cramp man, explained to Dana Mayer of *Options*, "and that's what I think we are."

"We've taken a lot of psychedelics, and you're never the same after you do," Interior told Juan Suarez in *The Music Paper*. "We're acid casualties," added Cramp guitarist and Lux-lover Poison Ivy Rorschach. "I guess bop pills created something in our music; maybe acid added something different."

Their image and sounds, totally alien to moral mortals, reek of sleazy, sweaty sex. Cramps call their perverted presentation psychobilly, voodoo rock, the latter, Interior told Mayer, "because voodoo does happen at our shows; it's a kind of natural, animal, raw-power thing—being in a trance state and having something extraordinary happening." Their intimate manhandling of fifties rock and roll and seventies punk energy with scraps of comics, B movies, monsters, hot rods, burlesque queens, and the trashy and the dark side is way-out weird. Cramps gigs—among them a stay-over at the Napa State Mental Hospital—include "I Was a Teenage Werewolf," "Strychnine," "What's Inside a Girl," and "Can Your Pussy Do the Dog?" Insiders can't get enough of their intense disregard for "normals" and the music mainstream.

The original lineup—Interior (né Erick Purkhiser, vocals), Rorschach (née Kirsty Wallace, guitar), Bryan Gregory (guitar), Miriam Linna (drums)—first appeared on audition night at New York's CBGB club in January 1976. While developing a fanatical fan following on the New York circuit, the Cramps appeared in Amos Poe's flick *The Foreigner* as a gang of thugs. Just prior to the creation of their limited-release label, Vengeance, and their debut disc, a reworking of Jack Scott's "The Way I Walk" recorded at Sun Studios, CBS News packaged "Raunch and Roll," a special featuring Poison Ivy, Lux, and the rest.

IRS heard a five-song demo made of the group by guitarist Chris Spedding and signed them in 1979. *Gravest Hits*, produced by Alex Chilton, included remarkable renditions of the Trashmen's "Surfin' Bird" and Rick Nelson's "Lonesome Town." The next year, after touring with Iggy Pop, the Police, and the Clash, they issued their first complete album, *Songs the Lord Taught Us.* Gregory, who collected soil from graveyards of every town the Cramps would play, left—reportedly to become a warlock.

Numerous Gregory replacements, limited-edition oddball singles, foreign-only albums, and legal difficulties have passed through the Cramps, yet they victoriously persist.

"Rock 'n' roll is a lifestyle, an attitude," explained Interior to Suarez. "I'm tired of seeing rock 'n' roll being respectable. People when they think of rock 'n' roll don't think of the negative; they have this image of Bruce Springsteen saving starving children somewhere."

KEY RECORDINGS: *Gravest Hits* (EP, 1979), *Songs the Lord Taught Us* (1979), *Psychedelic Jungle* (1981), *Smell of Female* (EP, 1983), *Bad Music for Bad People* (1984), *A Date with Elvis* (1986), *Stay Sick!* (1990); "The Way I Walk" (1977), "Goo Goo Muck" (1981), "The Crusher" (1981), "Can Your Pussy Do the Dog?" (1985).

THE CRAZY WORLD OF ARTHUR BROWN

They only had "Fire," one hit, but the phenomenal effect of the Crazy World of Arthur Brown on the course of rock and roll is incalculable. With the exception of Screamin' Jay Hawkins's coffin, skulls, and voodoo mumblings, rock musicians had only toyed with the idea of merging rock and the visual world of the theater. With the introduction of Arthur Brown (b. Arthur Wilton, on June 24, 1944, in Whitby, Yorkshire, England) and psychedelics, the rock and roll circus would hit town for good;

there were David Bowie's Ziggy Stardust, Alice Cooper, Kiss, and the MTV generation.

Brown's persona of the "god of hellfire" and his pioneering rock theatrics (i.e., outlandish costumes, hideous face-painting, and helmet-head ablaze) were, he claims, due to his overblown involvement with the search for ontological reality.

Brown forfeited his young years to study the supreme subject at both Reading University and Yorkshire University. Reportedly he was a teacher when "discovered" by the Who's Pete Townshend. Brown, Vincent Crane (keyboards), and Drachian Theaker (drums) were indulging in their unique blend of sight and sound production at the underground UFO pub when Townshend spotted their act and got them a recording contract.

"Fire" was their debut stateside disc and their only offering to chart either here or abroad. Brown has admitted that success came much too quick; constant touring and the ingestion of huge amounts of mind-altering substances took a heavy toll. Crane, for one, was dosed on LSD at a party. "For a long number of years," Brown told the Chicago *Tribune*'s Dave Hoekstra, "he never came back. He talked in numbers for a day and a half. He had to return to England for mental attention." Theaker was not without damage. "He used to kick his drums offstage during the act; he would run around hotels, pressing his vital parts against the windows! After that, we became unmanageable."

Things ended quite abruptly. Only one other single was ever issued. Crane and his tour replacement, Carl Palmer, formed Atomic Rooster. Theaker reportedly worked as a percussionist with the Scottish Symphony Orchestra and toured Europe as a part of a band of Indian artists.

As for Brown, well, he's never been at a loss for odd projects. After a trilogy of electronic outings with Kingdom Come, Brown did some studio work with Alan Parsons, appeared in the Who's flick *Tommy*, recorded some increasingly obscure solo sides issued in Europe only, and spent some years with Klaus Schulze, a technologically attuned noisemaker.

In the late seventies, Brown claims to have been located in Burundi, Africa, where he taught music history and directed the Burundi National Orchestra. A decade later, Brown was taking guitar lessons from King Crimson's Robert Fripp and fronting a keyboard band in Austin, Texas. Such maneuvers proved unsatisfying, and Brown was next a carpenter and painter with Jimmy Carl Black, an ex-Mothers of Invention drummer.

Brown has never stopped inhabiting that crazy world. About fifteen albums of his stuff are available somewhere in the known universe. By his own description most vary between "sheer electronic, industrial electronic, and electronic synthesized" stuff.

KEY RECORDINGS: *Crazy World of Arthur Brown* (1968); "Fire" (1968), "I Put a Spell on You" (1968).

THE CURE

Shock-haired leader Robert Smith gives the Cure's dense musical melancholia its pained voice: a distinctively forlorn, breaking quaver that infuses even the band's cheerier songs with a sense of underlying angst.

Before the Cure tapped into the troubled psyches of its many adherents, they were the pub-crawling band Easy Cure in the Sussex town of Crawley in the mid-seventies, and Smith wasn't yet the singer. "I was the drunk rhythm guitarist who wrote all these weird songs," he told *Musician*'s J. D. Considine. "I hated my voice."

It took him until 1977 to perform his first concert as the Easy Cure's vocalist. "I was paralyzed with fear," he said. "I was singing the wrong song . . . They carried on playing. No one even noticed. So I thought, 'If I can get away with that, I can be the singer.' I've worked on that basis ever since."

A 1978 debut single ("Killing an Arab") and 1979 album garnered the newly named Cure its first positive notices as intelligent deliverers of short, punchy rock in the post-punk mode. From there, they developed a signature sound of panoramic but gloom-infused mood rock (called "mope-rock" in *The New York Times*), with Smith-penned lyrics plumbing alienation, emotional detachment, disintegration, and fear, and his look—facial pallor, blackened eyes, smeared lipstick, and dark garb—presenting a kind of living image of clinical depression. "We've really always done pop songs," he said in a 1992 *Spin* interview. "It's just sometimes they're way too down—sort of desperate."

Ongoing personnel upheaval has made Smith the one consistent Cure member, seeing the band through mid-eighties stardom in the U.K. and, initially, cult-level recognition in the U.S. As the lineup solidified to a core of Smith, Simon Gallup (bass), Boris Williams (drums, from late 1984), Porl Thompson (guitar), and Lol Tolhurst (drums, then keyboards after mid-1982; replaced on keys by Roger O'Donnell, then Perry Bamonte), the band's stateside penetration deepened. Their album *Kiss Me Kiss Me Kiss Me* became a best-seller in 1987 and "Lovesong" came close to topping the pop charts two years later.

The Cure paradox is that wide popularity has resulted from a deep, ruminative sound rooted in notions of personal solitude and detachment. "There's two types of getting famous," said Smith. "There's one where you struggle to, and there's one where you struggle not to. We've fallen into the second category. We've become sort of well-known and popular despite ourselves."

KEY RECORDINGS: *Three Imaginary Boys* (1979), *Seventeen Seconds* (1980), *Faith* (1981), *Pornography* (1982), *The Top* (1984), *The Head on the Door* (1985), *Kiss Me Kiss Me Kiss Me* (1987), *Disintegration* (1989), *Wish* (1992), *Show* (live, 1993); "Boys Don't Cry" (1979), "In Between Days" (1985), "Lovesong" (1989), "Friday I'm in Love" (1992).

DICK DALE

"Let's get it straight: People call Dick Dale the King of Surf Music 'cause I was blowin' out amps in '57, '58; but Dick Dale don't play that wimpy reverb stuff," says Dale. "I play with power, amplified noise, amplified blues. Dick Dale melts two, three picks per song. I'm on fire and out of control. I've got punk and metalheads following my tour van around the country. And when they ask me, I tell 'em Dick Dale is burnin' and I don't play no surf shit; I play Dick music!"

Dale was born Richard Anthony Monsour in Beirut, Lebanon, in 1938. His parents immigrated to the United States and settled in Quincy, Massachusetts. In his teen years the family moved to El Segundo, California. Dale was going to be a singing cowboy.

Monsour became Dick Dale, because, says Dale, "this four-hundred-pound L.A. disc jockey named T. Texas Tiny thought it was a good name for a country singer. Seein' that the only person I ever idolized was Hank Williams, I thought it was a good idea." Dale won talent contests, made club dates, and appeared on country TV shows like *Town Hall Party* and *The Spade Cooley Show.*

At one of his club dates, in the Rinky Dink Ice Cream Parlor in Balboa, California, someone asked him if he'd keep his mouth shut and just pick. Dale thought about it and the next day came back with some instrumentals. The audience approval was great, and grew. In 1960, Dale and his Del-Tones took up a residency at the Rendezvous Ballroom, where they quickly became one of the most popular draws in the area.

After a few bum starts, Dale clicked in '61 with "Let's Go Trippin'," a guitar instrumental that some proclaim the first surf single. The inspiration for the surf sound, Dale says, came from experience. "When a wave would build up over me and come crashing down on me, breaking my ten-foot surfboard in my skull, the sound would be so powerful and fat. That was the feeling and the sound that I had to get out of my guitar." As for the high staccato notes Dale is known for machine-gunning: "I was imitating the hiss of my pet seven-hundred-pound mountain lions." Issued on his own label, *Surfers' Choice* charted midway in *Billboard*'s top 100 albums list.

Capitol Records signed Dale to a seven-year contract in mid-1963. No one could have foreseen the coming of the Beatles and the death of surf music. Four albums were issued, and in 1966 Dale retired, then suffering from intestinal cancer.

Dale moved to Hawaii, where he married a Tahitian dancer and recuperated. In the 1980s he returned to local performances and an appearance in the Annette Funicello and Frankie Avalon flick *Back to the Beach*. A duet cut for the film with Stevie Ray Vaughn was nominated for a Grammy.

Dale lives in an undisclosed desert with his wife, son, and a collection of jungle beasts.

"I still have fear even after playing for over thirty years," says Dale. "When I am up on the stage I pray to the good Lord to guide my fingers and get me through the night. Then I get off the stage swearing I'll never do that again!

"I'll never die. I'll just explode, right there before your eyes, onstage."

KEY RECORDINGS: *Surfers' Choice* (1963), *King of the Surf* (1963), *The Tiger's Loose* (1986), *Tribal Thunder* (1993); "Let's Go Trippin'" (1961), "Miserlou" (1962), "Surf Beat" (1962).

THE DAMNED

In 1976, Rat Scabies joined with Captain Sensible, onetime gravedigger Dave Vanian, and Brian James. The goal: to make the Damned the fastest and the loudest band in Britain . . . and maybe the world.

Playing live to crushes of pogoing skinheads, post-adolescent leather boys, and rainbow-haired punklets, the Damned delivered the demanded decibels while getting pummeled with substances dry and wet, soft and hard. "We're the only band that's got real communication between the stage and the audience," boasted Sensible to *Melody Maker*'s Carol Clerk in 1981. "People know they can come and talk to us and pour beer over us, buy us a drink and spit at us."

Drummer Scabies (b. Chris Miller), bassist-guitarist Sensible (b. Ray Burns), singer Vanian (b. David Letts), and guitarist Brian James (b. Brian Robertson) have been credited with several punk firsts. They issued what are regarded as the first U.K. punk single and album. They were the first British punkers to play New York's CBGB (in mid-1977), where they reportedly outweirded the Dead Boys and triggered a shift from the Apple's artsy-poetic style (Television, Patti Smith) to a harder, rougher mode—leading later to thrash. They also played at London's legendary, punk-incubating 100 Club and were part of the Sex Pistols' notorious Anarchy in the U.K. tour with the Clash and the Heartbreakers.

Shifting personnel kept the Damned's output uneven and their career rocky. The original lineup split in 1978 and then re-formed without songwriter James. Bassists came and went—there were Algy Ward (on the standout *Machine Gun Etiquette* LP), Paul Gray, and finally Bryn Merrick. A keyboardist, Roman Jugg, was added in 1982. And Captain Sensible departed in 1984 to concentrate on a previously launched solo effort. All seemed to end with the 1989 live *Final Damnation*, compiled from reunion shows of the four founders. (The 1993 CBGB's twentieth-anniversary celebration hosted yet another Damned reunion.)

The Damned are fondly remembered not only for sound but for sight: Scabies setting fire to his drums or using his head as a drumstick; Vanian appearing as a vampire, Sensible in a tutu. "One minute we're all nobodies on the dole, the next we're all famous," explained Scabies to writer Mat Smith. "People wanted us to be outrageous."

KEY RECORDINGS: *Damned Damned Damned* (1977), *Music for Pleasure* (1977), *Machine Gun Etiquette* (1979), *The Black Album* (1980), *Strawberries* (1982), *Phantasmagoria* (1985), *Anything* (1986), *Final Damnation* (live, 1989); "New Rose" (1976), "Neat Neat Neat" (1977), "Love Song" (1979), "Smash It Up" (1979), "Noise Noise Noise" (1979), "Eloise" (1986).

DEAD BOYS

Stiv Bators, Cheetah Chrome, Jimmy Zero, Johnny Blitz, and Jeff Magnum—the living Dead Boys—were sonic hellions among many hurtling through the graffitied corridors of punk-rock pleasure domes in the late seventies.

New York's decaying CBGB's was their haunt, and through its

crush of leather-bound, safety-pinned bodies, the emaciated-looking Bators could be seen giving new meaning to the phrase "hardest-working man in show business." Onstage, smashing his face against amplifiers, drooling bananas, hanging himself with a microphone cord, jamming his head into a pounding bass drum, he gave and gave and gave till there was nothing left to—you know the rest. The beer bottles and lit cigarettes thrown from the audience let him and the Boys know they were wanted.

For people rejecting the day's slicker, sleeker sounds, the Boys' scrappy overkill—even if a career-minded put-on—met an urgent entertainment need. "We're making them laugh," Bators once said. "We want to shock people into seeing themselves."

Slightly less jolting was the Boys' music—an assault of either cutting-edge hard-punk or low-grade heavy metal, depending on the listener's level of sedation. Its decibels, pleasing to punk ears, fell on deaf ones among the planners of commercial fare for surface-world consumption. So while clubmates like Blondie, Talking Heads, and a few others managed to slither out of the Lower East Side scene that spawned them, Stiv Bators and his Dead colleagues rattled, rolled over, and finally stiffed, leaving only a smattering of sonic artifacts—and many happy punk memories.

They rose out of Ohio at a time when the Buckeye State had its own active underground. Singer Bators entered it with a mission to shake the shackles of Catholic schooling and embrace shock and roll as practiced by the almighty Iggy Pop. (Bators proudly claimed to have supplied the peanut butter that Pop smeared on fans at one 1970 concert.) Stiv's search for those of like mind led him to Cleveland, where guitarist Gene "Cheetah Chrome" O'Connor and drummer Johnny Blitz (b. John Madansky) were fusing art and raunch in the band Rocket from the Tombs. Buried in 1975, the Tombs yielded the Chrome-Bators-Blitz group Frankenstein (and, led by David Thomas and Peter Laughner, the later-acclaimed Pere Ubu).

Frankenstein, lacking local outlets, morphed into the Dead Boys, who made their way to the musically vibrant New York Bowery in 1976. As scene stealers stoked by the fast and frantic likes of Britain's the Damned and the Sex Pistols, the Boys proved more explosive than most, marking the shift from punk's poetic early phase (Patti Smith, Television) to the thrashing, hardcore eruptions to come.

Young Loud and Snotty, produced in 1977 by singer-rocker Genya Ravan (of Ten Wheel Drive, Goldie and the Gingerbreads), packed the most punch of the Deads' three albums. Peak rawness and volume levels were matched with the Boys' best songs, of which several—including the aggressive, sloppy "Sonic Reducer"—were holdovers from Rocket days. To critic Lester Bangs, the album contained "classic trashy American garage rock which you ought to take about as seriously as it takes itself."

Follow-up studio and live discs preceded a dissolution of the Dead-men in 1979. Bators moved on, waxing a solo album (*Disconnected*, 1980) and a 1981 LP with the widely unnoticed Wanderers. He then formed Lords of the New Church with Brian James of the Damned, issuing three records between 1982 and '84. The Boys briefly reunited in 1987 for a single, and in that same year a solo Bators released the twelve-inch "Have Love Will Travel" b/w "Story in Your Eyes."

But none of these post–Dead Boys spasms reached quite the frenzy level of the originals. And none left as indelible an image as that of Stiv Bators in an apparent epileptic seizure at the microphone, shrieking above the squall of face-contorting Cheetah Chrome and their band of punk zombies in a crazed, *Zap Comix* exaggeration of mom and dad's worst rock and roll nightmare.

The Dead might have lived. But Stiv, in Paris in 1990, was struck by a car and killed.

KEY RECORDINGS: *Young Loud and Snotty* (1977), *We Have Come for Your Children* (1978), *Night of the Living Dead Boys* (live, recorded 1979, released 1981); "Sonic Reducer" (1977), "All the Way Down" (1987).

DEAD KENNEDYS

At the punk peak in San Francisco, crazed crowds crammed the cramped quarters of club Mabuhay Gardens to feed off the thrashing chaos of the latest rage—the Dead Kennedys. Lead vocalist Jello Biafra—in his signature angry quaver—revved them to frenzies with politicized, black-humored rants against the forces of oppression, greed, war, and good taste. Guitarist East Bay Ray, bassist Klaus Flouride, and drummer Ted issued sound in ultrafast-loud-short blasts to hammer home his point.

For a time, the Dead Kennedys were hailed and reviled as the most abrasive and politically aggravating U.S. band to appear in the wake of England's Sex Pistols. Biafra emerged as a unique rock activist—a kind of radical-punk Lenny Bruce or Mort Sahl—and one of San Francisco's most colorful characters when in 1979 he ran for mayor with the slogan "There's Always

Room for Jello." (He came in fourth out of ten with the proposal—among others—that downtown businessmen be required to wear clown suits.)

The Kennedys story dates back to the cynical, post-Watergate seventies. Trapped in a Boulder, Colorado, high school, Biafra—then named Eric Boucher—found comfort in the antipop of used Stooges albums before departing for the University of California at Santa Cruz. "When I went to college for two-and-a-half months," Biafra told Lynden Barber in *Melody Maker,* "I found that all the people were into was bragging about their fancy stereos, getting stoned and drunk, and getting rich."

Repulsed, Biafra traveled north to roil rebelliously amid San Francisco's newly bubbling cult of brash punk-rockers. Encouraged by others, he formed a band and chose a name guaranteed to suggest American decline. "There was a 'this wide American empire can't possibly shrink' type attitude," Biafra said. "The straw which broke the camel's back and sent Americans into this antipolitical, escapist, apathetic attitude started with the Kennedy killings."

The DKs' initial single—"California über Alles," issued in 1979—lampooned then-governor Jerry Brown and pictured a zen-fascist state ("Mellow out or you will pay"). It became their anthem and earned spins on many an underground turntable.

"Some people in high positions of power with no sense of humor didn't seem to understand," Biafra told writer Gregg Turkington. More receptive were fringe audiences in England, whose support pushed the next single, "Holiday in Cambodia," to the top of the U.K. alternative-music chart in 1980. Both songs were among fourteen included on the DKs' debut album, *Fresh Fruit for Rotting Vegetables,* an acclaimed artifact of raw punk sound and radical but rib-tickling verbal venom.

Subsequent albums—in which lyrical sights remained trained on such targets as the religious right (the 1981 EP *In God We Trust, Inc.*) and so-called Nazi punks (who, ironically, had embraced "California über Alles" as a call to arms)—were released on the DKs' own Alternative Tentacles Records. The label played a role in furthering the careers of other unusual bands: Butthole Surfers, Flipper, and NoMeansNo among them.

Inevitably, counterforces closed in on the DKs. In 1986 they were charged by authorities with "distributing harmful matter to minors" after packaging their *Frankenchrist* album with a poster—by widely hailed artist H. R. Giger—that some deemed offensive. The case was ultimately dismissed. But during the energy-draining year it took to reach resolution, the Dead Kennedys disbanded.

Separately, they've remained active, Biafra issuing acerbic social-political commentary on such discs as 1989's aptly titled *High Priest of Harmful Matter* and working with Ministry, Mojo Nixon, and other left-fielders.

As a controversial, high-profile personality—and a successful one—Biafra became the target of so-called punk fundamentalists. In 1994 he was badly beaten in a Berkeley club, the multiple attackers reportedly decrying him as a "sellout rock star."

KEY RECORDINGS: *Fresh Fruit for Rotting Vegetables* (1980), *Plastic Surgery Disasters* (1982), *Frankenchrist* (1985), *Bedtime for Democracy* (1986); "California über Alles" (1979), "Holiday in Cambodia" (1980), "Moral Majority" (1981), "Rambozo the Clown" (1987).

DEVO

Devo was different, avant-garde and definitely a noncommercial entity of stellar proportions. "We were a *devo*-lving three-prong attack," says Jerry Casale, the act's bassist and cofounder with keyboardist-guitarist Mark Mothersbaugh. "We had a *devo*-lving look, a sound, and the answers. Devo was an all-out assault on nothingness."

First spotted in the mid-seventies, Devo was perceived as an alien entity, faceless and bone-chillingly cool. "In a six-week period in our initial *de*formation we had *de*scended to this look that stuck on us," says Casale. "We wore paper yellow suits with paper 3-D eye wear. Put five guys in such and the look was of uniformity. We were replaceables, totally alike, yet different from the abyss."

Later Devo would further their visual *de*cline into pseudo J.F.K.-Reagan wigs (Devo-dos), flowerpot hats (energy domes), and toilet-seat collars.

Their movements on stage were jerky, their sounds sterile, convoluted, industrial. Devo "singing" was at great effort emotionless, though tension was ever present. "We were not musicians," Casale explains. "We were users of instruments."

Devo lyrics were apocalyptic jabs at contemporary society, with asides to lust and contorted sexual activities. "We were

students and humans—angst-ridden—and had steeped our-selves in Nietzsche and Ronald McDonald and punk science."

Devo handouts and album inserts propagated an ambitious philosophy. Mankind, Devo declaimed, had finally reached the omega point and all was now falling apart, *devo*-lving. "We were spuds *devo*-lving from a long line of brain-eating apes," adds Casale.

Fans became *Devo*-tees. Their sizable though never main-stream numbers are now—nearly two decades later—*devo*-lving, though Casale assures there is an ever-dutiful cluster of cult cling-ons that are vigilant for new and further *devo*-lved Devo product and performance.

The Devo tale dates back to the dark mid-seventies and Akron, Ohio, a town Casale describes as "industrial, gray, hideous—culturally, a black hole. Nothing inside of nothing."

Casale and Mothersbaugh met at Kent State University, where both were aspiring visual artists. "We were doing more or less what we wanted visually, using a lot of printing techniques," he says. Soon there were five spudsters—added were Jerry's brother Bob Casale (keyboards, guitar) plus Mark's brother Bob Mothersbaugh (lead guitar) and Alan Myers (drums). Their outlandish getup and tongue-in-cheek musical approach accrued notice; they played in Cleveland and at New York's CBGB, then relocated to L.A. Iggy Pop spotted Devo's act and brought them to the attention of the proper authorities, David Bowie and Brian Eno; the latter produced the group's debut album.

Two swell-selling singles were issued on Devo's own Booji Boy label, including a strangely syncopated version of the Rolling Stones' "Satisfaction." Warner Bros. signed the band in the hopes of capturing a mutated mainstream audience for Devo's quirky music.

Says Casale, "Warner Bros. had this attitude: 'Okay, you guys are totally bizarre. We don't get it, but somebody does. Do what you want. Hang yourself.'"

Despite the S&M connotations, "Whip It"—a cut off *Freedom of Choice,* their third LP—received a massive amount of airplay and a lone gold disc. Two other mainstream bids—"Working in the Coal Mine," a herky-jerky remake of the Lee Dorsey classic, and "Theme from Doctor Love"—followed. But all was not well with the mating of the nine-to-five surface world and these robotic spuds.

"We frightened normal people," says Casale. "There was this strong reaction. Radio hated us. We didn't fit the demographics." In 1985, after seven albums, Warner Bros. dropped the group.

Capitol Records subsidiary Enigma revived the act in 1987. Before the label's demise in 1990, Devo issued three further album adventures. More recently the act has returned to live performances and has been recording for Rykodisc, both as Devo and their alter-ego Dove the Band of Love, a strictly mundane Muzak-making concern.

"What could be more *devo*-luted than our becoming a Muzak

band?" asks Casale. "Like the Bible, *devo*-lution is basically an extended joke. One man's doughnut is another man's death."

KEY RECORDINGS: *Q: Are We Not Men? A: We Are Devo* (1978), *Duty Now for the Future* (1979), *Freedom of Choice* (1980); "Satisfaction" (1978), "Whip It" (1980).

THE DICTATORS

"We were doing the leather jacket thing before the Ramones— *that* shtick," recalls Dictators founder and bass-and-keys man Adny Shernoff. "Makes you feel like an old Catskills comedian: *'They stole our shtick!'*"

Not a comedy act—but close to it—the Dictators had a shtick that went well beyond leather jackets. There was other tough-guy stuff. There were dark shades. Frizzed-out heads of hair. Gang-style nicknames.

They stood astride the stage of the New York club CBGB when punk was at a peak, their main mouthpiece, "Handsome" Dick Manitoba (the "handsomest man in rock and roll" by his own assessment), a belly-shaking mass of ranting and rasping rock overkill.

The Dictators were different, injecting the scene with a mixture of power, punk, and parody that could only have been drawn from the fantasy of an addled rock critic. Which in a way it was: Shernoff had been a rock writer; cult critic R. Meltzer and former *Creem* scribe Sandy Pearlman had championed and shaped them. Thus spawned, the Dictators were a caricature, a nutty ideal of a band sending up—and celebrating—rock's rawest, most heavy-metallic, trash-cultural aspects.

It was Shernoff who first noted the need for the Dictators, putting aside his copublishing of the *Teenage Wasteland Gazette* to take action with guitarists Scott "Top Ten" Kempner and Ross "the Boss" Funicello. "I was attending a school in New Paltz.

Roberta Bayley

We dropped out, got a little farmhouse, and started rehearsing every day," he remembers. "Richard [Blum—a.k.a. Dick Manitoba] was a character who would sort of hang out with us. Richard was coming up on the weekends. I think he was working for the post office."

Pop pensman Meltzer introduced the fledgling band to those who would matter. In no time the group had an Epic-released debut disc—a punk predater called *The Dictators Go Girl Crazy!* (produced by Pearlman and Murray Krugman, the team behind Blue Öyster Cult)—and were power-blasting their way into the receptive brains of New York City's punks and bridge-and-tunnel fans.

Like others of the day, they were fashioning an answer to rock's recent artsy excesses. The largely Shernoff-penned tracks on *Go Girl Crazy!* boiled everything back down to teen-dream essentials: burgers, TV, cars, pro wrestling, and other bits of pop iconography.

"Before we made a record and I was just a fan going to concerts and buying records, I just thought a lot of it was stupid and pretentious, and I didn't think it was real rock and roll," says Shernoff. "My attempt was making an album that was real rock and roll.

"I was friends with the Ramones. A few miles away they were attempting to do the same thing, and also in London there were people feeling the same way. We just got an album out a year or six months before anybody else."

The band's number soon expanded to include bassist Mark "the Animal" Mendoza and drummer Ritchie Teeter (replacing Stu Boy King). Handsome Dick was boosted from roadie to frontman—despite his noted vocal limitations. "He sang a few songs, and then he started singing more and more and more as we went on," explains Shernoff. "We were pretty young. You do things. You don't think, 'Oh, it can't be done.'"

Although accolades flowed from the press, and even though loyal minions jammed New York's small spaces to witness the act in action, none of the Dictators discs—four in all—ended up selling much. The 'Tators thus toppled after but a brief rule, leaving others of their time, if not entirely of their ilk—notably the Ramones and the Sex Pistols—free to reap credit for exerting greater influence.

Following the band's dissolution in 1978 (having been dumped by both Epic and Elektra), members insinuated their way into other, in some cases more marketable, musical entities. But they continued to reconvene periodically—in late 1980 for gigs that ended up preserved on an album, again in the mid-eighties, and in late 1993, when they played for CBGB's twentieth-anniversary celebration.

The Dictators may yet be tagged as the band that bridged CBGB and the Catskills. "We were irreverent," says Shernoff. "We thought it should have been three-chord fun, a little bit irreverent, a little on the edge. Maybe we were right. Maybe we weren't. I don't know."

KEY RECORDINGS: *The Dictators Go Girl Crazy!* (1975), *Manifest Destiny* (1977), *Bloodbrothers* (1978), *Fuck 'Em If They Can't Take a Joke* (live, 1981); "Master Race Rock" (1975), "Teengenerate" (1975), "(I Live for) Cars and Girls" (1975), "Faster and Louder" (1978).

BO DIDDLEY

He is the original electronic experimenter, a class-A songwriter, and surely one of the founding fathers of rock and roll. Big Bad Bo, the legendary "Bo Knows" spoken of in Nike shoe ads, the "Black Gladiator," Ellas Bates (né Ellas McDaniel, b. December 30, 1928, McComb, Mississippi), is still mad as hell.

"I want my money," says Diddley. "I don't wanna be no cult figure, y'understand. I made rock 'n' roll what it is; not Elvis Presley."

Despite claims, Diddley was not born with an electric guitar in his hands.

"Mama Gussie [McDaniel, a first cousin] raised me from eight months on, and my mother [Ethel Wilson Christopher], too," he adds, once calmed. "Mama was a hardcore Baptist. She didn't like my music; thought it was the Devil's music. But she went along with it later and was kinda proud of me, but she had her doubts."

Diddley moved to Chicago at age seven, and his musical training started early on violin, under the close watch of Professor O. W. Fredericks, music director at Chicago's Ebenezer Baptist Church.

"I found out that [violin] wasn't really what I wanted," Diddley says. "Man, I used to play all this funny music, like Tchaikovsky. I wanted to play some jazz and get down . . . I found out I couldn't play blues. I could not play like Muddy Waters . . . I was cut out to be just what I am, Bo Diddley. No one influenced Bo Diddley. I didn't copy no one, y'understand."

Diddley quit school in 1944, at sixteen. "I got ambitious, and my head got a little too fat," he says. "It was a big mistake, but would I be here talking to you as Bo Diddley if I'd stayed in school? I ask ya."

Diddley picked up a cheap guitar and his lifelong nickname. He worked as an elevator operator, drove a truck, made punchboards, and had some bouts as a semipro boxer. All the while, Diddley and his band, the Langley Ave. Jive Cats—Jerome Green (maracas, tuba), Roosevelt Jackson (washtub), sometimes Billy Boy Arnold (harmonica), Normagene "The Duchess" Woffard (guitar), and Frank Kirkland (drums)—worked streetcorners passing the hat and playing the dives with names like the Sawdust Trail and Castle Rock.

Vee-Jay Records turned him down, but Chess didn't. "They listened and liked this song 'Uncle John.' They had me change the words, and that became my first hit, man, 'Bo Diddley.'"

Diddley didn't have many hits but has always been legend for his arrogant stance, that "Diddley walk," his black getup, and most particularly for that primitive, hypnotic, and trademark rhythm he'd ceaselessly grind.

"It was nice what Nike did for me," says Diddley. "I mean, I don't play no basketball, nor all that sport stuff. Somebody musta spoke up for me."

After more than a decade, Diddley is back with new releases for Triple X.

"I never got my money, but I still love what I'm doing," he says. "It's the world to me to still perform for my Bo Diddley fans and loving them and having them love me in return. I ain't retiring. Bo knows, man. I still got people out there looking for Bo Diddley, and I wanna be there when they find me."

KEY RECORDINGS: *Bo Diddley* (1957), *Go Bo Diddley* (1958), *Have Guitar, Will Travel* (1959), *Bo Diddley in the Spotlight* (1960), *Bo Diddley Is a Gunslinger* (1961), *Bo Diddley Is a Lover* (1961), *Bo Diddley and Company* (1963), *Two Great Gui-*

tars (with Chuck Berry, 1964), *20th Anniversary of Rock 'n' Roll* (1976); "Bo Diddley" b/w "I'm a Man" (1955), "Diddley Daddy" (1955), "Pretty Thing" b/w "Bring It to Jerome" (1955), "Who Do You Love" (1956), "Mona" (1957), "Crackin' Up" (1959), "Say Man" (1959), "She's Alright" (1959), "Road Runner" (1960), "You Can't Judge a Book by the Cover" (1962).

THE DOORS

"The Doors wasn't just guys playing as loud as they could with fuzz and giant amps," said Doors guitarist and creator of "Light My Fire," "Love Me Two Times," and "Touch Me," Robby Krieger to Alan Paul of *Guitar World*. "Our music was more like jazz in the way it fit together."

Others would claim the Doors were like nothing before nor since. With their lyrical lines of sex, death, and reptiles; their aura of profundity; their integration of psychedelic jazz, rock, and blues; and Jim Morrison's charismatic long-haired and leathered posing, the Doors left an impact that a quarter century hence has yet to fade.

Morrison (vocals) and Ray Manzarek (keyboards) attended UCLA film school together in the mid-1960s. "We hung out together and became friends," Manzarek told Sandy Stert Benjamin in *Goldmine*. "At the time of graduation, Jim said he was going to New York to pursue a career in avant-garde experimental film." Six weeks later, while Ray was sitting on a beach in Venice, California, who happens along but James Douglas Morrison. He'd had a change of mind and laid about writing songs instead.

"I knew Jim was a poet and he knew I was a musician," Manzarek continued. "So I asked him to sing me something he wrote, and he launched into a verse from 'Moonlight Drive.' When I heard those words, I said, 'Holy cow! This is incredible.'"

On the spot, Manzarek suggested the two form a rock band. And right there, Morrison suggested the band be called the Doors, after a line in a William Blake poem and the title of Aldous Huxley's book about his mescaline experiences, *The Doors of Perception*. John Densmore (drums) and Robby Krieger (guitar)—both members of a group, the Psychedelic Rangers, and a Maharishi Mahesh Yogi meditation class attended by Manzarek—were enlisted.

By the summer of 1966 they were the house band at the Whiskey-A-Go-Go, ending four months later when owners objected to Morrison's parent-slayer song, "The End." By this point, Elektra Records had signed the act. Their debut album and second single, "Light My Fire," each topped the pop charts in 1967. Until the end four years later, the Lizard King and his band charted well with everything issued. Morrison became an idol, noted for his eccentric, sensuous, rebellious, and disorderly behavior.

Morrison turned attention to writing poetry, collaborating with Michael McClure on a screenplay and directing a play. After the release of *L.A. Woman*, Morrison took an extended leave of absence from the group. With Pamela, his wife, Morrison moved to Paris, where he died of a heart attack in July 1971.

"When Morrison took off for Paris, the Doors were not through," claimed Manzarek. "We were just a band on an extended vacation," he said. "Still are."

KEY RECORDINGS: *The Doors* (1967), *Strange Days* (1967), *Waiting for the Sun* (1968), *The Soft Parade* (1969), *Morrison Hotel* (1970), *L.A. Woman* (1971); "Light My Fire" (1967), "People Are Strange" (1967), "Hello, I Love You" (1968), "Love Her Madly" (1971), "Riders on the Storm" (1971).

DR. JOHN

Utilizing the visual persona of Dr. John Creaux the Night Trip-per, the alleged nineteenth-century New Orleans King of Voodoo, Malcolm "Mac" John Rebennack, Jr., concocted a fren-zied and yet to cease musical melting pot of creole soul and psychedelic rock and roll.

Rebennack (b. November 21, 1940, New Orleans, piano, guitar, bass) grew up surrounded by music. The family had a grand piano, and Rebennack's Uncle John and Aunt Odetta of-ten would have jam sessions with local musicians.

"I took guitar lessons formally—maybe two, three years—under studio cats like Walter ['Papoose'] Nelson, Ralph Montell, and Paul and Al Bowman," says John. "Never learned to read music; I just watched.

"Word of mouth got me in to making records. Montell and 'Papoose' let me sit in on [commercial] jingle dates that they didn't want to do, see. One thing led to another, and I started doing sessions for Chess Records and some of the other labels that didn't mind using me."

By the mid-fifties, Rebennack was doing sessions for small independent labels, writing tunes, arranging, producing, and touring in support bands for Joe Tex, Jerry "Lights Out" Byrne, Professor Longhair, and second cousin Frankie Ford. Some overlooked solo sides as Mac Rebennack were issued by Rex, A.F.O., and Ace.

Rebennack, after a shooting incident Christmas Eve 1961 that left one finger severely injured, switched from guitar to keyboards as his predominant instrument. With the session scene in New Orleans largely shut down by 1962, he moved to the West Coast to continue his behind-the-scenes recording activities, working for Sonny Bono, H. B. Barnum, and Phil Spector.

Rebennack, a member of Phil Spector's legendary "Wall of Sound" sessions responsible for such girl-group classics as the Ronettes' "Be My Baby" and the Crystals' "He's a Rebel," didn't like the recordings. "I thought they was paddin' the payrolls or something," says John. "I didn't realize they were using five piano players and six guitar guys cause it was something they dug."

With the help of producer "Dr. Battiste of Scorpio of bass clef," "Dr. Poo Pah Doo," and others, Rebennack came up with an otherworldly musical concoction and visual conception known as Dr. John Creaux the Night Tripper. In 1968, Atco Records issued the results as *Gris-Gris*.

The album cover visuals were far-out, even for the times. The Night Tripper was conceived to be the self-proclaimed "Grand Zombie," complete with witch-doctor digs, weirdly feathered headdresses, and as later airbrushed out of the debut disc's cover, a finely rolled marijuana joint.

The Summer of Love had happened. Love-ins and mind-expanding drugs were everywhere. The album sold well. But Rebennack didn't approve. "I thought I was doing something that was against all that. When I did the record I never had any idea that it would get denoted as something psychedelic. But most of the gigs we picked up were a result of that association; you know, psychedelic-type joints, be-ins and all that.

"I didn't like that psychedelic music. I thought it was real jive. It didn't have any hip rhythms, and maybe with just a few exceptions like Jimi Hendrix, there wasn't anything happenin' with the music. It was a lot of excuses for long extended jams that wasn't goin' nowhere. I got real bad vibes about it all. I thought we was doin' a parody on the scene and people just took us as bein' it. Nobody ever saw us for the parody that we thought we was."

With some spiritual guidance from Eric Clapton and Mick Jagger, two further musical trips were made to the other side— *Babylon* and *Remedies. The Sun, Moon, and Herbs* returned the good doctor to the charts. *Gumbo* did even better. The "Grand Zombie" was turnin' 'em on and gathering a hippie-trippy following, whether he liked it or not. All he needed was a hit single to consolidate his base. And with "Right Place, Wrong Time," a track cut with the Meters/the Neville brothers as accompanists, Dr. John had it made.

"I had that line about the right place and all in my songbook since 'bout 1959, but I couldn't come up with anything to put it together. I guess, ha, I was in the right place, but it musta been the wrong time, you know?"

With "Right Place" in the charts, the doc was told to get commercial-sounding. "We really wanted to do something fresh that no one else was doin'. So, we got into experimentin', and as a result they weren't knocked out with it. Due to that they fired me as an artist."

John picked up his gumbos and conqueror roots and all and made a number of largely one-off LPs for Columbia (as part of the Michael Bloomfield–John Paul Hammond Triumvirate), United Artists, DJM, Horizon, Demon, Street Wise, and Clean Cuts. In 1993, Dr. John's *Back to New Orleans* album won a Grammy Award for Best Ethnic Album.

Despite all the offbeat albums, Dr. John is probably best known to mainstream Americans as the heavy singin' that Popeye's Chicken jingle. "I got no problem with that," says John. "They're using the same jingle I wrote when they started out in New Orleans years ago. Those jingles kept my kids in school. If it wasn't for them, I'd be scufflin' like a dawg."

KEY RECORDINGS: *Gris-Gris* (1968), *Babylon* (1969), *Gumbo* (1972), *In the Right Place* (1973), *Desitively Bonaroo* (1974), *City Lights* (1978), *Dr. John Plays Mac Rebennack* (1981), *The Brightest Smile in Town* (1983), *Back to New Orleans* (1993); "I Walk on Gilded Splinters" (1968), "Iko Iko" (1972), "Right Place, Wrong Time" (1973), "Such a Night" (1973).

IAN DURY & THE BLOCKHEADS

He sang "I dribble when I nibble and I quibble when I scribble" in the funk tune "Spasticus (Autisticus)." And because he was Ian Dury (b. May 12, 1942), there was a chance it would be heard.

For a thin slice of time in the late 1970s, Dury—the short, slightly crippled survivor of a childhood bout with polio—stood at the height of celebrity in his native England. An art teacher who had shifted to rock and roll at age twenty-nine and then spent six years in pubs and clubs with a rowdy crew called Kilburn and the High Roads, singer-songwriter Dury had initially issued a memorable but unsuccessful single called "Sex & Drugs & Rock & Roll." A debut album—*New Boots and Panties!!*, which grooved with ebullient R&B and tales of working-class oddballs—then broke Dury to the public in the midst of the burgeoning new-wave movement.

Thereafter he was embraced by countrymen as a beloved spinner of skewed witticisms with a touch of the grotesque, a kind of mutant vaudevillian backed by a band of loony but able groovemeisters dubbed the Blockheads.

Idiosyncrasy and punkishness anchored Dury's appeal. But people also sensed that underneath, he was a self-effacing, warm, and likable sort. That, along with his overall enthusiasm and often cozy, whimsical humor and wordplay, made him especially endearing.

The regionalism of his lyrics—and perhaps the English music-hall tinge in his sound—never quite tempted the Yank mainstream, where his undiluted Cockney accent made him— as Mick Farren of the protopunk band the Deviants once put it—"a candidate for subtitles." But the stateside punk explosion ensured that a healthy cult contingent would be inclined toward his weirder aspects—the freakishness, the antiheroism, the shock-and-roll touches.

When the heyday ended—after "Hit Me with Your Rhythm Stick" left the top spot on the British charts and a couple of LPs failed to match the acceptance of the first—Dury successfully diversified into TV and movie acting. He also wrote a musical, *Apples*, that had a run in London in 1989.

The "Spasticus (Autisticus)" song—released in 1981 and rejected as a contribution to the U.N.'s Year of the Disabled— never did make it past the BBC and radio censors. But that mattered little to hardcore Block-heads, whose Dury-directed affection, if not their numbers, remained undiminished.

"There's always one person on every gig who does your secret sign to you," Dury once murmured to *Melody Maker*'s Brian Case. "They come up afterwards and get hold of you—always here, on the elbow, where it's really secure—and go, '*I know*.'"

KEY RECORDINGS: *New Boots and Panties!!* (1977), *Do It Yourself* (1979), *Laughter* (1980), *Lord Upminster* (1981), *4,000 Weeks' Holiday* (1984), *Apples* (1989); "Sex & Drugs & Rock & Roll" (1977), "Hit Me with Your Rhythm Stick" (1978), "Spasticus (Autisticus)" (1981).

JOE ELY

He's packed honky-tonks and nightclubs from coast to coast, opened for the Clash and Merle Haggard, guested with Bruce Springsteen and personal icon Jerry Lee Lewis, and received rave reviews for nearly everything he's ever recorded, though none of it has sold a lick. Joe Ely is caught on the categorical fence—too rock for country folk and too country for rock-and-rollers—and die-hard Ely addicts like it fine that way.

Ely was born in 1947 in Amarillo, Texas, raised in Lubbock, and spent his later teen years hopping trains, hitchhiking, drifting, and dreaming.

"I constantly reflect on the moment it all began. The vision is so vivid," explains Ely of the mystical meeting with his calling. "It was at this automotive dealership in Amarillo; a Pontiac dealer. FREE HOT DOGS FOR THE KIDS, the sign read. Dust was blowin' forty miles an hour. My dad an' I wore bandannas over our faces. You could hardly see this wild guy up there on a flatbed trailer. It was Jerry Lee Lewis; just him an' a piano. I can't never forget this madman wailin' and playin' in this dust storm. His mike keep blowin' over and he keep pickin' it up and screamin'. I knew that instant that I needed to be like this lunatic."

By 1972, Ely had befriended fellow songsmiths Jimmie Dale Gilmore and Butch Hancock and formed a short-lived flaky folk band called the Flatlanders. A Lubbock deejay put them in touch with famed producer, iconoclast, and current owner of Sun Records, Shelby Singleton. One eerie, otherworldly album was issued, eight-track only and in very limited numbers.

"Fifty copies were put out," says Ely. "We were different, loose and crude. Stevie Wesson played saw. We sounded like a flying saucer landing."

Ely and company toured some but received no royalties or even session pay and soon disbanded. "After that I got the rambling itch," Ely adds, "and went around the country with an acoustic guitar, making up songs, and spending about six months in New York City just singing up on the streetcorners, down in subway stations, and over on the Staten Island Ferry." After a quick run as a hand with the Ringling Bros. Circus in 1974, a janitor's job, and a stint as a fruit-picker, Ely was hit with a career-changing thought while slurpin' a soda in a drugstore.

" 'I need to go home,' I thought, 'and I need a band.' I had all these songs I'd written; so I just called up some old buddies of mine and we started working the bars around Lubbock."

Ely and crew started amassing a huge local following, and word spread back to Nashville and the offices of MCA Records. The time must've seemed right. The "outlaw" crop—Waylon, Willie, David Allan Coe, and Hank Williams, Jr.—was scoring country hits, as were even the pop-based Olivia Newton John and John Denver.

MCA signed Ely. His well-thought-out lyrics and eclectic Texas blend of country, rock, blues, Cajun, Mexican, and whatnot seemed ideal for the tremendous crossover possibilities now offered acts in pop and country.

Three albums were issued. Sales were disappointing, but something was happening. Robert Christgau, a *Village Voice* critic, proclaimed, "There hasn't been anything like this since Gram Parsons," and *Stereo Review*'s John Swenson wrote, "This is about as good as country-rock playing gets."

While on a European tour in '79, the Clash showed up backstage at a couple of Ely's performances. "I was really surprised," says Ely. "I had heard of them but I had never gotten around to see what was going on in London in modern rock 'n' roll." The Clash took Ely around, and when they were in the States on their first tour, Ely reciprocated. The following year the Clash invited Ely over to tour with them on their *London Calling* outing. During this tour, Ely recorded a no-frills, rock-oriented live album, *Live Shots*.

Country listeners shuddered. "It was the kiss of death," Ely says. "I don't have hits. I'm not in the spotlight. But it's all right. People tell me I've influenced a lot of the younger country singers and I'm very grateful that I get to keep on doing whatever I'm doing."

KEY RECORDINGS: *Joe Ely* (1977), *Honky Tonk Masquerade* (1978), *Down on the Drag* (1979), *Musta Notta Gotta Lotta* (1981), *Live Shots* (1981), *Lord of the Highway* (1987), *Dig All Night* (1988), *Live at Liberty Lunch* (1990), *Love & Danger* (1994); "All My Love" (1972).

BRIAN ENO

"Look, I'm not a musician," Brian Eno told *Musician* magazine's Lester Bangs. "If you like what I do, it stands in defiance to that."

He's the apostle of art rock; the creator of a whole subgenre of pre–New Age sounds, variously called ambient or sound-

Roberta Bayley

scape music. And while a tremendous influence on pop music for the last quarter century, Eno is chart-free, never selling many records. He's a "rock star" who never tours, a serious composer who is incapable of reading music, a synthesizer player who hates his instrument.

Raised in Woodbridge, Suffolk, England, he was born Brian Peter George St. John de Baptiste de la Salle Eno, May 15, 1948. His early years were spent near a U.S. Air Force base, where he was exposed to rock and roll. While interested in music, Eno never got down to learning how to play an instrument, preferring to paint and draw. In the mid to late sixties, Eno attended the Convent of Jesus and Mary at St. Joseph's College and Winchester and Ipswich art schools.

Inspired by serious composers Cornelius Cardew, John Tilbury, Christian Wolff, and Morton Feldman, Eno began messing with tape recorders and modifying sounds; his first experiments involved striking a metal lampshade, then slowing down the tape and having associates read poetry as a voiceover. For a moment he performed with the Portsmouth Sinfonia, a full concert orchestra made up of improvising musical illiterates, and in a rock band called Maxwell's Demon.

"Avant-garde music," he told *Q*'s Robert Sandall, "is sort of research music. You're glad someone's done it but you don't necessarily want to listen to it."

By accident, in 1971, Eno met saxophonist Andy Mackay on a subway train. They had met previously at a musical event at Reading University. Mackay talked of wanting to make a demo of Roxy Music, a new group that he was a part of. Eno agreed to drop by and help with the recording. A synthesizer was present, Eno touched it and was asked to join the band. "Roxy Music was a rock band with a rather peculiar perspective," Eno told Sandall. "It was all about creating a collage of popular cultural elements. And it was a group based on a complete confusion of musical personalities."

After Roxy Music's second album, *For Your Pleasure . . .* , in 1973, Eno departed for further auditory experimentations that have yet to subside. As "treatment artist," producer, or "musician," Brian Eno has worked with Robert Fripp, Robert Wyatt, separately with Velvet Underground's John Cale and Nico, on three albums each for David Bowie and the Talking Heads, with David Byrne solo, on both Ultravox's and Devo's debut discs, with Hawkwind's Robert Calvert, and on Phil Manzanera's *801* and U2's Grammy-winning *Joshua Tree*.

A true believer in the power of doing things improperly, Eno told Sandall: "I'm interested in making things with the wrong people or the wrong tools."

KEY RECORDINGS: *Here Come the Warm Jets* (1973), *Taking Tiger Mountain (By Strategy)* (1974), *Another Green World* (1975), *Before and After Science* (1977), *Music for Airports* (1979), *More Blank Than Frank* (1986), *Desert Island Selection* (1989).

ESQUERITA

"I was in Dallas with my backup band and a beautician," Esquerita told Miriam Linna in *Spin*, "and a white woman done fainted! She looked at me and said *'Lawdy,'* and down she went. I asked, 'How come she fainted? I don't look that bad, do I?' And they said, 'Esquerita, it's the first time they've seen anything like you.'"

It was the late fifties, and Esquerita was like a rock and roll groovy from a bad B movie—dangerously out of control, time, and touch—just too damn much for nearly anybody. He was huge, nearly seven feet in patent-leather Cuban heels, mile-high pompadour, wraparound rhinestone-studded sunglasses, and lacy things real fifties men only bought for their mistresses.

In the early fifties, he first spotted Little Richard, then billed as Princess Lavonne. Richard's red sequined gown, wig, and makeup left a permanent impression on Esquerita. They forged their relationship in the Macon Greyhound Bus Terminal, where Esquerita was selling blessed bread with a preacher named Sister Rosa.

Said Richard of this magic meeting, in the Charles White biography: "Esquerita and me went up to my house and he got on my piano. He had the biggest hands of anybody I'd seen. I said, 'Hey, how do you do that?' and he says, 'I'll teach you.' And that's when I really started playing. He's one of the greatest pianists, and that's including Jerry Lee Lewis, Stevie Wonder, or anybody I've ever heard. He really taught me a lot."

He was born Esker Reeder, Jr., in Greenville, South Carolina. He fiddled on neighbors' keyboards, took lessons for a while, and by age nine or ten he was playing in church and accompanying a female trio called the Three Stars. In his teens he lived in Brooklyn and was a member of a gospel group, the Heavenly Echoes. It's his piano banging that is heard on their lone single for Baton.

It was while hitting the keys at the Owl Club back in Greenville that he was "discovered" by Paul Peek, guitarist with Gene Vincent's Blue Caps. Peek, blown away by Esquerita's torrid sounds, told Vincent of this wild man billed as Professor Esker Reeder. With country singer Dave Dudley's supervision, Vincent dashed off a couple of demos on Reeder for his label, Capitol. Reeder became "Esquerita."

Over the next fifteen months, Esquerita and an assortment of Blue Caps laid down the bulk of the wild man's legacy—twenty-eight tracks. Three singles and an album of yells, screams, horn honkings, insipid lyrics, and piano punching were issued by Capitol; all passed largely unnoticed. Thereafter Reeder was reduced to a number of one- and two-off singles with various independent labels. "The Green Door," recorded as an instrumental under his given name, charted, becoming his only "hit."

By the seventies the travails of Esquerita were becoming legendary first in England, later France; a double-album package was issued there in 1976. After dark times and the recording of four sides for Berry Gordy—yet to be issued—Reeder, calling himself "Mark Malochi," spent the early eighties jailed at Rikers Island.

The legendary Esquerita died of AIDS on October 23, 1986.

KEY RECORDINGS: *Esquerita* (1990); "Oh Baby" (1958), "Rockin' the Joint" (1958), "Laid Off" (1959).

FAIRPORT CONVENTION

They were the first group to integrate British folk music into the electric rock and roll format successfully. Although Fairport Convention rarely charted, even in their homeland, they've continued to the present as nonstop innovators—with a dozen or more different lineups and twenty-some rotating members.

Fairport was formed in North London in 1967 as a quartet: Ashley "Tyger" Hutchings (bass, vocals, guitar) and Simon "Sime" Nicol (banjo, dulcimer, viola, guitar, vocals)—former members in the Ethnic Shuffle Orchestra—plus Richard Thompson (guitar, vocals) and Shaun Frater (drums), soon replaced by Martin Lamble. After a few appearances, Judy Dyble (vocals, piano) and Ian Matthews (né Ian Macdonald, vocals, guitar) were added.

Joe Boyd, an American manager and producer, secured some gigs and a contract. With the release of their self-titled debut album, Dyble was gone to work with the pre–King Crimson group Giles, Giles and Fripp and to form Penguin Dust. Sandy Denny (guitar, vocals, keyboards), her replacement, had sung with the Strawbs. Matthews left in 1969, after *What We Did on Our Holidays*, to form Matthews Southern Comfort—noted for the tribute hit "Woodstock"—and to pursue a still viable solo career. Before the issuance of their first homeland charting album, *Unhalfbricking*, Lamble was killed in a motoring accident; Dave "Swarb" Swarbrick (vocals, violin, mandolin) replaced him.

Fairport Convention's popularity peaked at this point with the release of *Liege & Lief*—critically billed "the definitive British folk-rock album." Denny and Hutchings, disagreeing on the band's direction, both took leave, the former to found Fotheringay, the latter Steeleye Span. With new members Dave "DM" Mattacks (drums, keyboards) and Dave "Peggy" Pegg (bass, vocals) they carried on, well into the 1970s. Thompson left in 1971 to duet with his wife Linda and to establish himself as a premier songwriter and guitarist.

"When you're youngsters, twenty years old, you don't care too much, all you want to do is play your music," said Pegg of the band's little financial gain to *Q*'s Mat Snow. "When Fairport were at their height of their success in '68 to '70, they were each earning twenty-five pounds a week."

The by-then legendary Sandy Denny returned to the fold in

1973 for *Rosie* and in 1974 for the stellar performance *Rising for the Moon*. Denny died in 1978 of head injuries suffered in a fall.

Lineup changes have continued since. Recordings became more sporadic as the group entered the 1980s.

Reunions are now annual forty-eight-hour events in Cropredy, England. "We've survived, we have our place," Nicol told Snow. "We're a big fish in a fairly small pond, but we like it that way."

KEY RECORDINGS: *Fairport Convention* (1968), *What We Did on Our Holidays* (1969), *Unhalfbricking* (1969), *Liege & Lief* (1969), *Full House* (1970), *Angel Delight* (1971), *Babbacombe Lee* (1971), *Rosie* (1973), *Fairport Nine* (1973), *Gladys' Leap* (1986); "Si Tu Dois Partir" (1969).

MARIANNE FAITHFULL

From naive-sounding folk-pop and the *"Umbrellas of Cherbourg Love Theme"* to the stark, war-torn rock vocals and X-rated vitriol of *Broken English*—that's the vast distance traveled by Marianne Faithfull.

Fresh out of convent school at age seventeen, Faithfull (b. December 29, 1946, London) caught the eye of Rolling Stones manager Andrew Loog Oldham at a party. He invited her to a recording session. She agreed, showed up, and recorded the Jagger-Richards song "As Tears Go By" in a thirty-minute session. The song became a hit, Faithfull became Mick Jagger's girlfriend, and for the latter part of the sixties she ran with the Stones in a free-form stumble through the drug-drenched, glittering corridors of swinging London.

There were several innocuous, folk-infused Marianne Faithfull albums along the way, and a couple of acting roles. But a 1969 drug overdose/suicide attempt, a breakup with Jagger, a divorce from husband John Dunbar, and a battle with heroin ad-

Marianne Faithfull

diction brought it all to a halt. Dropping out, she left behind the dim image of a mere Rolling Stones footnote, a pop minor-leaguer shaped by others. "It was like all the work that was done was nothing to do with me," she told J. D. Considine of *Buzz.*

Faithfull's own cult-acclaimed moment came a full ten years later with *Broken English,* one of rock's standout comebacks— a career jump-starter that she still calls her "masterpiece." Unexpectedly, it revealed not the mythic sixties innocent but a damaged-yet-intact survivor of a long stretch of bad road, her voice now travel-weary and raw and her songs shot through with lacerating bitterness. Life and art seemed inescapably intertwined on the disc: on tracks like "Why'd Ya Do It?" a brutal rant about sexual betrayal, the cracked vocal, harsh sounds, and tacit autobiography all commingled, yielding a brain-searing acid bath of authentic psychodrama.

The catharsis, however, was all the listener's. "The whole thing was still too cloudy with pain and anger and pride and chemicals," said Faithfull. "It didn't really go anywhere, for me. There was no kind of real healing done. It was good for me but it really, in the end, it was just the same."

Recovery continued; Faithfull became a respected post-punk torch singer, a rock doyenne. A string of albums followed, none more acclaimed than 1990's *Blazing Away,* a retrospective live set that included—in a bit of "Thanks for the Memories" nostalgia—a rendition of her 1969 Jagger–Richards collaboration, "Sister Morphine." "Maybe the most you can expect from a relationship that goes bad," she wrote in her 1994 autobiography, "is to come out of it with a few good songs."

KEY RECORDINGS: *Marianne Faithfull* (1965), *Broken English* (1979), *Dangerous Acquaintances* (1981), *A Child's Adventure* (1983), *Strange Weather* (1987), *Blazing Away* (1990); "As Tears Go By" (1964), "Come and Stay with Me" (1965), "Working Class Hero" (1979), "Why'd Ya Do It?" (1979), "Sister Morphine" (1990).

THE FALL

Out of Manchester, England, fell Mark E. Smith (b. March 5, 1957) and his creation the Fall, the band embraced by fanatical followers as the real item in beyond-the-fringe noise-rock circles. They're "the one punk band that never reneged on the promise," according to the *Village Voice*; "the only one that's created its own sound-world," per England's *Melody Maker*; the ones who droned on long after less committed acts nodded out, in the view of partisans.

In true cult-band fashion, the Fall escaped mainstream notice by being a bit too idiosyncratic—unlistenable, to resisters—which in their case meant teetering always toward the avant-garde edge while anchoring their sound to a populist beat.

But sonic Fall-out has been absorbed over the years across a wide swath of the rock landscape, helping to spawn such mutant forms as industrial punk, thrash metal, hardcore, aggrodrone, and grunge.

"I like music primitive," Smith once said to *Musician*'s John

Leland. "I like it experimental." And with the exception of some forays into skewed, near-melodic material, "experimental" is pretty much the way it's been through several lengthy career phases.

It was in 1977 that he first loosed its grinding dissonance, wrapping the sound around his vocal signature of spoken/chanted cryptic-poetic declamations marked by occasional shrieks, end-of-phrase hiccups, and other uttered oddities. With that as the nucleus, the Fall tried different coatings. From record to record, they dragged in scraps and bits from all sectors of the rock junk heap—garage, metal, disco, funk—using them all to their own often cacophanous ends. In a wink, the band—at first a quartet of keys, guitar, bass, and drums behind Smith—attracted fierce phalanxes of anarchy-enamored Fall-people. Popularity centered in England, but with the odd pocket elsewhere—Iceland and New Zealand, for example.

In 1983 Smith met Laura Salinger—a.k.a. Brix—in a Chicago bar. They argued at first. Then they married. She joined the band, for what would be a lengthy initial stint. Many, remembering the Fall's former Smith-led autocracy, cite this as a period of relatively democratic productivity. With Brix adding brittle guitar and a contrasting vocal melodicism, and with new material mating her music with Smith's verse, the sound bridged the discordant and the accessible. "Pat—Trip Dispenser," from a 1984 twelve-inch 45, dispensed a dense, plodding groove—suggesting Hendrix on a downer—interrupted by a Beefheart-angular guitar figure and then some jagged-metal guitar slashings. "C.R.E.E.P.," from the same disc, is an apparent play off pop pap, Brix shouting and spelling out the title in teenybopping Bay City Rollers style. "No Bulbs" from 1984 notes grim bummers in a lightless flat ("when your home is a trash mound," Smith sings) against a hypno-driving back-groove.

The Fall's personnel changed constantly. Its members over the years have included early guitarist Martin Bramah and keyboardist Una Baines (both later to form Blue Orchids), longtime drummer Karl Burns, other drummers Paul Hanley and the recent Simon Wolstencroft, guitarist Craig Scanlon, and guitarist/synthesist Simon Rogers.

Brix Smith (who at one time said of Smith, "He's a genius; no one else can write words like he can") herself bowed out in 1989 as both Smith wife and Fall collaborator.

Undeterred, the Fall continued to issue discs to its ever-receptive but still narrow public, Mark Smith's reputation spilling over into "serious" performance art circles via the late-eighties production of his play, *Hey! Luciani*, and music written for an experimental dance piece.

In summer 1994, Brix returned to active Fall duty.

KEY RECORDINGS: *Live at the Witch Trials* (1979), *Grotesque (After the Gramme)* (1980), *Perverted by Language* (1983), *The Wonderful and Frightening World of the Fall* (1984), *This Nation's Saving Grace* (1985), *Domesday Pay-Off* (1987), *Seminal Live* (1989), *Extricate* (1990), *Code: Selfish* (1992), *The Infotainment Scan* (1993), *Middle Class Revolt* (1994); "Repetition" (1977), "C.R.E.E.P." (1984).

FEELIES

Told of their inclusion in *Cult Rockers* and of the planet still being populated with needy Feelie fans, guitarist, songwriter, cofrontman, and founding Feelie Glenn Mercer responds, "Really."

They were born in the punk era, but played quirky rhythms and mumbled nonsense lyrics over frantically strummed guitar noises. Post-punk is what pundits called their sound. "Really," says Mercer. "I don't know what it was." Suggests Mercer: "Psychedelic surf rock?"

Mercer and fellow frontman-guitarist-songwriter Bill Clayton (a.k.a. Bill Million) met while attending high school in Haledon, New Jersey, in the late sixties. In 1976, with the DeNunzio brothers, Keith (a.k.a. Keith Clayton) and Vinny—bass and drums respectively—they formed the Feelies, a name for a virtual reality–like movie device utilized in Aldous Huxley's *Brave New World*. Vinny left, and for a while drummer extraordinaire Andy Fisher (a.k.a. Anton Fier)—later of the Electric Eels, Lounge Lizards, and the Golden Palominos—filled in.

Numerous recordings were cut but not released by Ork Records. Stiff Records of England commissioned the self-produced album *Crazy Rhythms*. Critics fell over themselves praising the product, but sales were minimal. Stiff wasn't pleased, and the Feelies were without a label. "They were promoting the label more than they did us," says Mercer of their meager commercial showing. "They actually sold more T-shirts than records and were proud of it."

For the next six years the Feelies seemed to have vanished. "We never disbanded," says Mercer. "Really. We just sort of got into other projects." In 1981, Mercer and Million composed music for the flick *Smithereens*. Mercer began playing with the Trypes, a sixties-type band made up of old high school buddies. Million later joined; both soon concurrently performed with the Willies and Yung Wu. Other projects reportedly included Dr. Robert, Foggy Notion, and Mr. Baxton. Says Mercer of the group diversification, "The various bands gave us a way to experiment. Besides, they were fun."

In 1986, the Feelies, as a group, returned with the Peter Buck–produced *The Good Earth*. Two major-label albums were issued by 1991, after which the group disbanded.

KEY RECORDINGS: *Crazy Rhythms* (1980), *The Good Earth* (1986), *Only Life* (1988), *Time for a Witness* (1991); "Raised Eyebrows" (1979).

THE FLAMIN' GROOVIES

"They have been and remain the very picture of a cult band, ignored by the world at large, but positively revered by a small but discerning group of loyal fans," wrote rock critic Carl Cafarelli.

For nearly three decades the Flamin' Groovies were out of step and marching to their own drummer. The rock media labeled and dismissed them as anachronisms, revivalists, and worse. "It's amazing to me that any of this [music] is looked upon as nostalgia," frontman Cyril Jordan told Cafarelli of *Goldmine*, in defense of Groovie turf. "Whether we're doin' the DC5 [Dave Clark 5] or the Beatles it's the greatest stuff that's ever come down the pike. This is timeless music."

In 1965, Roy A. Loney (vocals, guitar) and Tim Lynch (guitar), both folkies in the Camptown Singers, decided to form a Bay Area rock and roll outfit. Jordan (vocal, guitar, mellotron), George Alexander (bass, vocals), and Ron Greco (drums) were added, and born was the Chosen Few.

The name sucked, all agreed. "One day, I was stoned on acid," said Jordan of the birth of the group's new moniker, "and I was running around the house just saying 'Groovy!' to everything."

With the peace and love scene still happening in San Francisco in 1968, the Groovies were forced into self-promotion to exist. *Sneakers*, their self-produced, pressed, and hand-delivered ten-inch sold 2,000 copies. Epic Records was impressed and issued *Supersnazz* and "Rockin' Pneumonia and the Boogie Woogie Flu." Neither received much notice outside of the Midwest. *Flamingo* and *Teenage Head* likewise sold poorly though pundits trembled with delight, and the Groovies' fan following grew.

In 1971 Lynch was arrested for drugs and draft evasion. Loney later left to form the Phantom Movers. With a move to England by the remaining members, phase one—the manic fifties-oriented period—of Groovie history was complete.

After a one-off single for Greg Shaw's Bomp, the Groovies were discovered by Dave Edmunds and given a second airing by Sire Records. With James Farrell (guitar), Chris Wilson (vocals, guitar, harp), Beatle boots, velvet jackets, and remakes of Beatles, Byrds, and Stones cuts, the Flamin' Groovies finally found a more receptive home in England. Three albums and numerous singles followed. Nothing sold particularly well here, there, or anywhere.

"The idea was always to ape the Beatles," explains Wilson. "We were good, but we never were what was happening at the moment. If we goofed, it was that we did too many cover versions. We didn't trust our own songwriting abilities."

A limited-edition album was issued in 1986. By that point nearly all members but Jordan and Alexander were gone. At decade's end the flame went out, and there were Groovies no more.

"There's magic in our music," says Chris Wilson, phase two Groovies guitarist. "It's sloppy, mixed poorly, and we coulda tightened some lyrics, but we still got a hundred thousand fans that want us back."

KEY RECORDINGS: *Supersnazz* (1969), *Flamingo* (1970), *Teenage Head* (1971), *Shake Some Action* (1976), *Now* (1978), *Jumpin' in the Night* (1979); "Teenage Head" (1971), "You Tore Me Down" (1974).

FLIPPER

"As a member of Flipper, I live in an insane little world," drummer Steve DePace told Chuck Cristafulli in *BAM*. "I could never say my life is boring."

The four-piece noise-assault band, initially led by two bassist-singer-writers, has antagonized or riled rock fans of many a varied stripe in clubs across the land. It's been a source of pride—to bandmember and Flipper loyalist alike.

Mohawked slamdancers at Flipper's mid-eighties gigs hated the band's medium paces. Others simply fled in disgust and rage. Friendlier forces were seen taking to the stage, passing around Flipper's microphones, grabbing the instruments, or barking new lyrics into the P.A. Flipper seemed not to care, or they offered active encouragement.

In their native San Francisco, where they surfaced in 1979 amid an explosion of post-punk hardcore bands, Flipper stood apart. Others were emitting sound in fast-loud-short bursts of anger. But Flipper—comprising, at the time, DePace plus bassists Bruce Lose and Will Shatter and guitarist Ted Falconi—approached its anarchy with a slower, Grateful Dead-ish, lazy-man kind of looseness.

Tempos were slow, anchored by the heaving, plodding twin fuzz basses. Ever-present were squealing feedback; squalling, chaotic guitar; screaming chants on lyrics like "If I can't be drunk, I don't want to be alive." Song durations stretched into endless, lobotomizing repetition.

The band issued records of this stuff on the left-field Subterranean label through much of the eighties. They scored cult points (not chart hits) with such fare as "(There's No Place as Bad As) Southern California" and "Life" (chorus: "Life is the only thing worth living for"). A 1986 live album had a Flipperish extra: its jacket unfolded into an "On Tour" board game—a cartoon of the U.S. as a land mass of urban decay, toxic waste dumps, nuclear test sites, Bible-toting book burners, armed survivalists, and weird cult members.

Against that psycho-setting, Flipper pursued its real-life road trip right up to Shatter's death of a heroin overdose in 1987. The surviving members then submerged themselves in normal, day-job life, remaining furtively incognito for the next five years.

They returned in 1993 to find that antagonism toward Flipper hadn't waned. "It's great to be hated intensely," said a relieved DePace. "We get people very upset," added Lose. "It's nice to know we've still got the knack."

KEY RECORDINGS: *Album*—*Generic Flipper* (1982), *Gone Fishin'* (1984), *Public Flipper Limited Live 1980–1985* (1986), *Sex Bomb Baby!* (1988), *American Grafishy* (1993); "Love Canal" (1980), "Ha Ha Ha" (1980), "Sex Bomb" (1982), "Flipper Twist" (1993).

ROBERT FRIPP

Rock Research and Development. Experimental Division. Frippertronics Project. Output: One "small, self-sufficient, mobile, intelligent unit"—Robert Fripp—periodically released to surface world to "work in the marketplace" and test new ideas about music and performing. Objective: Expand the creative and economic parameters of rock and roll and promote sanity and reason in a field marked by "madness," anti-intellectualism, and "wholly false values."

Master plans, grand schemes, and a matrix of rationales and

theories have bolstered British guitarist-composer Fripp's major career moves, including a long-term musical-political-philosophical campaign to effect change in the music industry. His forays have largely slipped past the radar sensors of the mass media, but Fripp himself—as guitar guru, solo avant-gardist, and revered brain-rock pioneer—is all but guaranteed a slot in the rock firmament, somewhere amid the Enos, Zappas, and other boundary benders.

Groomed to take over his father's real-estate firm, Fripp (b. 1946) first attracted notice as a musician for his catalytic role in the heavy-progressive band King Crimson. Starting in 1969, he guided that intermittently active act through various lineups and evolving sounds, from mellotron-soaked sonic epics on the first album to adventurous, pan-ethnic energy blasts in the early eighties.

"One of the ideas that was important to me," Fripp told *Creem*'s Richard Grabel, "was that you could be a rock musician without censoring your intelligence. Rock music has a very anti-intellectual stance, and I didn't see why I should act dumb." Fripp has railed about music-industry control, "madness in the marketplace," the rock-stardom thing in which large-scale shows separate performer from audience and encourage passivity, false adulation, "vampirism."

His answer to the problem began to take shape around the time of Crimson's first extended layoff. In 1974, Fripp vowed to continue in music as a "self-sufficient, mobile unit." It was in part to survive what he told *Rolling Stone*'s Ian Dove would be "a decade of considerable panic in the 1990s—collapse on a colossal scale . . . [that would make the Depression era] look like a Sunday outing."

The self-propelled Fripp Unit entered the market in 1979 on an international "antitour" of museums, record stores, pizza parlors, and small clubs. The odyssey launched the first of several announced three-year "campaigns" in the marketplace, this one called the Drive to 1981—the Year of the Fripp. In this first phase he would explore his "political and economic theory of the industry"; test alternative "ways of relating to the audience, new places to play"; and experiment with Frippertronics and Discotronics. Hypnotic in sound, the Frippertronic technique—developed by ambient-sonicist Brian Eno—allowed Fripp to record layers of guitar melody into hooked-up tape decks, have them play back repeatedly, and then create soaring improvisations over the result.

The album *Exposure* was the first artifact of Campaign Phase One, which ended—on schedule, in 1981—with his Discotronic dance-rock band the League of Gentlemen. Fripp described his next three-year marketing phase as "discipline, my first step on the incline to 1984." It evolved—not as planned—into a new edition of King Crimson (their first album of this period titled *Discipline*).

With its demise, Fripp instituted Guitar Craft, a mode of instruction that's attracted hundreds of student-disciples over the years, and which he's called "more akin to yoga than formal guitar technique. Actually an approach to living." A Guitar Craft performing group, the League of Crafty Guitarists, spins out mesmerizing audio abstractions using acoustic—not electric—guitars. "The electric guitar is an instrument of schizophrenia," Fripp explained to *Musician*'s Ted Drozdowski. ". . . it's schizo-phonic." Another offshoot: the California Guitar Trio, heard with Chapman stick player Trey Gunn (the "stick" is a stringed "touchboard" fingered with two hands) on Fripp's 1994 *String Quartet* album.

Outside Craft, Crimson, and the Unit, Fripp has turned up on duo discs with Eno and guitar colorist Andy Summers; as guitar soloist with David Bowie and vocal group the Roches; as a producer; and in collaboration with his wife, singer Toyah Willcox.

Final Fripp Unit observation: "It helps to have it dressed in Spandex."

KEY RECORDINGS: *Exposure* (1979), *Under Heavy Manners/ God Save the Queen* (1980), *Let the Power Fall* (1981), *Network* (EP, 1985), *Robert Fripp String Quartet* (1994); **with Brian Eno**—*No Pussyfooting* (1973), *Evening Star* (1975); **with the League of Gentlemen**—*The League of Gentlemen* (1981); **with Andy Summers**—*I Advanced Masked* (1982), *Bewitched* (1984); **with the League of Crafty Guitarists**—*Live!* (1986); **with Toyah and Fripp**—*The Lady or the Tiger* (1986); **with Sunday All Over the World**—*Kneeling at the Shrine* (1991).

FUGAZI

They sound like open warfare. Or peak activity at a construction site, with pumping jackhammers, pummeling pile drivers, and a frenzied foreman ranting over the top. Such noise is Fugazi's main sonic building block. They arrange it, shape it, modulate it. They stop it on a dime, leaving chasms of silence.

They contrast it with scraps of melody or moments of soft sound, building back to a cathartic roar of blaring, distorted guitars and cataclysmic rhythm.

Refiners of the faster-louder post-punk style called hardcore, the four-man Fugazi backs its decibels with a populist ethic, avowed social activism, and disdain for the rules of the mainstream music business. They issue albums on frontman Ian MacKaye's own independent Dischord label, sell well into six figures with each release, and refuse to sign with the majors. "We're just not interested," MacKaye said in *Spin* magazine. "There's nothing the labels can offer us that would be worth the loss of control over our own music." True to their anti-commercial word, they sell their albums at low prices and won't play at clubs that exclude minors or charge more than five dollars a ticket. Such practices have made Fugazi near-heroes in the far fringes of the rock underground.

Singer-guitarist MacKaye, the son of a *Washington Post* religious editor, had attracted similar notice in the early 1980s as the leader of Minor Threat, a band that defined Washington, D.C.'s hardcore style while also denouncing the scene's drugs-and-violence ethic. Singer-guitarist Guy Picciotto had led the similarly dissenting mid-eighties outfit Rites of Spring. When they merged in Fugazi in 1987 with bassist Joe Lally and drummer Brendan Canty, they embraced the full-frontal intensity of that rock genre and rejected its nihilism, using their songs to vent rage over a range of issues, from exploitation of Native Americans (in "Smallpox Champion") to drug use (in "Shut the Door") to sexual assault (in "Suggestion").

In live shows, a substantial network of Fugazi adherents ensures packed houses, where near-religious fervor fuels throbbing masses of slam-dancers, stage divers, and crowd surfers. That many ignore MacKaye's occasional pleas to "be respectful" and "just act like human beings" (the band discourages slamming and diving) suggests that a conflict between message and mayhem may continue to be an ironic mainstay of the Fugazi attraction.

KEY RECORDINGS: *Fugazi* (EP, 1988), *Margin Walker* (EP, 1989), *Repeater* (1990), *Steady Diet of Nothing* (1991), *In on the Kill Taker* (1993); "Suggestion" (1988), "Waiting Room" (1988), "Shut the Door" (1990), "Reclamation" (1991), "Rend It" (1993), "Smallpox Champion" (1993).

THE FUGS

Despite their inability to sing in key or play an instrument with a minimum of expertise, the Fugs created their own brand of music—porno rock—making offensiveness fashionable. The band broke the moral ground for Zappa's Mothers of Invention, the Stooges, the sixties' flower power, and eons later the anarchy and anger of the punk and rap movements.

Thirty years later, the original recordings of the Fugs slamming social mores and taboos, politics, hippie metaphysics, and rock and roll are still embraced by a swelling under-nation of Fugheads.

"We were freeing everything up. There was nothing subtle about us. We were raising consciousness, warning people to watch out for the bastards of power," explained core Fug Tuli Kupferberg. "No one was talking about masturbation, drug addiction, oral sex, the killings in Vietnam."

Ed Sanders, founder of *Fuck You: A Magazine of the Arts*, opened the Peace Eye Bookstore in a onetime Kosher meat mart in New York's Lower East Side. Kupferberg lived next door above the Lifschutz wholesale egg market. Since the late fifties, the "I Like Ike" era, Kupferberg had operated as a one-man street crusader, printing pamphlets calling for an end to racism and the flowering of free sex.

Tuli and Ed met in late '64, and soon there were the Fugs, a random collection of word-slingers out to shock the respectable community with poetry and satire. After rehearsals at the Peace Eye, the Fugs—a fornicatory euphemism Norman Mailer had

used in his novel *The Naked and the Dead*—began regular performances at the Players Theatre on MacDougal Street in Greenwich Village. Membership fluctuated, but the Fug core included Sanders (vocals), Kupferberg (vocals), and Ken Weaver (vocals, drums); numbered as semi-Fugs were Peter Stampfel and Steve Weber (concurrently billed the Holy Modal Rounders), Charlie Larkey, and "amphetamine flute" players and poets Al Fowler and Szabo.

The idea was totally unique: poets with electric instruments. The *First Album*, issued in 1965 by ESP Records, has been called the first release of what came to be called "underground" music. A second album was rejected by ESP as "too offensive"; *The Fugs* was a substitute release.

With "I Feel Like Homemade Shit," "Boobs a Lot," "I Couldn't Get High," "Coca Cola Douche," and "Kill for Peace" in the Fugs repertoire, the public response was immediate: silence. Mass America never acknowledged the existence of these revolutionary hippie dippies.

In '67, Kupferberg, Sanders, and their Fug-brethren conducted an exorcism of the Pentagon from a flatbed truck.

"We had absolutely no sense or belief that there would be an interest in this stuff thirty years later," Sanders wrote in a recent group biography. "It didn't occur to us at all, otherwise we might have paid more careful attention to recording techniques."

Surprisingly, a major label decided to sign the Fugs. Reprise issued three studio albums and a live package before the group folded. None of their wares proved inoffensive enough to attract approving mainstream attention.

In 1969, the self-proclaimed All-American-Skin-Rock-Peace-Sex-Psychedelic-Tenderness-Society-Group ended.

"We were testosterone-maddened, driven to meet girls, and playing music let us do that," said Sanders. "Besides, we all felt we were geniuses with a message for the world. On a primitive level the Fugs were good. We turned on a bunch of kids to look at the world from a rebel stance. A lot of people were touched by our songs."

Sanders issued a couple of solo albums and went on to write *The Family*, a successful documentation of Charles Manson; *Tales of Beatnik Glory*; and *Chekhov*, a book-length biography in verse. Volumes of poetry have been published, winning Sanders Guggenheim and NEA fellowships. Kupferberg, who wrote the anti-Vietnam text *1001 Ways to Beat the Draft*, formed the Revolting Theatre and became a political cartoonist with works collected in five anthologies. Presently he fronts Tuli and the Fuxxons. Larkey married singer-songwriter Carole King.

KEY RECORDINGS: *The Fugs First Album* (1966, reissue of *The Village Fugs*), *The Fugs* (1966), *Virgin Fugs* (1967), *Tenderness Junction* (1968), *It Crawled into My Hand, Honest* (1968), *The Belle of Avenue A* (1970); "I Couldn't Get High" (1966), "Slum Goddess" (1966).

GRATEFUL DEAD

A splash of color hits a touch-of-grey cityscape: The Deadheads are back in town. And they're not hard to spot. Out on the street, batches of tie-dyed fuzzballs are seen scattering as cops order them to "keep on truckin'." Down in a crowded rush-hour subway, roving packs of patchouli-scented flower kids are given wide berth. Elsewhere, carfuls of "traveling heads" are stopped and strip-searched, the cause for suspicion their skull-motif Deadhead stickers.

So goes the reception for the modern Deadhead in lame corners of the world at large. Today, the power of the hippie flower has mostly faded, now relegated to a torn page in a social history of the sixties or periodically revived as a retro-fashion trend. But wherever Grateful Dead tickets are sold, a brand-new love generation boogies on to its own good-time beat, perpetuating a tradition that dates back, roughly, to 1966. Incredibly, the Deadhead numbers continue to make their favorite performers one of the top concert draws in the world, confounding industry "experts" who bank their futures on more conventional box-office fare.

The Dead are "old, slow, and ugly as sea slugs feeding on fungus," according to the *Village Voice*. They've had but one top-forty tune in nearly three decades. On bad nights, they sound as loose and loopy as a pickup band at a suburban beer blast. Even on good ones, they fall out of any current-trend mold, their signature improvisations—long, sinewy, and evolving—testing the limits of MTV-shortened attention spans.

Yet the following they've amassed over the years—now including the offspring of original Deadheads—is massive indeed. And not every "head" resembles the stereotypical stringy-haired peddler of "doses and crystals" seen skulking on the fringes of a typical gathering. Three-piece suits have been spotted among concert crowds. At least one Republican governor has openly declared his Dead fealty.

The network of Deadheads is as connected and organized as a mini-industry, built on a shared penchant for making, collecting, cataloging, and trading homemade recordings of live shows—with the Dead's blessing. "The 'tapers' are actually a very important aspect of the Deadhead community," says Toni Brown, editor of the Dead-oriented magazine *Relix*.

Hardcore nomads exist. "There's a huge number of traveling Deadheads," Brown reports. "You have the younger kids taking a year off from school, going off and following the Grateful Dead. There is that faction of people who actually have built careers around the Grateful Dead. Everybody's ideal is to make a career of going on the road with the Grateful Dead."

Why? How can it all be? Nobody's certain. But commentators continue to credit the Dead's charismatic combo of sound, durability—and some ineffable mystique. "The Grateful Dead is only fifty percent music," said a loyalist to one Dead doubter. "The other half you will *never* understand."

They were linked in the mid-sixties with Ken Kesey's communal Merry Pranksters and the emerging San Francisco counterculture. Today they're the nucleus of a large assortment of loosely connected musicians, lyricists, visual artists, roadies, spinoff groups, and hangers-on.

Principal players are known by now to all but the most culturally insulated. Jerry Garcia (b. 1942, d. 1995) was the longtime Dead figurehead. From early involvement in jug-band music via Mother McCree's Uptown Jug Champions (with future mates Ron "Pigpen" McKernan, Bob Weir, and lyricist Robert Hunter) and rock in the Warlocks (adding Phil Lesh and Bill Kreutzmann), Garcia fused his quavering, reedy voice and signature guitar style—bubbly, oblique, and busy—into an unmistakable, largely AM radio–resistant sonic stamp.

The others have aided and abetted. Anchoring, of sorts, has come from second guitarist Bob Weir in the form of Dead-jam counterpoints and up-tune vocal leads. Lanky Phil Lesh has seemed more an intellectually inclined product of his early classical composition studies than a body-throbbing, beat-booming bassist. The two drummers, Bill Kreutzmann and (starting in 1967) Mickey Hart, are known for rolling, interactive convulsions rather than the backbeat-heavy grooves of most rock and roll. Keyboard players have changed over the years, from original member Pigpen (died 1973) to Tom Constanten, Keith Godchaux (died 1980), Brent Mydland (died 1990), Bruce Hornsby, and Vince Welnick of the Tubes. Donna Godchaux supplied backup vocals from 1972 to 1979.

The sound that brought them their early popularity—barband boogie spiked with electronic psychedelia and jazzlike experimentation—has remained intact but with additions. Mixed in are hints of Indian rhythm, Indonesian gamelan, and the avant-garde.

The Dead are known for the fact that no two shows—and no two live versions of a song—are exactly alike. A typical set will really be a suite of songs connected by free-form group improvisations. The results vary widely: On one night it may seem as if the band is falling apart and widespread torpor has set in; on another the music achieves a trancelike, timeless quality, morphing and evolving subtly in the manner of minimalist sounds by such as Terry Riley, Philip Glass, and Steve Reich.

The approach—and its attendant fan acclaim and taping habits—has spawned legions of musical emulators over the years, from 1990s "neo-retro" jammers like the Spin Doctors to cult cultivators Phish, often seen as a mini-Dead.

En route, the Dead seem to have gone through three distinct phases. From 1965 to 1969 they were charter contributors to the burgeoning San Francisco sound, serving as a focal point of the anti-establishment drug culture that had a base in that city.

When the movement faded, the Dead survived. Their audience expanded and their cult core solidified with the 1970 releases of the carefully crafted *Workingman's Dead* and *American Beauty*, albums full of vocal harmony and country-rock appeal that have remained their most popular discs. The band then spent the next fifteen years building a reputation—little noticed by the mainstream—as a live act.

Early in their third decade they finally scored a top-ten hit in 1987's "A Touch of Grey." From that point on, the Dead were acknowledged as a phenomenon, uniquely successful, one of the last holdovers of a legendary era, yet still vital and still evolving—and always on their own terms.

The experts and emulators have all taken note: that it's possible, with enough core adherents, to break the standard rules about image, polish, and strategy and still end up in *Forbes* magazine's list of the forty highest-paid entertainers in the world.

KEY RECORDINGS: *The Grateful Dead* (1967), *Anthem of the Sun* (1968), *Aoxomoxoa* (1969), *Live/Dead* (1970), *Workingman's Dead* (1970), *American Beauty* (1970), *Grateful Dead* (live, 1971), *Europe '72* (live, 1972), *Wake of the Flood* (1973), *From the Mars Hotel* (1974), *Blues for Allah* (1975), *Terrapin Station* (1977), *Shakedown Street* (1978), *Go to Heaven* (1980), *In the*

Dark (1987), *Built to Last* (1989); "Dark Star" (1968), "St. Stephen" (1969), "Truckin'" (1970), "Uncle John's Band" (1970), "Sugar Magnolia" (1970), "Friend of the Devil" (1970), "Playin' in the Band" (1971), "A Touch of Grey" (1987).

SCREAMIN' JAY HAWKINS

He's never had a hit record. Yet Screamin' Jay Hawkins is a rock and roll legend, known world 'round for his precedent-setting flamboyant dress and voodoo-vermin stage antics—coffin-encased stage entrances, skeletons, snakes, capes, shrunken heads, and gunpowder flashes. There're bones up the nose, creepy mascots, and outrageous mumbo-jumbo jive about the "Feast of the Mau Mau," "Alligator Wine," and "Constipation Blues"—all generously seasoned with inhuman yelps, grunts, and groaned incantations.

Without Screamin' Jay, Alice Cooper, Kiss, David Bowie, and the course of rock and roll would have been different.

"My mama told me, 'Jay, you got an ugly look,'" explains Hawkins on the formation of his life's work, his crazed music-making voodoo persona. "'You wash it, get out here, and put a smile on it. Now, I gonna tell you a secret to keep you the rest of your days. You smile and laugh, from the bottom of your gut—even if you got to lie—cause that's the best you're gonna get. Life's gonna give you hell, son.'"

Jalacy J. Hawkins was born (July 18, 1929) in a bus terminal in Cleveland—or thereabouts. "There was seven of us with one mother and different daddies," explains Hawkins. "My father was from Arabia." As a newborn he was placed in an orphan-age; later—depending on the interview—he was placed with well-to-do members of a tribe of Blackfoot Indians, or raised a hoodlum in a hellish neighborhood. He fought in the Cleveland Golden Gloves as a teenager, took a few piano lessons, toyed with a sax, quit high school, and joined the military, where after suffering a wound in Korea, he worked as an entertainer in the Special Services Division. Hawkins continued his career as a boxer until 1949, when he fought Billy McCann, the middleweight champion of Alaska. "He beat the hell out of me," says Hawkins. "I still fight, but now it's on the street."

In the early fifties, a kilt-clad Hawkins was the piano and sax man for Tiny Grimes and His Rockin' Highlanders. "I was his chauffeur, bodyguard, and dog walker, too," he adds. With Grimes and later Johnny Sparrows and His Sparrows, Hawkins recorded some career-defining sides: "Baptize Me in Wine," "She Put the Whammy on Me," "Screamin' Blues." Jay Hawkins was to be no run-of-the-mill rock-and-roller.

He had recorded under his given name but became Screamin' Jay one dark night in the early fifties. "At this one club there was this woman that weighed seventeen tons," says Hawkins. "She sat all by herself at a small table with a bottle of Johnny Walker Red. That woman would pound on that table with her fists and yell, 'Scream, Jay, scream.' I did, and she liked it, and after that I'd look for the ugliest woman in the audience and sing to her; I'd scream my songs; I'd torment 'em."

Glitz aside, it was one song that made him and maintains him an embedded rock landmark, the 1956 almost-hit, "I Put a Spell on You." Screamin' Jay, Sam "the Man" Taylor, Mickey "Guitar" Baker, Panama Francis, and the rest of the historic session cast were blind drunk when Hawkins laid out his immortal nonsense. Explains Hawkins: "Arnold Matson, the A&R man, says, 'Jay, do you drink?' 'Yeah, I drink.' 'Do you get drunk?' 'Yeah.' 'How do you sound?' 'How the hell do I know, I'm drunk.' So he went out and got a case of Italian Swiss Colony Muscatel. For damn near twenty years whenever I sang 'I Put a Spell on You' I was drunk. It damn near killed me.

"I just can't understand how a song like that can continue this long. I first recorded it as a love ballad in 1948, and it ain't left me yet. I've no qualms and didn't get ripped. And I'm grateful for 'Spell,' cause the checks keep coming."

"Spell" was banned from most "decent" radio programs. "I wish they'd ban everything I do," says Hawkins. "That record sold a half-million more once they did that." Hawkins's subsequent singles for Okeh were arguably equally great. "Person to Person," "Frenzy," "There's Something Wrong with You"—nothing got airplay; nothing clicked, saleswise.

"I got fed up and went to Honolulu for ten years," he says. "Alice Cooper, David Bowie, and these other guys were makin' the money doin' what I'd been doin' for years."

In 1994, after numerous one-off singles and marginally produced albums, Hawkins, backed with the Buddy Blue Band, recorded *Somethin' Funny Goin' On,* his finest work in twenty-five years.

"If it had worked out right—but life don't—I wouldn't be Screamin', I'd be an opera singer. I love classical music," says Hawkins. "I got a voice. I wanna do *Pagliacci, Carmen, Figaro,* 'Ave Maria' . . ."

KEY RECORDINGS: *At Home with Screamin' Jay Hawkins* (1957), *What That Is* (1969), *Screamin' Jay Hawkins* (1970), *Somethin' Funny Goin' On* (1994); "I Put a Spell on You" (1956), "Frenzy" b/w "Person to Person" (1957), "Alligator Wine" b/w "There's Something Wrong with You" (1957), "Stone Crazy" (1969), "Constipation Blues" (1969).

HAWKWIND

Hawkwind has been a cult act since its inception. Their performances were "happenings." There were strobes, lasers, and a far-out light and smoke show. Gobs of multicolored goo were projected on cinematic screens, lightly dressed bandmembers, and seminude expressionists. Sporadically, there were fire-eaters, explosions, and random gunshots. They were Hawkwind, a band of rebellious hippies on the run and with a purpose. But that was twenty-plus albums and twenty-plus years ago, before the drug busts, constant personnel shake-ups, and numerous life-inducing adventures.

"We're not hippies anymore," says Dave Brock, Hawkwind's leader and only constant through all the years, "maybe never were. I mean, who is a hippie? We were stoned freaks. Noise-wise, we're sonic warriors working the outer limits of sci-fi rock. And actually we were revolutionaries—still are—involved in the White Panthers, free concerts, ecology, and charities." A portion of the profits from their recent albums, including *Space Bandits*, are to go to the Royal Society for the Protection of Birds. "We've raised funds for brain scanners," adds Brock, "and actually saved four rhinoceroses in Zambia. The game warden sent us pictures. We've yet to meet them, but look eagerly forward to it."

Brock (guitar, synthesizer, vocals) and Nik Turner (flute, sax, human sounds) put the initial collection of freaks together in 1970 in the Nottingham area of London. Initially there was a strong association with an alternative society called Group X. From the beginning they engendered a fanatical following via loose lifestyle and their willingness to perform anywhere, any-time—for free. While Dylan worked the paying crowd at the Isle of Wight Festival, Hawkwind appeared outside the festival fence to work their aura and sounds to those unable to get in.

A quarter of a century ago, their music and that of Amon Düül, Can, Neu, and Tangerine Dream was called "space rock." It was a European response to America's psychedelic scene. As a form its fame has been eclipsed, though its influence lives in part in New Age music. "It is similar," Brock admits. "But we use our computers as a barbarian would. Our music often has a metal edge and remains experimental. It can be frightful. The music moves, you know, like a ship—a spaceship—sailing along the seas from one setting to another. Like life itself, it's all alike. But everything is different. I don't know if there's a pro-gression. We've been at sea now for what seems light-years. I hope there is progress, but sometimes I wonder."

The music's intent then as now is to compel its listeners to s–p–a–c–e o–u–t. "Yeah, that's it," Brock says with childlike glee. "You got it. If it's a really good light show, you understand, and the band's all right and you've got your sense about you, you won't need any drugs. I'm not bothered by people being stoned out, but we're not encouraging it. Personally, I don't need them. Life is a trip."

KEY RECORDINGS: *Hawkwind* (1970), *In Search of Space* (1971), *Space Ritual* (live, 1973); "Silver Machine" (1972), "Urban Guerrilla" (1973).

RICHARD HELL AND THE VOIDOIDS

He was a leading figure—a visionary, some say—in early punk rock. His appearance, music, even name were emblematic of the New York scene. He wore ripped shirts and spiked hair. His songs were nihilist rants with shots of humor, played raw, fast, and loud. As a showman he was a whirling rock dervish, as a bassist-vocalist barely competent and proud of it. He was Richard Hell, former problem teen turned rock antihero, co-founder of two seminal punk bands, the leader of a third, and the writer of the underground anthem "Blank Generation."

"I was sayin' let me outta here before I was even born!" he howled in that song. Born Richard Meyer in Kentucky on October 2, 1949, he first showed up in New York after letting himself out of his Delaware high school in the mid-sixties. Inspired by nineteenth-century French wordsmiths Rimbaud, Baudelaire, Verlaine, and Huysmans, Meyer output his own poetry first in a journal he published called *Genesis: Grasp* and then, with former schoolmate Tom Miller, in the book *Wanna Go Out?* under the fictional name of Theresa Stern.

"I get off on getting attention," he told *Melody Maker*'s Chris Brazier. "Poetry was a dead end." But he noticed at the time that

Roberta Bayley

the glam-rockin' New York Dolls seemed to be having better luck in their chosen medium. Meyer tested out those waters by joining guitarist Miller and drummer Billy Ficca in a group dubbed the Neon Boys. It was a short-lived unit for which he shared vocals, played bass, and wrote an explosive song, "Love Comes in Spurts," that would become a Richard Hell standard.

The Neon Boys evolved in early 1974 into the four-member Television, the band that inaugurated the Bowery club CBGB's and in effect launched the punk movement. It was in this setting that Meyer began to exert outer-world impact. He changed his name to Richard Hell (while Miller became Tom Verlaine) and adopted an attention-getting visual image that was ragged, anti-glam, flash-negating. (Entrepreneur Malcolm McLaren allegedly picked up on the look and applied it to the Sex Pistols).

Hell's rudimentary bass playing helped trigger a key punk concept: that anyone can do it; you don't have to be a musical expert. "Everybody has the capacity to create himself," he said.

"Creating yourself is the most important kind of art of all; there doesn't have to be a product." Slopped-out rock was but Hell's platform for a kind of me-decade, Warholian art of the personality, the point being not to refine sound but to reshape the self—to redesign, say, a struggling poet named Richie Meyer into a more heroically proportioned Richard Hell—and project it into the public eye. "The art form of the future is celebrity-hood," he wrote in *Hit Parader*.

That orientation clashed with Verlaine's growing song's-the-thing focus, and Hell was squeezed out of Television by March 1975, before their first album. He quickly responded to the suggestion of ex-Dolls Johnny Thunders and Jerry Nolan that he join with them to form a new band. The resulting Heartbreakers loomed large on the Manhattan punk scene for about a year, but their relentlessly slam-dunk attack left little moving room for a thinker's misfit like Hell. He quit in April 1976, still albumless, finally to front his own act.

They were the Voidoids, a strangely mixed set of players that placed Hell's by now hysterically overwrought garage-rock vocals in a junkyard of avant-punk, spazz-funk sonics. Dissonant, angular guitar came from the older, balding Robert Quine while a second guitarist, Ivan Julian, played with more Hendrixlike fluidity; drumming issued from the sticks of Marc Bell, a future Ramone. Their artifact was *Blank Generation*—"the ultimate CBGB cult record," according to the *Village Voice*—whose grooves combined reworkings of prior Hell-raisers (the title song and "Spurts") with newer nuggets of No Wave negativism.

Whether due to lack of stamina, road burnout (heads pummeled with beer cans on a U.K. tour with the Clash), or simply waning interest, the Voidoids let it all implode, even as kudos came their way for originality and songcraft. They recorded the 1978 single "Kid with the Replaceable Head" produced by Nick Lowe (with replacements Jerry Antonius on bass and Frank Mauro on drums), toured with Elvis Costello, and then voided out in late 1979.

There was Hell product—the album *Destiny Street*—in 1982 and there were appearances in the films *Smithereens* (1982) and *Desperately Seeking Susan* (1985). Otherwise, the self-creation called Richard Hell lowered his profile, perhaps content to let ambitious others—Madonna, for example—take the art of the celebrity all the way. "Success is a record company's top priority," he said in Clinton Heylin's *From the Velvets to the Voidoids*. "I just wanted to sleep late more often."

KEY RECORDINGS: *Blank Generation* (1977), *Richard Hell/Neon Boys* (EP, 1980), *Destiny Street* (1982), *R.I.P.* (miscellanea, recorded 1975–83, released 1984), *Funhunt* (live items, recorded 1978, '79, '85, released 1990); "Blank Generation" (1977), "Love Comes in Spurts" (1977), "The Kid with the Replaceable Head" (1978).

JOHN HIATT

Praised by his musical peers, tapped for tunes by performers as disparate as the punkoid Iggy Pop and the top-fortyish Three Dog Night, and adhered to by those who favor raunchy, gut-bucket rock and roll served with lyrics that don't insult their intelligence, John Hiatt—singer, songsmith, life survivor—is a kind of cult-rocker prototype. The very qualities that have kept frenzied mass mania an impossible dream are what have tightened the bond to a deeply devoted core audience.

Hiatt's voice is unconventional—gritty, loose, hound-dog sloppy. His songs are low-tech in a high-tech world: gutsy, barebones American rockers, or blues and R&B extrapolations of such, the lyrics matching the music with the snug, comfortable fit of a funky old shoe. Though often leavened with wry wit, they tend toward portrayals of tattered lives or journeys back from some personal abyss—troubled tales of barroom down-and-outers, regretful loners viewing the damaged past in "some

cracked rearview," and romances fading to dark in a "lipstick sunset." All have been rendered with an ear for the effective nonrhyme and an eye for the vivid metaphoric image.

Visually, Hiatt's notably MTV-resistant, well past the days when industry image-makers could pawn him off as an idiosyncratic new-wave quirkball in the Elvis Costello mold—as was once attempted. He's a Joe Average, his craggy, shopworn features protruding from Mr. Blanding clothes draped over a lanky frame.

Onstage, the frame jumps to life as a rockin' herky-jerky man, doing the monkey with gangly neck and arm motions when not busy playing guitar or piano or yodeling an ending to a bluesy turn of phrase. Unselfconsciously loony, he's a reveler in human imperfection, a one-man answer to the studied poses of techno-rocker cool.

Born in 1952 the sixth of seven children and raised in Indianapolis, Indiana, Hiatt wrote his first song when he was eleven.

He dropped out of high school and, at age eighteen, migrated to Nashville, where he landed a job as a staff writer with the Tree Music Publishing Company and later moved to sell himself as a solo act. Between 1974 and 1980 he issued a quartet of albums—*Hangin' Around the Observatory* and *Overcoats* on Epic and *Slug Line* and *Two Bit Monsters* on MCA—that earned pundit praise while making nary a dent in the record-store racks.

In the early eighties he shifted to the Geffen label and recorded *All of a Sudden* against an incongruous synth-rock setting. Then it was on to more compatible pairings with producers Nick Lowe, Scott Mathews, and Ron Nagle for *Riding with the King*. But drug-and-drink problems kicked in, and as Hiatt struggled to catch the sobriety wagon, his estranged second wife hanged herself. "That was the bottom," he told *Musician's* Mark Rowland. "It was the end. It was the point at which something had to give." Geffen then dropped him when the 1985 album *Warming Up to the Ice Age*—a mix of guitar-powered rock, funky R&B, and a soulful duet with Elvis Costello—failed to sell.

A moment of the kind that feeds legends followed. Offered a deal by the English Denon label, Hiatt gathered guitarist Ry Cooder and bassist Nick Lowe (both cult figures of no mean repute) along with drum star Jim Keltner and—in four days—recorded *Bring the Family*. Production was ragged, but the loose sound nailed his raw rootsiness dead on. A&M Records bought the rights to the disc. Ears in unusually high numbers heard, liked it, and wanted more. Meanwhile, singer Rosanne Cash scored a country hit with Hiatt's song "The Way We Make a Broken Heart." Bonnie Raitt covered his "Thing Called Love" and included it on *Nick of Time*, a 1989 Grammy winner.

Hiatt kept the classic-rock sound rolling on his follow-up,

Slow Turning, and 1990's *Stolen Moments.* Then in 1992 he joined Little Village—considered a kind of supergroup of cult rockers—comprised of his bandmates from the *Bring the Family* recording.

"It's freed me up," he said of his late-arriving public acceptance. Hiatt's eleventh solo album, *Perfectly Good Guitar,* found him "feeling a good wind at my back," he told *People* magazine. He was enough at ease to mess with the sonic formula a bit—throwing in a touch of punk rock, a taste of grunge, a hint of the garage. "My attitude these days is, if you write a bad song what are they gonna do, throw you in songwriter jail?"

KEY RECORDINGS: *Slug Line* (1979), *Riding with the King* (1983), *Bring the Family* (1987), *Slow Turning* (1988), *Stolen Moments* (1990), *Perfectly Good Guitar* (1993); "Thing Called Love" (1987), "Have a Little Faith in Me" (1987), "Paper Thin" (1988), "Child of the Wild Blue Yonder" (1990).

HÜSKER DÜ

The three-man Hüsker Dü packed every decibel of hardcore, slamdance-inducing, crush-rocking power that mohawked post-punks of the early eighties required as they exploded in frenzies of stage diving, head cracking, and mutually assured destruction. The band was thoroughly accommodating, thanks to (1) the sheer velocity of its sound, often at "fastest band on earth" levels; (2) Bob Mould's roaring, heavily distorted buzz-saw guitar; (3) Mould's potato-bland look and nondescript, portrait-of-a-serial-killer vocal; (4) drummer Grant Hart's more melodious but frequently howling voice; (5) songs about sociopaths ("Diane"), cadavers ("Pink Turns to Blue"), and feeding dead cats to rats ("How to Skin a Cat").

But Minneapolis-based Hüsker Dü was more than just an ear-pounding blitzkrieg unit. They also trafficked in pop songs

with real melodies. Mould's occasional power-folk tracks (1985's "I Apologize") and Hart's hook-heavy, mixed bag of tunes added to a musical diamond in the rough—a core of accessible garage rock wrapped in layers of raw sonic texture. It's what set Hüsker Dü apart from other surrounding thrash-punkers and shot them, in a near-decade, to the front lines of the underground army, where they joined R.E.M. and the Replacements as alternative-rock progenitors and put down pavement for battalions of grunge-rockers yet to come.

The varied tastes of the three Hüskies are what did it. Mould, a consumer of punk, weird fringe music, and his father's collection of classic jukebox singles, moved from his home in Malone, New York, to attend college in St. Paul before connecting with drummer Hart (a connoisseur of pop) and bassist Greg Norton (big on the jazz end) in the late seventies. They started out on Ramones tunes in Norton's basement and made rough four-track demos before rising to the surface world with a moniker borrowed from a Danish board game (translation: "do you remember"). With abrasiveness and Mach speed as early goals, the band drew quick flak for Ramones resemblance, but the Düs thought different. "The way we spit things back out," Mould told *Rolling Stone*'s David Fricke, "a lot of them came out backward, upside down and sideways."

Mayhem reigned at a Chicago performance in 1981 that brought them to the attention of hardcore originators Black Flag, who helped get the first Hüsker album, the live *Land Speed Record*, released on the New Alliance indie label run by fellow radical rockers the Minutemen. That record, along with a studio follow-up on Hüsker's own Reflex label and an EP, *Metal Circus*, on Black Flag's SST label, cemented the trio's initial cult following of punk-metal heads. But buried in the audio onslaught of *Circus* were lyrics that indicated a creeping strain of sensitivity, later to alienate core skinheads while endearing the band to college crowds.

Critical consensus points to the follow-up double album *Zen Arcade* as the Hüsker Dü groundbreaker, the one in which their eclectic-pop leanings became especially audible in songs that tempered sonic blasts with touches of folk and psychedelia. Velvet hammerings continued on 1985's *New Day Rising*, with Mould's dense wall of guitar and his cathartic assaults ("Whatcha Drinkin'," "Plans I Make") counterbalanced by Hart's catchier rockers ("Books About UFOs" and the Dylan-meets-garage-rock "Terms of Psychic Warfare").

Noting Hüsker's brushfire of grass-roots popularity, major labels began circling in the mid-eighties. Mould, Hart, and Norton signed with Warner Bros., but they retained creative independence, ensuring that their label debut, *Candy Apple Grey*, was no brighter, cheerier, or less apocalyptic than discs that preceded.

Self-immolation brought the Hüsker heyday to a halt in early 1988. Grant Hart went on to release two solo discs and to form the group Nova Mob. Bob Mould, who had at one time expressed frustration with Hüsker Dü's fuzz-guitar bag, calling it a "claustrophobia in sound," cut a largely acoustic album and a noisier follow-up before assembling Sugar, a return to the surging power-trio format of . . . Hüsker Dü.

KEY RECORDINGS: *Land Speed Record* (1981), *Everything Falls Apart* (1982), *Metal Circus* (1983), *Zen Arcade* (1984), *New Day Rising* (1985), *Flip Your Wig* (1985), *Candy Apple Grey* (1986), *Warehouse: Songs and Stories* (1987); "Diane" (1983), "Eight Miles High" (1984), "Recurring Dreams" (1984), "Pink Turns to Blue" (1984).

IRON BUTTERFLY

"I don't understand all the interest, what the big deal is about this band," said guitarist Danny Weis to Marc Shapiro in *DISCoveries* magazine of the continued Iron Butterfly mania. "Honestly, it just sounds like crap to me."

Now largely dismissed as an acid-era bad trip—historically, "the original really heavy-metal band" and for a moment the biggest-selling act on Atlantic/Atco Records—the Iron Butterfly revolutionized rock and roll with one drug dirge, the heaviest freak-out auditory hallucination of the sixties, "In-A-Gadda-Da-Vida."

Formed in San Diego as the Pages in 1961 by Doug Ingle (keyboards) and Ron "the Bush" Bushy (drums), the Iron Butterfly—with members Jerry Penrod (bass), Darryl DeLoach (vocals), and Danny Weis (guitar)—turned a one-night gig, late in '66 at L.A.'s famed Whiskey-A-Go-Go, into a three-week stay, a three-month stop opening for the Doors and Jefferson Airplane at the Galaxy, and a spot on the Atco label.

Heavy, their album debut—*the* Butter-head classic—caused little stir in the music world and the loss of DeLoach, Penrod, and Weis (the latter two formed Rhinoceros). With the addition of child actor/violinist Erik Keith Braunn (né Rick Davis, guitar, vocals) and accordionist Lee Dorman (né Douglas Dorman, bass, guitar, piano), Butterfly took flight; in rapid succession—a national tour, a spot with Cream in the B flick *The Savage Seven*, and the creation of their magnum opus, the seventeen-and-a-half-minute "In-A-Gadda-Da-Vida."

On the creation of the classic bash, Bushy said: "I came home one night and found Doug. He had been working on a song and polished off a whole gallon of Red Mountain wine. What he had been working on was this thing to be called 'In the Garden of Eden,' but he was so drunk that when he sang it to me he slurred the words into 'In-A-Gadda-Da-Vida.' I thought it was real clever and wrote it down exactly as it sounded—and it stuck."

In-A-Gadda-Da-Vida remained in the nation's top ten for eighty-one weeks and became a "progressive"/underground radio staple, the first album in the modern era to sell a million copies. *Ball*, likewise, sold quite well; Braunn left to form Flintwhistle with ex-Butterflies DeLoach and Penrod. Ingle, Bushy, and Dorman fleshed out the band with former Blues Image and future New Cactus Band guitarist Mike Pinera and the aborted Second Coming stringman, Gregg and Duane Allman roommate, Larry "Rhino" Reinhardt. This revised lineup recorded *Live* and *Metamorphosis;* sales were slower, and in the summer of 1971 the Butterfly crashed in a pool of bad vibes.

"I don't know where my brain was when I was playing that stuff," said Weis. "It was basically LSD-orientated stuff and nothing else."

Braunn and Bushy reformed Iron Butterfly in the mid-seventies for tours and two LPs with MCA.

KEY RECORDINGS: *Heavy* (1968), *In-A-Gadda-Da-Vida* (1968); "Possession" b/w "Unconscious Power" (1968), "In-A-Gadda-Da-Vida" b/w "Iron Butterfly Theme" (1968).

JOE JACKSON

A songcraft specialist whose sophistication and taste permeate many an album's worth of original sound, British-born singer-pianist Joe Jackson (b. August 11, 1954 or '55) has attracted a claque of Jack-rabid fanatics ever attuned to his style-hopping ways.

Look Sharp!—a new-wave-era dose of smart power-pop and lyrical bite, with a catchy hit, "Is She Really Going Out with Him?"—brought Jackson initial notice in 1979. Later came *Night and Day* and *Blaze of Glory*, the former a shot of sleek urbanity tinged with Latin rhythm, the latter a concept-linked set, precision-tooled.

Along the way, there've been departures, experiments, and a commercial flop or two. *Beat Crazy* roiled in a set of reggae grooves. *Jumpin' Jive* was a fling with forties jump blues and swing. *Big World* traded studio perfection for the ragged rightness of a live performance recorded direct-to-digital-master. The all-instrumental *Will Power* contained orchestral works, one a symphony originally written for a film. (Jackson has composed numerous other movie scores since.) Nineteen ninety-four's *Night Music* mixed instrumental "nocturnes" with songs.

To some, Jackson has been a puzzlement, a chameleon whose mutations have slithered him out of every grasping attempt to define or label. "I [now] see myself as a composer who uses little bits of all kinds of musical styles and puts them together in my own way, to try to create my own little musical world."

Some seeds of Jackson's complex little world sprouted from his studies at London's Royal College of Music and "mostly just from listening and studying scores," he says. "I've been doing that since I was about twelve. I've studied jazz quite a bit, as well, but I suppose most of my training is more on the classical side . . ."

His "thinking-man's rock" has triggered some not entirely frictionless exchanges between Jackson and the outside world. Says he: "I've been asked in interviews a couple of times—more than a couple of times—over my career: 'Do you think that you're overqualified for rock and roll?' Sometimes I think, well, why? Do you have to be a moron to be in rock music? Now I just think the question is kind of irrelevant, 'cause I don't even think that I am in rock music particularly."

"It's this rock 'n' roll way of thinking," he told *Musician*'s Scott Isler, "[like] 'We'll just get together and get blasted and we play, man, and what comes out, that's the music, man.' To me, that's like fucking hippies high on acid in the sixties. It's so stupid to me. I wrote out the parts 'cause I knew what I wanted. It's my music; why shouldn't I?"

On hiatus from his own music in 1980, Jackson enlisted a few musicians to play Louis Jordan tunes on some pub gigs. The project snowballed, yielding the *Jumpin' Jive* disc and a supporting tour.

It was in the earliest phase of fame that Jackson was lumped in—mostly by the U.S. press—with Elvis Costello and Graham Parker as a kind of British angry young singer-songwriter. "Everyone has to be compared to someone else," he says. "I mean, no one can be so brilliantly original that they don't sound anything like anyone else, and will never be compared to anyone else—no matter who you are.

"I think someone once said that as we get older we don't change, we just become more like ourselves," he says. "I don't feel part of any particular genre or movement or scene, and I just want to be myself and be as unique as I can be. I feel more confident about that now than I ever have."

KEY RECORDINGS: *Look Sharp!* (1979), *I'm the Man* (1979), *Beat Crazy* (1980), *Jumpin' Jive* (1981), *Night and Day* (1982), *Body and Soul* (1984), *Big World* (1986), *Will Power* (1987), *Blaze of Glory* (1989), *Laughter and Lust* (1991), *Night Music* (1994); "Is She Really Going Out with Him?" (1979), "Steppin' Out" (1982).

WANDA JACKSON

Rockabilly fanatics pay hundreds of dollars for her original records, jam her near-annual European concerts, and reverently call Wanda Lavonne Jackson the Queen of Rock and Roll.

In the fifties it was a no-no and unheard of for anything in lipstick, nylons, and heels to do what this Jackson lass (b. October 20, 1937, Maud, Oklahoma) would freely do. "Honey Bop," "Fujiyama Mama," "Mean Mean Man," "Let's Have a Party"—with accompaniment often provided by Gene Vincent's Blue Caps—are among the most uninhibited rockabilly ever unleashed. Wanda Jackson is without peer.

Jackson's daddy—a fiddle-playing barber and used-car salesman—gave her a worn guitar when she was seven years old. When thirteen and attending Capitol City High in Oklahoma City, Jackson had a fifteen-minute radio spot on KLPR. In 1954, western swing leader Hank Thompson caught a performance and asked her to record with his band, the Brazos Valley Boys.

The following year Jackson joined country legend Red Foley in the "Ozark Jubilee," a TV show and touring company. It was at this time that she became involved with the King of Rock and Roll.

"I was doing country, 'cause that was all I knew until I met Elvis," says Jackson. "This is 1955. I was actually a bigger name than he was. I'd had a hit with Billy Gray [vocalist with the Brazos Valley Boys]. Elvis introduced me to rock 'n' roll and encouraged me to try it. I was eighteen, dating him, and working shows with him. He was different and cute; always laughing and singing. When he walked into the room you knew it.

"He told me I had a feel for it. He took me in his home, played some 78s for me, and got his guitar and showed me how to do it. He told me this is gonna be great music. I loved it right off; heck, I was a teenager myself."

With her first disc for Capitol Records in August 1956—"Hot Dog! That Made Him Mad" b/w "Silver Thread and Golden Needles"—it was clear that Jackson had the potential to be an exceptional rock and roll stylist. Over the next couple of years, she toured with Presley, Carl Perkins, Jerry Lee Lewis. As if possessed, her voice could be harsh, purr, scream like a banshee.

"I was the only girl who sounded like that," she says. "I didn't realize that then. It all seemed so natural. I wanted to be different, but I needed to be liked. I got into a lot of trouble just by the way I looked and moved. I wore high heels, long earrings, and wanted to be glamorous. When I did my rock stuff I wanted dresses that had some movement, and I had these tight skirts, sexy-type outfits with silk fringes; long before the go-go dancers in the sixties. I'd sing and just shake my leg a bit, and it looked like I was doing something."

Capitol Records didn't have a hunch, and one glance must have convinced some executives that Wanda was too hot for mass acceptance. By the time she hit the pop charts with her wild rockin' "Let's Have a Party"—a four-year-old album track—Jackson had already returned to sweet country ballads.

"They had signed Gene Vincent about the same time they got me," says Jackson. "They knew a man could sell this, but they didn't think a woman could. They never knew what to do with me.

"In '71 my marriage, my life was in turmoil. My career was at its peak. I had my husband with me, two children, beautiful houses, but I was in serious trouble. The drinking, the night life, the road were taking a toll on me. I knew a change was needed, and I was scared."

For the next decade, Wanda Jackson remained active recording primarily gospel songs. More recently, she has returned to recording country and occasionally rock and roll albums, though most are issued only in Europe.

"It amazes me, thrills me that some stuff I did near forty years ago is still making people happy. I'm flattered that sometimes thousands will come out to hear me."

KEY RECORDINGS: *Wanda Jackson* (1958), *There's a Party Goin' On* (1961), *Right or Wrong* (1961), *Two Sides of Wanda* (1964); "Hot Dog! That Made Him Mad" (1956), "Let's Have a Party" (1960), "Right or Wrong" (1961), "Riot in Cell Block Number Nine" (1961).

THE JAM

A band that *mattered*—in the socially relevant manner of the Clash but less the crusading tone—the Jam wore their Englishness on their sleeves. That helped make them a full-blown British pop phenomenon in the early 1980s, racking up top-ranking hits and inducing heavy attachment among a largely working-class constituency. It also kept them a cult act in the U.S., a specialty item consumed mainly by rock-revved Anglophiles.

The three gents in the Jam—Paul Weller (singer, guitarist,

CULT ROCKERS

writer), Bruce Foxton (bassist), and Rick Buckler (drummer), all managed by Paul's ex-boxer father—started as mod-clad neatniks in the days of punk grunge. They debuted in the punk-explosive London of 1976 sporting unfashionably fab Carnaby Street gear and pointedly spike-free hair. Weller had a glistening Rickenbacker guitar, a taste for sixties pop and soul, and crystal-clear but punchy melodies that put the Jam somewhere to the right of the Sex Pistols' and Clash's far-out flailings. They were denounced as conservative at first, dismissed as "mod revivalists" in some rowdy quarters.

Dissenting voices faded as Jam fame spread. Over a six-album span, punctuated with EPs and a flurry of 45s, the trio zapped the masses with blasts of increasingly critical social commentary, all patriotically tempered. They cataloged the ups and downs of British proledom—with vignettes of kidhood, working life, faded U.K. glory, and more—while wrapping themselves and their audience in a comforting blanket of shared identity.

In 1982, at the pinnacle of the Jam's ascent, Weller announced the band's breakup, ostensibly to spare fans the spectacle of a prolonged burnout or an old-age sellout. "We could go on for the next ten years making records," he said in *Melody Maker*, "getting bigger and bigger and all the rest of it." Instead, Weller spent the next eight years fronting Style Council, an R&B-based duo with organist Mick Talbot. By 1992 he was issuing solo Paul Weller albums that melded the soul of Style with the pop of Jam.

Why the relative U.S. indifference to Weller's mod, pop, and soul infatuations? "I don't think you've had the same thing in America," he told *Musician*'s Vic Garbarini, "but we've always had these little fads based around music and clothes . . . It may seem strange to Americans, but in England there's a need for that kind of expression—because there's nothing else."

KEY RECORDINGS: *In the City* (1977), *This Is the Modern World* (1977), *All Mod Cons* (1978), *Setting Sons* (1979), *Sound*

Affects (1980), *The Gift* (1982), *Dig the New Breed* (live, 1982); "Strange Town" (1979), "The Eton Rifles" (1979), "Going Underground" (1980).

THE JESUS AND MARY CHAIN

Psychocandy landed on the record racks in 1985 and got tagged as punk rock's second coming. And shock-haired perpetrators Jim and William Reid—the brain trust behind Jesus and Mary Chain—fueled the media flame. Their sound assaulted with fuzzboxes and feedback. Their gigs were annoyingly short—sometimes only ten minutes in length. They were proudly unprofessional. "We're not exactly great musicians," says Jim, "so we're forced to use our imagination."

But punk rock—in sound and attitude—has proven but one link in the Jesus and Mary Chain. Along with the rough guitar distortion are catchy sounds drawn from pop of the mid-sixties: Phil Spector's "Be My Baby" beat; Brill Building melodies; echoes of the Stones, Them, the Doors, Iron Butterfly. Early on, Jesus and Mary Chain connected melodic garage rock with punk's white-noise sonics and coolly detached vocals. *Rolling Stone* called them "pioneers of noise pop." "But that's not where it stops," Jim claims.

Raised in the Scottish suburb of East Kilbride, guitarist William (b. 1958) and singer Jim (b. 1961) migrated to London in 1984 armed with new songs and age-old dreams. "We didn't want to be just another band," recalls Jim. "We wanted to grab people's attention rather than sit around and politely wait to be discovered." Entrepreneur Alan McGee took note, signed them to his small Creation label, and released a debut single, "Upside Down." When it topped the British independent charts, the Chain gang hooked up with the Warner conglomerate and embarked—initially with bassist Douglas Hart and drummer Bobby Gillespie—on an often controversial course.

Riots sometimes broke out at concerts. Songs were banned from the radio for offensive lyrics; a B-side, "Jesus Suck," was never manufactured; the band's very name provoked ire. "I don't know if things in pop can be shaken up," said Jim Reid to *Spin*'s Ted Mico, "but I believe if anyone's done it, we have . . . We don't deny we're shy people, but we give you honesty. There's no group that sounds like us, no group who ever have and no group who ever will again."

KEY RECORDINGS: *Psychocandy* (1985), *Darklands* (1987), *Automatic* (1989), *Honey's Dead* (1992), *Stoned and Dethroned* (1994); "Upside Down" (1984), "Never Understand" (1985), "Just Like Honey" (1985), "Some Candy Talking" (1986), "Reverence" (1992), "Far Gone and Out" (1992).

ROBERT JOHNSON

He is considered the greatest of all the Delta bluesmen, arguably the most noted of *all* bluesmen. Living a truncated life in dire poverty, prejudice, and pain, Robert Johnson had too much going for him: his taut, high-pitched voice screaming of teetering on the edge of the abyss, his guitar playing beyond skillful, his compositions—"Sweet Home Chicago," "Crossroads Blues," "I Believe I'll Dust My Broom," "Terraplane Blues"—immortal standards.

Those with wooden ears and little historic sense take the position that Johnson's status is due to an infernal tale that has the bluesman bartering at the crossroads with the Lord of Darkness.

Johnson died a half century ago, leaving behind only twenty-nine recorded tunes. Blues and rock buffs never forgot him. Mainstreamers never knew of him. Yet in 1990, when his legacy was reissued as a two-CD boxed set, sales totaled nearly half a million units, winning "the hottest bluesman dead" a Grammy award.

Johnson was born (May 8, 1911, in Hazelhurst, Mississippi) the illegitimate son of Julia Dodds and Noah Johnson. Before his fifth year he was sent to live with his mother's first husband, Robert Spencer (a.k.a. Robert Dodds). Over the years, Robert used the surnames Dodds and Spencer before finally taking his father's name, Johnson. Robert learned how to work a harmonica and watched brother Charles, Son House, and Willie Brown play guitar. Witnesses report Johnson was an adequate music maker, though no earthshaker.

When he was nineteen, Johnson's wife died in childbirth. For the next three years he wandered around the Delta region. On his return in '33, Robert Johnson was a blues master. Brown, Son House, and others who knew him were astonished at his newfound proficiencies. Johnson was a new man.

According to the thinking of the time and persistent blues folklore, Johnson had sold his soul to Satan in exchange for his godly gifts. The transformation was just too radical and accomplished in much too brief a time for any mortal. As he traveled to Memphis, Chicago, and New York, his legend dogged him and grew.

Johnson's sounds were only taped on two occasions, over a total of five days. The first was in a San Antonio hotel room, November 1936; the second session in a Dallas warehouse, June the following year. Months later, Robert Johnson was dead, poisoned with strychnine-laced whiskey after a fleeting flirtation with a juke-joint owner's lady.

Johnson was inducted into the Blues Foundation's Hall of Fame in 1980 and the Rock and Roll Hall of Fame in 1986.

KEY RECORDINGS: *King of the Delta Blues Singers* (1961), *King of the Delta Blues Singers, Vol. 2* (1970), *The Complete Recordings* (1990); "Crossroads Blues" (1936), "I Believe I'll Dust My Broom" (1936), "Terraplane Blues" (1936), "Rambling on My Mind" (1936), "Hellhound on My Trail" (1937).

LOUIS JORDAN

The Grandfather of Rock and Roll, jump-blues saxman, singer, and bandleader Louis Jordan had a direct and potent impact on music played by key members of rock's first generation. And influence aside, he was one of the great forties small-band showmen, a jesting, jiving, rhythm-and-blues version of top swing hepcat Cab Calloway. Blending rollicking boogie-woogie with humor-laden lyrics and raucous sax work, he packed houses across the country and scored hits with such classic recordings as "Caldonia" and "Choo Choo Ch'boogie."

Born in Brinkley, Arkansas, on July 8, 1908, Jordan played his first sax gig as a teen with Rudy "Tuna Boy" Williams and toured the South with the Rabbit Foot Minstrels before joining Chick Webb's jazz big band in 1936 as saxophonist and singer. Aiming to reach a broader audience, he struck out on his own two years later, signed with the Decca label, and mined gold with his band the Tympany Five.

"With my little band, I did everything they did with a big band. *I made the blues jump*," he told historian Arnold Shaw. "I decided that when you came to hear Louis Jordan, you'd hear things to make you forget what you'd had to do the day before and just have a good time, a great time."

Eventually, Jordan's sound turned up in the music of young up-and-comers, one of whom, Bill Haley, hit fame in 1954 with "Rock Around the Clock." As Haley and other rockers grew popular, Jordan's star began to fade.

Following Jordan's heyday (nineteen pop hits between 1944 and 1949, fifty-four top-ten R&B singles from 1938 to 1950), he spent the sixties and seventies performing sporadically and recording for small labels until his death of a heart attack on February 4, 1975. Today, Jordan's music and personality live on: cover versions of his material abound, and his recordings—

now on CD—sound as fresh and upbeat today as when first issued half a century ago.

In 1987 Jordan was inducted into the Rock and Roll Hall of Fame, in the Early Influences category.

KEY RECORDINGS: *The Best of Louis Jordan* (1975), *Five Guys Named Moe: Original Decca Recordings, Vol. 2* (1992), *Let the Good Times Roll: The Complete Decca Recordings 1938–1954* (1992); "G.I. Jive" (1944), "Caldonia" (1945), "Choo Choo Ch'boogie" (1946), "Let the Good Times Roll" (1946), "Ain't Nobody Here But Us Chickens" (1946), "Open the Door, Richard" (1947), "Saturday Night Fish Fry" (1949).

JOY DIVISION/NEW ORDER

Years after Ian Curtis's death by self-hanging in May 1980, the singer-poet is remembered as an intriguing cult figure, his band, Joy Division, an influential entity of near mythic repute. To add to the legend, his surviving cohorts—Bernard Sumner, Peter Hook, and Stephen Morris—went on to become the comparably acclaimed New Order, far exceeding the first band's level of fame.

Joy Division, of Manchester, England, connected powerfully with fringe batches of the young and perturbed in the post-punk late seventies. To fans, Ian Curtis was a charismatic model, a troubled antihero with psyche on display in the grand music-misfit tradition.

The band backed him with the kinds of desolate and eerie dronings deemed right for a decaying world. They combined some of the gray-shaded, art-rock minimalism of the Velvet Underground; a touch of David Bowie techno-decadence; and the roughness and intensity of the Sex Pistols.

In a voice like a less tuneful Jim Morrison, Curtis sang the plaints and dirges that doubled the irony of the Joy Division

moniker (a reference to Nazi concentration camp brothels). Their key early "upbeat" song was an insistent thing called "She's Lost Control" that spun the tale of a girl's mind that had gone on the fritz. Life itself was the apparent culprit, and it had left her dazed, confused, and a tad suicidal. Curtis, meanwhile, delivered the desperate ditty in a detached monotone that made the whole thing seem just one more glitch in a string of unremarkable daily events.

How real was all this gloom-and-doom stuff? "One of the popular conceptions, or misconceptions, about Joy Division [was] that we were dark and somber young men," says a laughing Stephen Morris, the drummer. "But the reality was completely the opposite of that. We weren't great intellectuals. I suppose Ian was really into that, into dark things. He was, he liked dark things, I guess."

Curtis was a poetry-writing fan of the Doors, Lou Reed, and Iggy Pop when he began singing with the band, initially called Warsaw, around 1977. With him were bassist Hook—"Hooky" to friends—and guitarist Bernard Albrecht (later Sumner; legal name Dicken), neither one a musician at the time, and both fresh from the inspiration of a Sex Pistols show. "They could play terribly, and so could we," Morris later explained to *Rolling Stone*'s Debby Miller.

The Joy Division sound consisted of Curtis's Lou Reed-ish ramblings, lead lines on Hooky's bass, a prominent role for the drums, and hints of the high-tech that would later drive New Order. They also absorbed a bit of Giorgio Moroder's sound; a dance groove crept into the mix. Later, onstage, it would offset the band's bleakness and provide a sort of discoid counterpoint to Ian Curtis's Iggy-inspired physical idiosyncrasies. ("Epileptic dancing," as one reviewer described it, not knowing he may have been referring to one of Curtis's real epileptic seizures.)

Joy Division impressed TV personality Tony Wilson at a Manchester audition with a batch of bands, and he signed them to his tiny Factory label. The album *Unknown Pleasures,* released in July 1979, would become a treasured artifact among the Joy-ful.

It was before the release of their follow-up, and on the eve of a U.S. tour, that Curtis's "dark things" went out of control. Age twenty-three at the time, he dangled himself from a noose, leaving behind a terse note. Nearby, some said, was a copy of Iggy Pop's *The Idiot* on the turntable and Werner Herzog's film *Stroszek* in the VCR.

That ended Joy Division, just as they were becoming known. It also spawned New Order. "We all said we'd always carry on," Morris recalled. They experimented with new roles: Bernard took over vocals; Morris's girlfriend, Gillian Gilbert, joined to play synthesizers and guitar. And they eased into what became the New Order sound: disco- and Kraftwerk-influenced technorock blended with Joy Division's stark moodiness.

Although six atmospheric New Order albums have been issued, critics have been duly impressed, and audiences have been won over, the ghost of Joy Division lingers still. "It was ridiculous, really, after Ian died," says Morris. "Like everybody wanted to sound like Joy Division for quite a while after that . . . I don't know if New Order have been, or will ever be as influential as Joy Division were."

KEY RECORDINGS: Joy Division—*Unknown Pleasures* (1979), *Closer* (1980); "She's Lost Control" (1979); **New Order**—*Movement* (1981), *Power, Corruption and Lies* (1983), *Low-life* (1985), *Brotherhood* (1986), *Technique* (1989), *Republic* (1993); "Blue Monday" (1983).

KING CRIMSON

Robert Fripp and his periodically reincarnated band King Crimson haven't sold as many records as some other graduates of the seventies progressive, art-rock movement.

Drummer Bill Bruford, in fact, has identified a "Crimson Curse": No record will be commercially successful if it's by King Crimson.

But for music, Crimson's been hailed where others from the same spawning ground have been counted out as rock "dinosaurs." Time has smiled on the King: While art rock as a genre slipped from critical favor—thanks in part to punk's devaluing of pop pomp in the mid-seventies—Crimson has continued on, assumed new forms, and seen its stock rise. Evidence of Crimson influence has surfaced across a broad segment of the rock field, from heavy- and punk-metal to jazz fusion and synth-pop. New releases of old work have revealed Crimson's early adventurousness and originality. An overlap has been discerned between Crimson and the avant-garde of contemporary "serious" music. All of which helps to explain the band's continuing cult status more than a quarter-century after its birth.

Led by Fripp, the charismatic British guitarist known for exploring rock's outlands, the band went through five different

personnel configurations—each carrying an experimentation gene—between 1969 and 1994.

Lineup One came together in England in the innocent days when minor modes and murky Mellotrons signaled seriousness of musical intent. King Crimson—a conglomerate of Fripp, drummer Mike Giles, keyboardist–wind player Ian McDonald, bassist-singer Greg Lake, and lyricist Pete Sinfield—made an atmospheric debut of their own in 1969 with *In the Court of the Crimson King*.

Later cited by Fripp as one of his favorite Crimson albums, *In the Court* introduced a few Crimson earmarks: instrumental pyrotechnics, sonic twists and turns, and lyrics leaning toward the mystical ("Return of the Fire Witch" a sample title), culminating in the cult-embraced jazz-metal fusion of the disc's "21st Century Schizoid Man" opening track.

After a two-album period of transition, Crimson's Main Lineup Two took shape; it included Fripp and Sinfield plus Mel Collins (saxes, flute), Boz Burrell (vocals, bass, later of Bad

Company), and Ian Wallace (drums, later with Bob Dylan) and yielded *Islands* as an artifact plus a live disc, *Earthbound.*

In Lineup Three, John Wetton (bass, vocals), Bill Bruford (drums, ex-Yes), David Cross (violin, keyboard), and Jamie Muir (percussion) joined Fripp for a harder, more explosive, further-out Crimson. Three studio albums were issued (Muir leaving to join a monastery after *Larks' Tongues in Aspic*); in 1993 *The Great Deceiver,* a release of mid-seventies live recordings, rekindled interest in this usually overlooked Crimson permutation.

In 1981, following a seven-year break, Main Lineup Four surrounded Fripp with guitarist-singer-lyricist Adrian Belew (former sideman with Frank Zappa, David Bowie, Talking Heads), bassist–stick player Tony Levin, and drummer Bruford. The unit recorded three discs of interlocking guitars (Fripp on repetitive hypno-lines; Belew on soaring wild-animal sounds), fevered rhythms in odd time signatures, and Belew's distinctive David-Byrne-meets-Boz-Scaggs vocals.

Ten years after the dissolution of this batch in 1984, a Lineup Five appeared—a "double trio" of Fripp, Belew, Levin, and Bruford plus drummer Pat Mastelloto and stick-ist Trey Gunn. As with other lineups, it arose, claimed Fripp, not for commercial reasons but because "when music appears which only King Crimson can play, then sooner or later King Crimson appears to play the music." Accompanied, no doubt, by the Crimson Curse—though to die-hard Crimsonites who saw it as a guarantee of cutting-edge sound, the Curse would always boil down to a blessing.

KEY RECORDINGS: *In the Court of the Crimson King* (1969), *In the Wake of Poseidon* (1970), *Lizard* (1970), *Islands* (1971), *Larks' Tongues in Aspic* (1973), *Starless and Bible Black* (1974), *Red* (1974), *Discipline* (1981), *Beat* (1982), *Three of a Perfect Pair* (1984), *The Great Deceiver* (1993), *THRAK* (1995); "21st Century Schizoid Man" (1969), "I Talk to the Wind" (1969), "Starless" (1974), "Frame by Frame" (1981).

THE KINGSMEN

In under two hours and for thirty-eight dollars, late in the spring of 1963, Jack Ely (lead vocal, guitar), Bob Nordby (bass), Mike Mitchell (guitar), and Lynn Easton (drums), a Portland-based band, recorded one of the most recognizable, raunchiest sounding, best-known, and most notorious records in the history of rock and roll—therein assuring themselves cult status into the next millennium.

Florence Greenberg, owner of Wand, the independent label that acquired "Louie Louie," refers to the rock perennial as "God-awful. Garbage! That thing is the shame of my life. It was also the most lucrative thing in my whole life. I didn't like it. It was just lousy. My distributor, Bob Silverman, forced me to issue it. And then it was a hit and a hit again. And that junk still sells."

Their musicianship was bareboned. The sound quality was attractively "horrid." The lyrics were slurred to incomprehensibility. But the Kingsmen cover, of a fifties Richard Berry (the bass voice on the Robins' "Riot in Cell Block #9") B-side and later local hit by the Wailers, sold—give or take a few million—eight million copies. It spawned a sea of cover versions and remakes and encouraged a constant stream of party-oriented youths to form frat bands. The idea of such a band was to get basic, sloppy, loose, and have fun.

The Northwest Recording Studio where the two-minute happening took place was hardly a studio. "Rugs and curtains were strewn about. It was poorly miked," said bandleader Easton. "They weren't used to working with rock bands." Ely added, "The recording room had sixteen-foot ceilings. The boom stand was as far up as it could go, and I stood underneath it and yelled the words."

Ironically, if the Kingsmen disc had not been recorded so "poorly" and the shouted lyrics so jumbled, "Louie Louie" undoubtedly would not have become the rock evergreen it has.

"I was shocked when some stations banned it," says Greenberg. "It was just an old song about a sailor! The FBI came to my studio, I swear. They sat around all day listening to Kingsmen tapes. They never found any obscenities in that thing."

In the six months it took "Louie Louie" to become a monster hit, all of the original Kingsmen but Easton had departed. A similar-sounding band was quickly constructed, and six albums were dashed off. A few hits—"Money" and "The Jolly Green Giant"—by this refurbished Kingsmen are still cherished, but nothing approached the etherealness of "Louie Louie."

It's estimated that four hundred versions of the old sailor song exist. A Los Altos radio station held a marathon playing seventy straight hours of nothing but "Louie Louie." Rhino Records has issued a compilation of some of the best, worst, and most bizarre renderings of the work. *Louie Louie*, the book by Dave Marsh, was unleashed in 1993.

KEY RECORDINGS: *The Kingsmen in Person—Featuring "Louie Louie"* (1963); "Louie Louie" (1963), "Money" (1964), "The Jolly Green Giant" (1965).

LITTLE FEAT

Lowell George—singer, songwriter, slide guitarist—gave Little Feat its initial impetus and, later, with his ballooning frame and ever-present overalls, an easy-to-recognize image. He also was thought to be its Achilles' heel: Without the distinctive print of his slithering bottleneck licks and velvet-hammer voice—a clean-toned tenor roughened with bluesy gravel—the band, it was felt, just wouldn't have been the same. So surprise was mild when, following his death in 1979 of a drug-related heart attack, the patter of Little Feat faded off into the white noise of rock and roll memory.

Sharper surprise came nearly a decade later. Longtime, long-dormant Feat footsoldiers stirred with a start at the returning sound of Little Feat. And Lowell loyalists took extra note: Live and on new vinyl, the fresh Feat retained much of the vintage act's cult-acclaimed flavor—the funk-tinged New Orleans rock and roll, the offbeat accents and boogie grooves, the instrumental interweave—only now with a high-tech gloss and density absent in the heyday. All original members were present. Veteran studio cohort Fred Tackett (guitar) was also there, plus—filling the key Lowell George slot—Craig Fuller (vocals), formerly of the hit-making Pure Prairie League. Downright ghostly, some felt, was the uncanny similarity of Fuller's voice to that of George.

George's shoes (small shoes, inspiring the name of the band) were not easy ones to fill. "The best singer, songwriter and guitar player I have ever heard, hands down, in my life," said Bonnie Raitt in *Guitar* magazine. "I don't expect to hear another like him."

Little Feat's musical trek began in Los Angeles, where George (b. April 13, 1945, Arlington, Virginia), after stints with the Factory, the Standells, and Frank Zappa (George debuted on *Weasels Ripped My Flesh*), heeded the advice of the latter and set out in 1970 to form his own band. He initially corralled Zappa's bassist Roy Estrada and pianist Bill Payne, who had been trying unsuccessfully to hook up with Zappa. With Richie Hayward (a bandmate from the Factory) on drums, the blues-infused, countryish quartet lined up a recording contract with Warner Bros. and issued an eponymous first album—a commercial dud—followed by a second disc, *Sailin' Shoes,* that became cult-attractive.

Estrada left to join Captain Beefheart. Bassist Kenny Gradney and his conga-pounding cohort Sam Clayton were hired, bringing in hipper rhythmic percolations. Guitarist Paul Barrere joined, fattening the guitar sound behind Lowell George. And with the "classic" six-piece Little Feat lineup in place they recorded *Dixie Chicken* in 1973—the group's defining recorded moment.

More than two decades after release, *Dixie Chicken* still stands as a classic of roots-rock with a progressive edge—starting with the title track's sonic gumbo and tall tale of a Dixie boy's dalliance with an intoxicatin' southern belle. It "takes a stand," George told Steve Weitzman of *Guitar.* "It makes a point; it cops an attitude; it tries to get funky; it does get funky. It backs off a little bit. It's white. It's black. All those entities make that song fluid or not fluid. And maybe the icing is a little too thick on it, so it's a little lopsided." Balanced by the disc's others—like the smoky Allen Toussaint blues "On the Way Down," the spare "Roll Um Easy," the funked-out "Fat Man in the Bathtub" (with its Zappa-zany touch), and the steamrollin' "Two Trains"—it added to a steeping soup of sound found nowhere else in rock and savored accordingly by the faithful. "If you knew who we were, you loved us," Paul Barrere told Weitzman.

For the next six years, Little Feat walked an obstacle-ridden road. George's involvement decreased. The other members' contributions increased. Frustration was voiced over George's growing drug-related unpredictability. But notice kept accruing—via the fan-fave-follow-up *Feats Don't Fail Me Now,* three more studio releases, and their biggest seller, the live *Waiting for Columbus*—right up until the band stepped into its final puddle of irreconcilable difference and de-shoed—permanently, it appeared. In June 1979, while touring in support of the solo album *Thanks, I'll Eat It Here,* George died in a hotel room.

Members dispersed. Barrere recorded solo albums and played with a band called Bluesbusters. Bill Payne worked sessions and backed such people as Linda Ronstadt and James Taylor. Hayward and Gradney toured with Warren Zevon. Clayton signed on with Jimmy Buffett. On a late-eighties tour behind Bob Seger, Payne and Fred Tackett (who'd been heard on Feat discs) hatched a plan to revive Feat—in part to counter the dry anonymity of sessioning. The other players were called back in. Several Lowell replacements were envisioned—Bonnie

Raitt, Robert Palmer—before Craig Fuller was settled on and the new Feat were off to recapture what Barrere once described as "magic night after night after night."

KEY RECORDINGS: *Little Feat* (1971), *Sailin' Shoes* (1972), *Dixie Chicken* (1973), *Feats Don't Fail Me Now* (1974), *The Last Record Album* (1975), *Time Loves a Hero* (1977), *Waiting for Columbus* (live, 1978), *Down on the Farm* (1979), *Let It Roll* (1988), *Representing the Mambo* (1990), *Shake Me Up* (1991); "Willin'" (1972), "Dixie Chicken" (1973), "Rock and Roll Doctor" (1974).

NILS LOFGREN

Nils Lofgren, eventual juggler of a dual career as sideman to the stars and solo performer of no mean cult repute, grew up in Maryland and squeezed his first sounds out of an accordion. It led to harder stuff: guitar when the Beatles and Rolling Stones first emerged, and professional musical aspirations after Hendrix rocked his world. At seventeen, Nils quit school and made a beeline for Greenwich Village—and a lifetime of guitar-infused rock and roll.

After recording a single with a band called the Dolphin and then forming the three-man Grin, he met Neil Young in a Washington, D.C., bar and soon found himself playing piano on the singer's 1970 *After the Gold Rush* album and being cited as a new "discovery." The resulting fame led to a label contract for Grin—and exposure of Lofgren's talents as a singer, songwriter, and multi-instrumentalist. After four albums, Grin broke up, and Nils went on to issue the first of many solo discs that mixed melodic pop with raunchy, blues-laced guitar and clean-toned vocals. Those albums never took off, but Nils built a hardcore following largely through famously incendiary live shows in which he would play searing guitar solos, full of pop-ping harmonics and high squeals—sometimes while perform-ing acrobatic flips, rolls, and trampoline jumps.

Among the fans of those shows—and a onetime show opener for Lofgren—was Bruce Springsteen, who hired the flipped-out guitarist for his E Street Band in time for the 1985 Born in the U.S.A. tour. When that arrangement ran its course, Lofgren moved on to Ringo Starr's All-Starr Band and, finally, to more action under his own name.

"I love the pressure of a live audience," he says. "It keeps me in the moment and turns my mind off, and for a while I get to be this kind of spiritual, instinctive creature . . . You don't need to be in a high-visibility, superstar band like the E Street Band. It can happen in a funky bar in Providence two nights ago . . . thank God."

KEY RECORDINGS: Grin—*Grin* (1971), *1+1* (1971), *All Out* (1972), *Gone Crazy* (1973); **solo**—*Nils Lofgren* (1975), *Cry Tough* (1976), *Back It Up!!* (1976), *I Came to Dance* (1977), *Night After Night* (1977), *Nils* (1979), *Night Fades Away* (1981), *Wonderland* (1983), *Flip* (1985), *Silver Lining* (1991), *Crooked Line* (1992).

LOUNGE LIZARDS

"My band was the hottest thing in New York," said Lounge Lizards leader John Lurie to the *Village Voice* in 1984. "Every-body knew who I was. But paranoia set in."

On the Lower East Side, amid tenements, urban grit, and night haunts of the hip and jaded, the Lounge Lizards served for a time as resident practitioners of what they called "fake jazz." They came on the tail end of the No Wave, the late-seventies movement-du-jour that valued concept over professional polish and craft and that issued such hybrids as funk and punk, rock and shock.

Skilled jazz players the Lizards were not, but they riffed on the jazzman's stereotyped image. Clad in drab suit-and-tie garb and fifties-hipster attitude, they amused post-punk listeners with smoke-ringed sonic ironies, juxtaposing cocktail music with cacophony, warped versions of tunes by Thelonious Monk with John Lurie's own crude (at the time) originals.

The Lizards idea came from downtown denizen Lurie, a lanky, reptilian sax player with a theatrical bent (he'd devised a 1978 performance piece called *Leukemia*, in which he'd soloed surrounded by flashing lights and taped sounds of shattering glass). The original Lizards—his brother Evan on piano, avant-rockers Arto Lindsay and Anton Fier on guitar and drums respectively, and Steve Piccolo on bass—debuted in 1979. Notice came quickly. "We did one gig and the next week we were in six newspapers," Lurie said. "People lined up around the block—you couldn't get in to see us."

But just as quickly, the novelty faded. Rock crowds retreated as the Lizards started becoming musically proficient and steadily losing their entertaining "fakeness." Critics bailed out. The rest of the United States had never much noticed in the first place.

The Lizards have proved durable. Europe and Japan became the band's strongholds—and remain so to this day. No longer quasi-jazz, the Lurie entity and its fluctuating membership (as many as nine pieces at times) play a much-evolved instrumental brew that draws skillfully from an intriguing array of influences.

Lurie, ever restless, branched out in the mid-eighties to score and act in noted films by Jim Jarmusch. "So I'm a movie star now," he said at the time. "So big deal."

KEY RECORDINGS: *The Lounge Lizards* (1981), *Live from the Drunken Boat* (1983), *Live 79/81* (1985), *No Pain for Cakes*

(1987), *Voice of Chunk* (1989); "Strangers in the Night" (1980), "Harlem Nocturne" (1981), "My Trip to Ireland" (1987), "My Clown's on Fire" (1987).

LOVE/ARTHUR LEE

Pioneers in the American response to the British Invasion, along with the Byrds, the Turtles, and the Mamas and the Papas, Arthur Lee and Love—one of the first true "underground" acts—forged what was to become the influential but short-lived folk-rock movement.

Arthur Lee (b. 1944, Memphis, Tennessee) moved to the West Coast prior to the British Invasion. As part of the nascent music scene in California, Lee first recorded in 1963 with the L.A.G.'s and the following year with the American Four. In 1965, when Lee happened onto a performance by the Byrds at Montebello Bowl, his world changed.

Lee quickly formed a new group with Byrds road manager Bryan Maclean (guitar, vocals), ex-Surfaris Ken Forssi (bass), John Echols (guitar), and Don Conka (drums), the influence behind Love's underground druggie dirge "Signed D. C."

As the Grassroots (not the late-sixties folk-rock group) they quickly developed a loyal L.A. following, holding down a residency at the ultrahip haunt Bido Lito's. Elektra's Jac Holzman, deciding his label's future was in rock and roll, signed them, the company's first rock group.

After Dunhill Records patented the name Grassroots—with another band—Lee, the self-proclaimed "king of the underground," came up with "the best name in the whole wide world." As Love, their self-titled debut album contained a pack of potentially classic singles—"Hey Joe," "No Matter What You Do," and "My Little Red Book." The latter charted, soon followed by Love's only top-forty entry, the ferocious "Seven & Seven Is."

Liquid Jesus, the Fuzztones, Billy Bragg, and Alice Cooper recorded their own renditions. "If I would've known there was gonna be this much eruption over 'Seven & Seven Is,' I would have wrote 'Eight & Eight Is' and everything else on down the line," he told Frank Beeson in *Goldmine*.

Numerous excellent singles and at the least two more classic albums—*Da Capo*, including the ground-breaking nineteen-minute full-sided cut "Revelation," and *Forever Changes*, fleshed out with an orchestra and Lee lyrics that he (then twenty-three) considered his "last and dying words"—were to be issued before Lee would linger on largely only in the hearts of his still stable Love cult. The Doors, whom he had recommended Holzman sign to his Elektra label, flourished; Love withered.

"Elektra didn't promote me like they did the Doors," said Lee, in response to questions of just why the singularly talented and expressive Arthur Lee never connected with a mainstream audience. "And then too," he said, "I wasn't white."

KEY RECORDINGS: **Love**—*Love* (1966), *Da Capo* (1966), *Forever Changes* (1967), *Four Sail* (1969); "My Little Red Book" (1966), "Seven & Seven Is" (1966), "Orange Skies" b/w "She Comes in Colors" (1966), "Alone Again Or" (1967); **Arthur Lee**—*Vindicator* (1970); "Everybody's Gotta Live" (1970).

DARLENE LOVE

"As far as 'He's a Rebel' was concerned, it didn't really do a lot for me; it did more for the Crystals," says Darlene Love of the 1962 girl-group classic on which she sang the lead vocal. Producer Phil Spector had hired Love and her group the Blossoms to record the song when the Crystals had proved unavailable; yet the label on the disc still listed the Crystals—not the Blossoms, and not Love. Fueled by Love's powerful voice, the song shot to number one on the pop charts—securing the Crystals' fame.

"He's a Rebel" was a career milestone for Love. Yet it remained a monument to her lack of fame despite style-defining activity during rock's formative girl-group era. That hit was but one of many vintage rock songs on which Love sang her gospel-bred heart out. But while her contemporaries made the history books, Love's own role as one of rock's founding voices has been recognized only by a select few: those who were there with her and a later sect of Love aficionados and pop history buffs.

It was the Spector association that laid the groundwork. Back in 1959, when her name was still Darlene Wright (born c. 1942, Los Angeles, daughter of a Pentecostal minister) and she was in her last year of high school, she was asked to join the Blossoms, a vocal group that had already been together under the name the Dreamers since around 1954. With Wright they released singles and sang behind such performers as Sam Cooke before coming to Spector's attention in time for the "Rebel" episode.

What followed was a period in which Wright recorded for Spector under a variety of artist names. There was a second Blossoms effort credited to the Crystals. Another song, "Zip-A-Dee-Doo-Dah," was issued in late 1962 under the name Bob B. Soxx and the Blue Jeans (featuring both Wright and male singer Bobby Sheen). Spector also produced Darlene on several solo singles, the first of which, "(Today I Met) The Boy I'm Gonna Marry," listed her name not as Darlene Wright but as Darlene Love.

Even though "Rebel" became a chart-topper, Love's participation was known by few beyond the people who were at the recording session—until about a year later when Murray the K at the Brooklyn Fox started spreading the news. But, as Love recalls, "it wasn't until many, many years later that people actually found out that it wasn't the Crystals."

Darlene and the unsung Blossoms made do with a two-year stint as singing regulars on the TV show "Shindig" supporting many a featured performer. "There were not any black artists on television yet at that time," says Love. "The Blossoms were really blazing a trail for black artists." They also added to the lengthy list of stars they backed up on record—a roster that ultimately included the Ronettes, Johnny Rivers, Paul Anka, Duane Eddy, Bobby Darin, B. J. Thomas, Buck Owens, Doris Day, and Jackie DeShannon. They toured with the Righteous Brothers and, in the late sixties, with Elvis Presley. "He was very nice," she remembers. "Very shy. Very friendly. And I think one reason we all got along so well together is because he loved gospel music."

Love went on to work as Dionne Warwick's backup singer for ten years before setting out to rev up her solo career. It started out with a dry spell, during which she reportedly cleaned houses to make money. But it picked up in the mideighties as sixties nostalgia kicked in and Love landed a leading role in a musical of Ellie Greenwich songs (some of which Love had sung for Spector) called *Leader of the Pack*, which ran at New York's Bottom Line and then moved briefly to Broadway. She followed that with film roles as Danny Glover's wife in the *Lethal Weapon* series. In the meantime, she recorded a live album, *Paint Another Picture*, that got lost in the shuffle of the Columbia Records purchase by Sony.

In 1993, the spotlight was finally trained directly on Love when she began a long-running engagement at the Bottom Line with *Portrait of a Singer*, showcasing her history-laden work of the preceding thirty years. It was her long-delayed opportunity to set the record straight about the true owner of the voice on all those variously labeled singles of the girl-group era and to reveal—if only to a small audience—one of the essential early components of Phil Spector's legendary Wall of Sound.

KEY RECORDINGS: *Paint Another Picture* (1990); "He's a Rebel" and "He's Sure the Boy I Love" (the Crystals, 1962), "Zip-A-Dee-Doo-Dah" (Bob B. Soxx and the Blue Jeans, 1962);

"(Today I Met) The Boy I'm Gonna Marry" (1963), "Wait Till My Bobby Gets Home" (1963), "A Fine Fine Boy" (1963); sang backup on "Chain Gang" (Sam Cooke, 1960), "Johnny Angel" (Shelley Fabares, 1962), "(Dance with the) Guitar Man" (Duane Eddy, 1962), "Be My Baby" (the Ronettes, 1963), "Shoop Shoop Song" (Betty Everett, 1964), many more.

NICK LOWE

If he'd done nothing but write "(What's So Funny 'Bout) Peace, Love and Understanding"—a cult classic of blazing rock energy recorded by Elvis Costello—Nick Lowe *still* would have been a gurulike figure to scads of music aficionados.

But "(What's So Funny)" was just a career highlight—a single blip in a steady surge of background and foreground involvement that's gone on for more than a quarter century.

Lowe's been a bass-playing, singing, and songwriting team player with some acclaimed groups, among them the short-lived Rockpile. He was a member of the noted English quintet Brinsley Schwarz in the early seventies, present and accounted for in the smoky, crowded pub scene that helped spawn punk rock.

As a producer he's shaped the sounds of such noted left-fielders as Elvis Costello, Graham Parker, and John Hiatt—nearly the full roster of cult-certified "angry young songwriters"—and such bands as the Damned, the Pretenders (their first single), and the Fabulous Thunderbirds.

He's issued sporadic salvos of solo discs, his compositions hailed as models of unfettered pop craft—"no hidden meanings," as he told *Rolling Stone*'s James Henke, "no songs about people getting eaten by their dog." They thinly veil references to rock's roots, each song a potential "name the influences" test for pop history buffs. "It's gotten to be like a rock critic's sport," he said. "Find out where [Lowe] nicked this lick from."

So why—given the cult assessment of his impact and the

sheer weight of his résumé—has Lowe managed to remain only a shadow figure in the minds of the mainstream masses?

His musical immersion began early. It was as a school kid that Lowe (b. March 24, 1949, Suffolk, England) first joined with guitar-playing pal Brinsley Schwarz to approach the beckoning world of rock and roll. Together they formed the Sounds 4 Plus 1. By 1966 they were waxing singles for Parlophone under the name the Kippington Lodge. Four years later they were Brinsley Schwarz (the band), for which Lowe penned much roots-rocking musical matter.

When Schwarz fizzled in '75, Lowe moved into his most influential role—as a producer of others. Graham Parker's *Howlin Wind* debut disc was an early effort. Then Lowe's manager, Jake Riviera, brought him in as producer and artist for the small but groundbreaking Stiff label ("If it's a Stiff, it's a hit"). He released the very first Stiff single, "So It Goes," under his own name; joined the label's package tour of 1977 that included Elvis Costello and Ian Dury; and produced Costello, staying with him for seven discs in all and contributing "(What's So Funny)" to 1979's *Armed Forces*.

Lowe's own album output began reaching the public in 1978 with *Pure Pop for Now People* (titled *Jesus of Cool* in the U.K.), followed a year later by *Labour of Lust*. The musicians on those discs were guitarists Dave Edmunds and Billy Bremner and drummer Terry Williams. In 1979 they officially became Rockpile, the promising, cult-acclaimed purveyor of a rockabilly-Berry-boogie trad-rock mix. There was but one album, *Seconds of Pleasure*, before they crumbled. "Being in a group is not a very dignified experience," he said later.

Lowe kept producing, lending his hand to projects by Dr. Feelgood, Paul Carrack, John Hiatt, and Carlene Carter (his wife at the time). He earned the nickname Basher for his notably unmeticulous studio style (motto: Bash it out now, tart it up later).

Product issued under his own name seemed to connect less with the record-buying public, although 1979's "Cruel to Be Kind" put him in the upper tiers of the top forty.

In the mid-eighties, a discouraged Lowe retreated a bit. Said he, "After all that activity, I just couldn't think why I should continue. I couldn't seem to find anyone who thought about music the way I did." John Hiatt was one, and Lowe accepted an invite to play on his rootsy *Bring the Family* album in 1987.

Following a solo disc, *Party of One,* Lowe appeared in 1992 with other veterans Hiatt, guitarist Ry Cooder, and drummer Jim Keltner in the group Little Village. "Those were my criteria [for continuing]: making grown-up music and not copping some silly pose," he said. "You never really know what's going to be a hit, and I'll go to any reasonable length to get one. But that doesn't include going on a kids' show and having green stuff poured on my head."

KEY RECORDINGS: *Pure Pop for Now People* (1978), *Labour of Lust* (1979), *Seconds of Pleasure* (Rockpile, 1980), *Nick the Knife* (1982), *The Abominable Showman* (1983), *Nick Lowe and His Cowboy Outfit* (1984), *The Rose of England* (1985),

Pinker and Prouder Than Previous (1987), *Party of One* (1990), *The Impossible Bird* (1994); "Cruel to Be Kind" (1979), "I Knew the Bride (When She Use to Rock and Roll)" (1985).

LYDIA LUNCH

Sonic terror struck fringe dwellers of the rock underground in the late seventies and 1980s, and its most extreme purveyor may well have been Lydia Lunch. As a dark-haired banshee howler, guitar-noise thrasher, performance artist, and unleasher of controversial verbal and video matter, she's spewed negativity to shocking effect—and with unmatched fervor—for nearly two decades. "I'm not in the entertainment field," she told *Melody Maker*'s Cathi Unsworth in 1993. "I'm in the confrontation field."

First evidence of her attack-dog artistry emerged amid New York's post-punk No Wave movement. Its prevailing audio ethic was "anyone can do it," and sounds were weirder and more outrageous than ever. Those emitted by Lunch's first group, Teenage Jesus and the Jerks, were more abrasive than most.

Then but seventeen, Lunch was fury-fueled by a history of "conflicts, abuses, and strife." A 1987 monologue called up wrenching early memories of "being rocked like a football in a cradle" and a home life that caused her to flee in her mid-teens "before somebody got murdered." In a later interview, she admitted having "hatred and vileness inside me from the age of six." With Teenage Jesus, formed in 1976 with combat sax player James Chance, she let it all vent.

Mixing free jazz and punk until Chance's departure, the Jerks under Lunch lurched toward a white-noise frenzy. Electronic squalls surged over plodding beats. Lunch played senseless slide guitar or loud chordal anti-harmony. Vocally, her verbal venom spilled in wailing one-note declamations on such "songs" as "The Closet" (conjuring claustrophobia and suffocation), "Orphans" (picturing footless children running through snow), and a flood of bloodcurdling others.

"I'm a very optimistic person," Lunch once claimed.

"My pessimism is optimism," she later explained to writer Caren Myers. "My negativity is positive. I'm not slitting my wrists or the throat of others. I am trying to make a positive format out of all this horror."

The Jerks' horror format—though positive—proved a fast fizzler. Recordings were few, limited to a couple of singles, two EPs, and some sounds on a 1978 album, *No New York,* that also showcased the Contortions, DNA, and Mars. (Ten Jerks tracks are included on Lunch's 1986 *Hysterie* compilation.)

Replacement formats followed in restless and rapid succession. A mysterious unit called Beirut Slump recorded a handful of brain-grating obscurities. Lunch waxed a variety-spinning solo album, *Queen of Siam.* She then assembled the soon-to-be-cult-favored 8 Eyed Spy—a near-accessible blend of swampy blues, jazz, and a sprinkle of surf-rock, all rendered bleak with Lunch's overriding caterwaul. The band—with drummer Jim Sclavunos (of the Jerks), saxist-guitarist Pat Irwin, guitarist Michael Paumgarden, and bassist George Scott (a onetime Contortion)—survived for a matter of months, folding in August 1980.

Through the eighties, Lunch circulated through the shock-noise underground, colliding and bonding with others of like mind. As its resident voice of doom, she emerged as a kind of den mother of din—an Ethel Merman of mayhem—figureheading collaborations with such noted antimainstreamers as

- Sonic Youth, noise-rockers from New York, on 1985's "Death Valley 69"; guitarist Thurston Moore on several discs; and bassist Kim Gordon as a member of Lunch's 1989 group Harry Crews.
- Birthday Party, the influential London-based abrasion unit, on their 1982 *Drunk on the Pope's Blood* EP

and Lunch's *Honeymoon in Red;* guitarist Rowland S. Howard on 1982's *Thirsty Animal* EP and other recordings; and singer Nick Cave in a band, Immaculate Consumptives, and on *The Agony Is the Ecstacy* and other discs.

• Jim Thirlwell (a.k.a. Clint Ruin), the brain behind the extremist entity Foetus Inc., on the 1988 EP *Stinkfist,* 1988's *The Crumb,* and as a shaper of industrial sounds for live Lunch monologues.

• Einstürzende Neubauten, Berlin-based avant-garde conceptualists and shop-tool noisemakers, on their 1982 *Thirsty Animal* EP.

• *No Trend,* Washington, D.C.–based post-punkers, on their 1985 *Heart of Darkness* EP.

• Exene Cervenka (of X), Henry Rollins (of Black Flag), Michael Gira (of the Swans), Debbie Harry (of Blondie), author Hubert Selby, Jr., and others on assorted printed, spoken, and filmed projects.

Stand-up tirade became a main Lunch performance art form, first committed to commercial tape on *Hard Rock* in 1984 and continuing through *Uncensored* and *Oral Fixation.* Lunch's bully-pulpit bummers have shoved audience faces and ears into her gruesome conception of a no-win world—where the subjects of her rants include the government, aggressors, victims, life in general, and even her fans ("I'm talking at idiots," she's pointed out).

"I'm positive that the world will end," she said, "that cancer will dominate, that everyone will get an incurable disease, that war will obliterate the earth, that man will become extinct . . . Sure there's hope. . . . There's plenty of hope. Hope for the weary."

Lunch's utterances have been preserved in readable form in the book *Incriminating Evidence* (1992) and on video in *The Gun Is Loaded.*

KEY RECORDINGS: *Queen of Siam* (1980), *13.13* (1982), *The Agony Is the Ecstacy* (EP, 1982), *In Limbo* (EP, 1984), *Hard Rock* (with Michael Gira, 1984), *The Uncensored Lydia Lunch* (1985), *The Drowning of Lucy Hamilton* (with Lucy Hamilton, 1985), *Hysterie* (compilation, 1986), *Honeymoon in Red* (1987), *Stinkfist* (EP, with Clint Ruin, 1988), *The Crumb* (EP, with Thurston Moore, 1988), *Oral Fixation* (1989), *Shotgun Wedding* (1991).

MAHAVISHNU ORCHESTRA

They were exotic, fiery. Using only instruments—no voices—they concocted a blend of screaming rock, jazz, Indian, and classical sounds that in the early seventies was entirely new. They were the five-man Mahavishnu Orchestra, and with their key discs *The Inner Mounting Flame* and *Birds of Fire*, they launched an army of imitators, spawned the jazz-rock "fusion" genre, and enlarged the audience for jazz. Adherents hailed their leader as "the most influential guitar player since Jimi Hendrix."

In the early sixties, guitarist John McLaughlin (b. January 4, 1942, Yorkshire), was an active denizen of the London R&B scene. He backed Graham Bond and, briefly, Brian Auger and Georgie Fame and the Blue Flames. In 1969, having issued a jazz disc, *Extrapolation,* he answered the call to play in the stateside Tony Williams Lifetime (on disc and at joints like Slug's saloon in New York) and on Miles Davis's pioneering *In a Silent Way* and *Bitches Brew* albums. McLaughlin's eclectic, multicultural tastes, rapid-fire riffs, and angular, slicing chord work set him apart. Encouraged by Miles, he assembled Billy Cobham (drums), Jan Hammer (keyboards), Jerry Goodman (violin), and Rick Laird (bass) to perform jazz-infused but rock-electrified compositions of his own creation.

Cobham had played with Billy Taylor and Horace Silver;

Hammer with Sarah Vaughan; Laird previously with McLaughlin and with Buddy Rich; Goodman with rock horn band the Flock. "I got the best musicians available at the time," McLaughlin told *Guitar Player.*

Dubbed Mahavishnu (after the name McLaughlin used as a disciple of guru Sri Chinmoy), the mini- "orchestra" opened with an extended stay at the tiny Gaslight club in Greenwich Village. Evident were dazzling interplay and wide technical range. Harmonies were advanced, complex; textures dense and electronic, with guitar and violin doubling melodies over a surging rhythm section at high decibels and occasional warp speeds.

The success of 1971's *The Inner Mounting Flame* gained the band access to larger rock-concert stages, where they were alien entities (McLaughlin short-haired, white-clad) in a world of fist-pumping metalheads and flamboyant glam-flashers. But their performances were explosive, apocalyptic. On double-necked six- and twelve-string guitar, McLaughlin would ignite one of the band's skyrocketing ensemble flights, a breakneck passage—of convoluted twist and hairpin turn—that the entire quintet would somehow survive without mishap and then deftly transform into a percolating groove behind one convulsive solo after another.

The mainstream was unaware. Those who cared about Mahavishnu were aficionados whose ears had been molded by the likes of Soft Machine, Cream, Hendrix, Zappa, and jazzmen Miles Davis and John Coltrane. They proved to be the seeds of a sprouting subcult—a rabble of guitarists, fretless bassists, and keyboard synthesists whose attempts to cross jazz and rock would, through the 1970s, be tagged and sold with the label *fusion.*

Not all of it met with approval. "How do I feel about jazz-rock?" McLaughlin later said to writer Julie Coryell. "Boring! It bores me to tears; it just doesn't go anywhere. I haven't heard any since the original band."

Among the handful of respected jazz-rock bands, Mahavishnu stood as the most idiosyncratic, passionate, and appealingly unpolished—compared to, say, the coolly abstract Weather Report or the precise and flashy Return to Forever.

Inner Mounting Flame and *Birds of Fire* remained the definitive Mahavishnu discs, the ones spun most frequently by band loyalists. The latter scored in the top twenty of the *Billboard* album chart—rare for jazz-tinged vinyl. But group inspiration began to wane. By the release of a live third album, the flame was out.

Keyboardist Jan Hammer became a fixture in fusion, recording with such as Jeff Beck, Santana, and Neil Schon and releasing solo albums. He eased into the world of TV background music and in 1985 scored a rare instrumental number-one hit with his theme from *Miami Vice*.

Drummer Cobham remained a jazz-rock figurehead—a bandleader, accompanist, and producer. Goodman and Laird pursued less visible activities.

McLaughlin kept the Mahavishnu name in play for several more albums with different personnel, in the process employing violinist Jean-Luc Ponty and drummer Narada Michael Walden (later a noted pop producer). In later years he solidified his reputation as one of the world's more adventuresome guitarists, duetting with Carlos Santana on *Love, Devotion, Surrender* in 1973, trio-ing with Paco DeLucia and Al Di Meola on two albums, and leading an acoustic, Indian-flavored unit called Shakti.

"What happened to the Mahavishnu Orchestra was a misunderstanding," McLaughlin told Don Menn and Chip Stern in *Guitar Player*. "It was the lack of mutual spiritual consciousness . . . complete artistic and spiritual liberation . . . And that's really all my goal is about."

KEY RECORDINGS: *The Inner Mounting Flame* (1971), *Birds of Fire* (1973), *Between Nothingness and Eternity* (live, 1974), *Apocalypse* (1974), *Visions of the Emerald Beyond* (1975), *Inner*

Worlds (1976), *Adventures in Radioland* (1987); "Meetings of the Spirit" (1972), "The Noonward Race" (1972), "Vital Transformation" (1972).

THE MC5

They were full of tension, teenage ire, and the naive rhetoric of the exploding sixties counterculture; they were precursors of the punk movement, the "first seventies band of the sixties." The Motor City Five—in brief, the MC5—were maniacs on a mission, with a three-point plan for impending rebellion: rock and roll, dope, and sex in the streets. No rockers had previously said it so explicitly: "Kick out the jams, motherfuckers!"

Rob Tyner (vocals), Pat Burrows (bass), Bob Gasper (drums), Wayne Kramer (guitar), and Fred "Sonic" Smith (guitar) joined forces as the Bounty Hunters in '64. All were sometimes attending a Detroit high school when Burrows and Gasper dropped out to be replaced by Michael Davis (bass) and Dennis "Machine Gun" Thompson (drums) and a name change to MC5.

From the onset, they blared rock noise louder than anyone. It was a wall-shaking assault on the senses—"guerrilla rock," critic Dave Marsh labeled it. Shouting slogans and obscenities and posturing with the American flag, their home-turf performances set off revolting reverberations. Opening for the Cream, Jimi Hendrix, and the Mothers of Invention, the MC5 became intensely embraced by the Motor City's growing hippie community.

By 1967 they found John Sinclair, a guru, a neobeatnik, a "psychedelic gangster," wrote Marsh, and fabricator of the so-called Trans-Love Energies organization and the White Panther Party. Sinclair became their culture-expanding guide, manager, and producer. With Sinclair, MC5 tripped to Chicago in 1968 to be the only band to play Lincoln Park during the confrontational Democratic Convention.

Their raw rock 45 "I Can Only Give You Everything" caught the attention of Elektra A&R man Danny Fields. The MC5's debut album—the only "live" rock debut LP ever—was taped October 30 and 31, 1968, at Detroit's Grande Ballroom in 1969. *Kick Out the Jams* was impassioned rock and roll. Lewd liner notes and an obscenity in the title cut embroiled their label in a controversy. One music chain refused to carry the disc. The Five placed a responding ad in underground papers and took it upon themselves to plaster "Fuck You" stickers over the offended store's windows. A sterilized single and revised album—minus the offending word and liner notes—were dispatched, but impressions were already formed; the label set the Five free.

Sinclair was arrested on a marijuana charge and sentenced to a nine-and-a-half-to-ten-year term for possession of two joints. The Five signed with Atlantic and, with rock critic/later Bruce Springsteen associate Jon Landau producing, created a package that annoyed fans and that pundits proclaimed the greatest rock and roll album of all time. Sales for *Back in the U.S.A.* were poor; after *High Time*, Atlantic dropped the Five.

MC5 moved to England in hopes of reviving their career. Such was not to be the case; Davis and Thompson were the first to leave the group. Davis formed the New Order. Smith worked with Sonic Rendezvous, married rock poetress Patti Smith in 1980, and died in 1994. Kramer, after spending two years in jail for cocaine dealing, worked with Johnny Thunders and Was (Not Was) and released a few singles with his band Air Raid.

"We symbolized the total rebellious underside of the youth revolution combined with the antiwar movement and the civil rights movement," Thompson told *Goldmine's* John Koenig. "We embroiled all of it."

KEY RECORDINGS: *Kick Out the Jams* (1969), *Back in the U.S.A.* (1970), *High Time* (1971); "Kick Out the Jams" (1969).

MEAT PUPPETS

Few of rock's fringe offshoots are as self-contradictory as the
punk-goes-progressive mix cooked up by the Meat Puppets, the
Phoenix, Arizona–based trio of guitarist-writer Curt Kirkwood,
his bassist brother Cris, and drummer Derrick Bostrom. As
"sick and weird" and raggedly raunchy as they first set out to
be—in keeping with much "indie" rock of the early eighties—
the Puppets pulled a reverse twist and ended up sounding not
unlike the early-seventies guitar-hero rock that punk had once
rejected. Propelled by Curt's fluid, Allmans-like picking and the
trio's adept interplay, the Puppets' music has veered widely from
fast-and-loud thrashing to psychedelia, country rock, and tones
of a more delicate hue, with Curt's and Cris's occasionally grat-
ing vocals often providing the one reminder of their post-punk
birth.

"Our original stage show was hopelessly torturous," Derrick
Bostrom says, "very loud and screamy, and it was real extempo-
raneous—kinda like a noise cover band. We started writing
original songs which were based on dissonance and intense
tempo change . . . We were into the idea that the nature of
punk rock was that it had a psychedelic side, as opposed to a
Black Sabbath side."

Signed to SST, the small label run by hardcore pioneers
Black Flag, the Puppets followed their punkish debut album
with a more country-flavored disc. "We'd had our fill of hardcore . . . We used to do Fleetwood Mac covers for skinheads to
see if we could piss 'em off," explains Bostrom. "It was kind of a
hoot to put out an album that had mellow country things after
we had arranged to put out records on Black Flag's label.

"Of course, the next album, *Up on the Sun*, was the one that
really brought us to people's attention. It wasn't really a country
thing. It was kind of a forerunner to what we all consider 'alternative' these days, although not very grungy."

Some of the Puppets' grunge-rock adherents have since proved chart-worthy. The Meats themselves have been with the major London label since 1991. So why hasn't Meat consumption spread past cult confines? "Probably because the masses just don't get it," shrugs Curt Kirkwood. "Whatever typical reasons—the same reason people get killed."

KEY RECORDINGS: *Meat Puppets* (1982), *Meat Puppets II* (1983), *Up on the Sun* (1985), *Out My Way* (EP, 1986), *Mirage* (1987), *Huevos* (1987), *Monsters* (1989), *Forbidden Places* (1991), *Too High to Die* (1994); "Backwater" (1994).

MEKONS

Their convoluted rock rantings defy classification. Elements of punchy polka are freely mixed with dub, punk, industrial, reggae, and hayseed country. The Mekons—totally passed over by the public, vigilantly adored by Mekonsphiles—have been cursed; yet they survive.

"The Mekons are not about formulas and not about hit-making," explained Mekon main man Tom Greenhalgh to Todd Avery Shanker in *Illinois Entertainer*. "That's what has sustained us. What's been called our curse—our terrifically bad luck with the major record labels and inability to get our music to the public—is in many ways our saving grace. We have never had to live up to the standards of a 'big hit' song. Eighteen years, we've never had a hit."

They were formed in the punk era in Leeds, England. Like their brethren, Greenhalgh (guitar, vocals), Jon Langford (guitar, vocals), Sally Timms (vocals), Sarah Corina (bass), Mark La Falca (drums)—the original Mekons—played abrasive guitar noise. Their name was pulled from a fifties British comic, *The Eagle*. Explained Greenhalgh, "The story revolved around these evil, intelligent aliens with little green heads and stout bodies—

Mekons—who zipped around in flying saucers and fought the ultraconservative 'heroes.' "

Time has touched these aliens. The punk purist stance of their virgin efforts has evolved into something of a country-punk hodgepodge that is still evolving into we know not what, and which true Mekonsphiles in hot anticipation can hardly control their desires to acquire.

As for the future: "We have no intention of ever returning to a major [label] unless, of course, they offer us a lot of money."

KEY RECORDINGS: *Fear and Whiskey* (U.K. only, 1985), *Honky Tonkin'* (1987), *The Mekons Rock 'n' Roll* (1989), *The Curse of the Mekons* (1991), *Retreat* (1994); "Chop That Child in Half" (1986), "Never Work" (1994).

MINISTRY

Alain Jourgensen's sonic-Satan image stands in gargoyle relief against Ministry's industrial-metal facade. The look is biker-bad: tattooed and goateed; black-clad. Pronouncements—on record or in print—aim to disturb and aggravate, via sick humor. Sounds are nightmarish, intense—"aggro," as he describes it. Guitars squall; beats bash; vocals rant. The act's methods ensure it: "Our studio techniques are legendary," Al told *Rolling Stone's* David Fricke. "Five-day sessions with strobe lights and psychedelic drugs."

Onstage, Jourgensen and his band of sometimes nine-strong Ministry-men have been known to play behind a giant chain-link fence. The purpose, as he told *B Side's* Sandra Garcia, has been "to cut down on the size of the objects being thrown" and to serve as giant "monkey bars" for stage divers.

Producer-guitarist-vocalist Jourgensen and his accomplice, bassist-producer Paul Barker—self-credited, respectively, as

Hypo Luxa and Hermes Pan—are Ministry's energy-infused brain trust.

Jourgensen launched the act in 1981. Two years later he had a bum brush with synth-popularity via the widely panned *With Sympathy* album on Arista. He persevered, returning as an uncompromising audio extremist on 1986's *'Twitch.'* In years since, with Barker on board, Ministry's deliverings of death disco spiked with shards of punk metal have brought pained pleasure to many a denizen of the dance-club underground.

Ministry is actually but one of numerous Jourgensen efforts—many associated with the Wax Trax label, home of thrash-dance and Chicago's influential house-music scene. The revered Revolting Cocks have been a long-term related project, as have collaborations with Jello Biafra (of the Dead Kennedys), Ian MacKaye (of Fugazi), and Cabaret Voltaire.

But Ministry has been the main aggro-vehicle. "I strut around onstage wearing a Nazi helmet, circling my head with two fingers," Jourgensen said to writer Fricke. "And people still think I'm a racist Nazi. That is what we're fighting against. But if we have five people who didn't get the joke before but they get it now, we've done a good job that night."

KEY RECORDINGS: *With Sympathy* (1983), *'Twitch'* (1986), *The Land of Rape and Honey* (1988), *The Mind Is a Terrible Thing to Taste* (1989), *In Case You Didn't Feel Like Showing Up (Live)* (EP, 1990), *Psalm 69* (1992): "Cold Life" (1981), "Stigmata" (1988), "So What" (1989).

MINK DEVILLE

Willy DeVille and his band first snagged attention in 1976 at the New York punk hangout CBGB's. Stylewise, they stood out: Songs like "Venus of Avenue D" and "Spanish Stroll" grafted urban myth and retro, Drifters-era R&B onto the day's standard chatter of ragged guitars. Critics lauded the mixture, seeing in the figure of Willy—a street-slick smoothie, tall and thin with high-top pompadour and occasional pencil-thin mustache—a promising new recycler of their beloved pop traditions. He was a "fabulous working-class folkie cum urban classicist" with an aptitude for "tenement naturalism," raved the pulse-fingering *Village Voice*.

"I'm a New York person. I've lived on the streets of New York since I was fourteen or fifteen," DeVille told *Crawdaddy's* Scott Isler in 1977. "We're a New York band." The nucleus of the act—Willy on vocals and guitar, Ruben Siguenza on bass, and T. R. Allen on drums—bonded in post-hippie San Francisco. It was after a move to the Apple and the addition of guitarist Louie X. Erlanger and keyboardist Robert Leonards that Mink began its plunge into the bubbling punk-rock cauldron.

Mink DeVille was one of the earliest of the bands to surface with a major-label deal, inking with Capitol while also contributing a couple of keen cuts to the now-historic *Live at CBGB's* compilation album. Veteran producer (and onetime Phil Spector cohort) Jack Nitzsche steered their first studio effort, and the result, 1977's *Mink DeVille,* winningly wove in many of those sonic threads of early-sixties urban R&B.

But neither *Mink DeVille,* nor its follow-up (the last disc with the original band), nor the albums that came after—including the fan-favored *Le Chat Bleu,* with its input from legendary song-scribe Doc Pomus—were able to create more than a ripple in the surface-world airwaves.

But continuing cult interest has since kept slick Willy active —although minus the "Mink" prefix. "Mink DeVille was my dream," he told *Musician's* Jimmy Guterman. "The dream is over." In 1990 he was living in New Orleans, blending measures of Crescent City spice into his already rich, rhythm-and-soul-stoked musical brew.

KEY RECORDINGS: *Mink DeVille* (1977), *Return to Magenta* (1978), *Le Chat Bleu* (1980), *Coup de Grâce* (1981), *Where An-*

gels Fear to Tread (1983), *Sportin' Life* (1985); "Let Me Dream If I Want To" (1976), "Spanish Stroll" (1977), "Each Word's a Beat of My Heart" (1983); **Willy DeVille**—*Miracle* (1987), *Victory Mixture* (1990), *Backstreets of Desire* (1992).

MOBY GRAPE

"They remain to this day the greatest band I ever saw," said veteran producer David Rubinson to writer Johnny Angel. "They were the American Rolling Stones."

Moby Grape dropped out, decades ago. Bob Mosley—the band's great bassist-singer—never caught the ear of the mass public. Legendary songwriter Skip Spence retreated to a life on the fringe, and by the mid-nineties was reportedly living in a residential-care home.

Yet Grape-ophiles haven't forgotten the act's sixties heyday, when it stood out amid San Francisco's crush of raga-rockers, electrified folkies, and hippified tie-dye heads. "The Moby Grape were the only one of those bands that could write pop hits," Rubinson said. "All the others, Big Brother, the Dead, they were murdering the blues; they stunk."

The Grape, claim those in the know, boasted better guitars, drums, bass—five musicians total, all singer-writers, and not one a weak link.

The band's debut album—three decades after its release—is still cherished, hailed as a classic of the hippie era. Its psychedelic country soul had impact—songs like "Hey Grandma" and "Omaha" became set-list centerpieces for scads of student rockers, some of whom later ended up in star outfits (Robert Plant in Led Zeppelin, for one).

But the Grape's own high time was brief. They fumbled and fell in a fracas of bad deals and bum trips now numbered among the key tragedies of sixties rock.

It began in '66 when guitarist Peter Lewis of L.A.'s Peter and

the Wolves (and son of TV's Loretta Young) shuttled up the western coast with Bob Mosley to meet a manager, Matthew Katz. He matched them with guitarist-singer Skip Spence, who was the former drummer of Jefferson Airplane (and writer of their song "My Best Friend"). The three then brought in blues-rockin' picker Jerry Miller and skin-basher Don Stevenson of a Seattle-spawned group, the Frantics.

The combination clicked, and Columbia Records signed them in 1966, amid a music industry frenzy to snag snippets of the Bay Area's booming new "sound."

"San Francisco was like heaven," Lewis told *Zigzag's* Mac Garry. "Everyone was stoned and happy and free" when the group began work on their album. "It was the heaviest, most intense rock music I ever played in my life. Everyone was in gear because we knew it was time to get it on or get off . . . and we got it on." The resulting grooves spewed intertwining guitars and multilayered vocals. Byrds-like country rock cut to melodic pop-soul, and powerhouse blues to electronic wall-of-sound.

There were shades of the Beatles, touches of Motown, tastes of Stax-Volt.

When issued, the album made the top forty, earned underground acceptance, and pleased the ears of pundits, who tagged it "one of the most impressive debut albums ever" (*Crawdaddy*) and "an American *Rubber Soul*" (*Rolling Stone*).

But that was as good as it got. Despite an all-stops-out promo binge (five singles, a lavish kickoff party, and "Purple Power" ads), songs failed to snag the mass market. And early Grape implosion loomed. "The band would go out on the road and wreck hotels like the Who," said Rubinson.

During sessions for the follow-up album, *Wow,* Spence went weird. "He started wearing upside-down crosses," Lewis told Angel. "He carved devil's horns into his Strat cutaways."

"Most of us came back to earth eventually," he added. "Skip hasn't."

The *Wow* disc proved wobbly. Bob Mosley quit to join the Marines. Later waxings—some with him—were uneven. Then a legal settlement, in the early seventies, fixed a flaky financial fate: then-estranged manager Katz reportedly was granted ownership rights to the first two albums—the only ones that sold— along with the band's Moby Grape moniker (to which he'd already laid claim).

Thereafter, members toiled infrequently, under pseudonyms like Maby Grope, the (Original) Grape, the Ducks, and the Melvilles. And royalties generated by the classic album found their way to pockets other than the artists'.

Katz, meanwhile, had put another group of musicians on the road and called them Moby Grape. "If I say a band is Moby Grape, then they are Moby Grape," he said in an *L.A. Weekly* article. "Who cares who the members of Moby Grape are? A handful of dumb rock fans? I own the name. It's mine."

Bona fide Grape squirtings in years since have been sporadic. There've been club sightings. A cassette—under the name Legendary Grape—found its way out of Miller's Seattle home base in 1990. Sony Music, who bought out Columbia, saw fit to issue a Grape boxed set in 1993.

But a return to the glory of yore hasn't happened. Concerned industry friends, however, banded together in the mid-nineties to unravel the Grape's longstanding legal tangle. The goal: Return to the "American Rolling Stones" the rights to their own classic music.

KEY RECORDINGS: *Moby Grape* (1967), *Wow* (1968), *Moby Grape '69* (1969), *Truly Fine Citizen* (1969), *20 Granite Creek* (1971), *The Very Best of the Moby Grape* (compilation, 1993); "Omaha" (1967), "Mr. Blues" (1967), "Truckin' Man" (1969).

MOTÖRHEAD

They're scuzzy and scary; tacky and tasteless, with a skull-and-crossbones insignia; they're "the worst band in the world," proclaimed the media.

Issued in the punk-powered mid-seventies, Motörhead had a mission described by front man Ian Frazier Kilmister: "We will concentrate on basic music. Loud, fast, city, raucous, arrogant, paranoid, speed-freak rock 'n' roll. It will be so dirty that if we moved in next door to you, your lawn would die."

True to word, Motörhead deed has been to pioneer a ferocious metal rock that untrained ears sense is one unending noxious noise.

Kilmister, "Lemmy" for short—derived from his penchant for borrowing money, as in "lemmie a fiver"—had toiled in the Blackpool-based Rockin' Vicars and the psychedelic fields of Sam Gopal's Dream and Opal Butterfly in the radical sixties. For a while he was a roadie for Jimi Hendrix, then Hawkwind; later, he was the latter's bassist. In 1974, he was removed from Hawkwind due to a drug bust at the American–Canadian border. Returning to England, in 1975, Lemmy (vocals, bass) formed Bastard with ex-Pink Fairies Larry Wallis (guitar) and Lucas Fox (drums).

After a few gigs, Bastard's name was changed to Motörhead—slang for speed freak. A Dave Edmunds–produced album, *On Parole*, was cut and shelved for a decade, and Fox and Wallis departed. Lemmy brought in guitarist "Fast" Eddie Clarke and drummer Phil "Philthy Animal" Taylor. *Overkill*, produced by the Rolling Stones' sometime-producer Jimmy Miller, and *Bomber* were issued in 1979; both proved top-fifty U.K. hits.

With ceaseless touring, a grassroots, convoluted, and unlikely following of metalheads and punk fanatics was forged. *The Golden Years,* a 1980 EP, made the British top ten; "Ace of Spades" and an album of the same name went top twenty. A live album in 1981 proved a first: *No Sleep Till Hammersmith* rocketed to the top of the charts the first week of its release.

Throughout the eighties Lemmy relentlessly continued on, recording successful duets with Girlschool and the Plasmatics' Wendy O. Williams. The latter, a reworking of Tammy Wynette's "Stand by Your Man," incensed Fast Eddie, who departed to form Fastway. With the release of *No Remorse*, in 1984, Lemmy was with a new lineup: Michael "Wurzel" Burston (guitar), Phil Campbell (guitar), and Pete Gill (drums).

In 1990, the band moved to the U.S. to take possession.

On their lack of financial success, Lemmy replies: "That's just the way it is. If I had more, I would have spent more, so it would still be gone." It's the misconceptions that bother Lemmy most. "People are under the misconception that we're stupid, that we ride motorcycles and we're Hell's Angels. That pisses me off."

In the minds of Motör-heads, Lemmy and band are an institution and fathers of speed-metal. Lemmy disputes: "We don't do heavy metal, we don't do punk, we don't do speed, black, death, doom, or scrap metal. Molten metal, home-baked cornbread metal."

KEY RECORDINGS: *Motörhead* (1977), *Overkill* (1979), *Bomber* (1979), *Ace of Spades* (1980), *No Sleep Til Hammersmith* (1981), *Iron Fist* (1982), *No Remorse* (1984), *1916* (1991); "Ace of Spades" (1980).

MOTT THE HOOPLE/IAN HUNTER

"That band could have been the biggest band that ever was," said main Mott Ian Hunter to Marianne Meyer in *Relix*. "It was all ass-backwards—it didn't make sense. We had success after we had given up."

With David Bowie handling things, Mott the Hoople—all quietly proclaimed heterosexuals—became a centerpiece in the short-lived early-seventies lip-gloss-'n'-mascara, glitter/glam-rock scene. "Instantly, we were considered fags," Hunter told Jon Young of *Trouser Press*. "A lot of gays followed us around, especially in America. We were scared, at first. We were small-town boys."

Verden "Phalley" Allen (keyboards), Dale "Buffin" Griffin (drums), Pete "Overend" Watts (bass), and Mick Ralphs (guitar) had performed together around the Hereford area as the Doc Thomas Group and Shakedown. In 1968, with the addition of Stan Tippens (vocals), they were Silence. The following year, Tippen's voice took leave and he was out; Ian Hunter (b. June 3, 1946, Shrewsbury, Shropshire, England, vocals, piano, guitar) in. Fresh from a jail stay, Guy Stevens, their manager and producer, renamed them Mott the Hoople, after Norm Mott, a peculiar Jewish character in a Willard Manus novel.

Hunter—along with Roger Glover, later of Deep Purple—had labored as a failed songsmith for Francis, Day, and Hunter, suppliers of pop pap for Tom Jones and Englebert Humperdinck. It was the existence of Sonny Bono that convinced Hunter to try singing. "When I heard him," he told Michael Davis of

Record Review magazine, "I thought, if he can do that and get away with it, I can do it too."

The day Hunter was tapped for Hoople, he had seven quid in his pocket. "The idea of joining was to get through the summer holidays without working in the factory," he told *DISCoveries*' Andrew Darlington. "I thought the group was terrible; but they were going to give me fifteen quid a week—for three months!"

Their self-titled debut featured photos of Hunter's trademark permed mane and aviator sunglasses and his distinctive Dylanesque vocalizations, the latter allegedly the result of Stevens lowering Hunter into a hypnotic trance. Sales were modest. Their live performances gathered the act some U.K. notice and mildly improved sales for *Mad Shadows* and *Wild Life*. Nineteen seventy-two's *Brain Capers* failed to produce any interest, and the band called it quits.

Among their loyal fans was David Bowie. His offer of a tune, "All the Young Dudes," brought the band back into the studio and for the first of numerous times to the top of the British charts. "Dudes" would become their only stateside top-forty entry. A Bowie-produced album bearing the same name sold quite well, even in the U.S.

This association with Bowie and the glitter/glam-rock niche didn't set well with Hunter. "I felt like a bricklayer's laborer in gilt," he told Darlington. "I felt particularly uncomfortable with the whole thing. I was just an ordinary working-class bloke; all this was a bit too effete for me."

During the "Dudes" tour, Allen left the group, to be replaced in mid-'74 by Love Affair keyboardist Morgan Fisher. Their *Mott* album reached the top ten in the U.K. Squabbles over leadership between Hunter and Ralphs encouraged the latter to leave to form Bad Company; ex-Spooky Tooth Luther Grosvenor, rechristened Ariel Bender, replaced him. *The Hoople* and *Live* charted well, though with the departure of Bender— momentarily replaced by Bowie's Spiders from Mars guitarist

Mick Ronson—the band split in two. Hunter and Ronson toured together in support of each other's solo efforts. The others recruited Nigel Benjamin (vocals) and Ray Major (guitar) to issue two albums as Mott. Two further albums were cut with Medicine Head vocalist John Fiddler as the British Lions.

Hunter's solo LPs, with Ronson appearing on five of the seven, have continued to feed the cult stream. *You're Never Alone with a Schizophrenic* proved a top-forty stateside album.

"We've always had that cult following and never the hits," Hunter told Darlington. "Mott was so good because none of us were particularly good. It just jelled."

KEY RECORDINGS: Mott the Hoople—*Mott the Hoople* (1969), *Mad Shadows* (1970), *Wild Life* (1971), *Brain Capers* (1972), *All the Young Dudes* (1972), *Rock and Roll Queen* (1972), *Mott* (1973), *Live* (1974); "All the Young Dudes" (1972), "All the Way from Memphis" (1973), "Roll Away the Stone" (1973), "The Golden Age of Rock 'n' Roll" (1974); **Ian Hunter**—*You're Never Alone with a Schizophrenic* (1979), *Short Back 'n' Sides* (1981); "Just Another Night" (1979).

BILL NELSON

A guitar-playing rock futurist gone over the avant-garde edge, Bill Nelson initially operated on the fringes of the pop mainstream with his mid-seventies British band Be-Bop Deluxe, whose art-rock, progressive sound and Hendrixy soloing got him tagged as an upscale guitar hero. He rejected the role, issued an experimental album called *Sound-on-Sound* (almost all solo, but credited to Bill Nelson's Red Noise), and got a quick taste of his future commercial fate when his U.S. label, Capitol, test-marketed the record to radio stations. "That album actually lost me my deal with Capitol Records," Nelson told *Down Beat*'s John Diliberto. "They actually photostatted all the comments and showed them to me. . . . They were so despairing they're hilarious. They [were] things like 'What is this crap?' 'Out-Devos Devo!' 'Too wacko for us.' There wasn't one station that said it was great."

Nelson retreated to the privacy of his home studio in Yorkshire, "Echo Observatory," and proceeded, over the years, to produce volumes of equally radio-resistant musical esoterica, generally dividing it up between "serious" electronic compositions and more consciously pop-oriented efforts. *La Belle et la Bête*, representing the former, is a loosely structured pastiche of atmospheric chords, melody scraps, environmental sounds, and pointillistic noises composed for a stage production of the classic Jean Cocteau film. On the pop side are *The Love That Whirls*, *Vistamix*, *On a Blue Wing*, and *Luminous*, on which Nelson sings with the cool of David Bowie over layers of mechanized drums and multicolored sound effects topped with fluid, violinlike guitar lines.

Released on his own Cocteau label, the one-man synthesized concoctions have reflected Nelson's interest in "automatic" composing techniques (essentially, unedited mind emissions), trance music, and "alchemy, Rosicrucianism, esoteric Freemasonry, Hebrew Kabala, tarots," and the fusion of sexuality and mysticism.

The original fist-pumping Be-Bop Deluxe fans have long since given up trying to understand.

KEY RECORDINGS: *Northern Dream* (1971), *Sound-on-Sound* (as Bill Nelson's Red Noise, 1979), *Quit Dreaming and Get on the Beam* (1981), *Sounding the Ritual Echo* (1981), *The Love That Whirls* (1982), *La Belle et la Bête* (1982), *Chimera* (EP, 1983), *Vistamix* (1984), *On a Blue Wing* (1986), *Chance Encounters in the Garden of Lights* (1987), *Luminous* (1991), *Blue Moons and Laughing Guitars* (1993).

THE NEVILLE BROTHERS

"We grew up in the [Calliope Housing] projects at a time when a black man couldn't walk the streets of the French Quarter," explained Aaron Neville to Michael Corcoran in *Request*, on roots that gave rise to the distinctive Neville sound. "I'd listen to Pookie Hudson sing 'Goodnight, Sweetheart, Goodnight,' and I knew that there was beauty in the world. Music gave me hope."

Together or apart, the four brothers have been making notable discs for forty years, toured with the Rolling Stones, and been proclaimed by more than a few astute critics "the most talented family in America." Aaron, third eldest, in 1987 boasted to *Spin*'s Bunny Matthews that the Neville Brothers were "the baddest fuckin' band in the world."

Despite talent, accolades, persistence, and a growing fan base, the Nevilles have only of late begun to sell more than a minor amount of recordings.

Before Art and Cyril—half the New Orleans–born siblings—joined forces in the late sixties as the funky-flavored R&B Meters, each brother had been accumulating diverse experiences. Aaron (b. January 24, 1941, vocals), who served six months for auto theft, worked as a dockhand and created the biggest mainstream splash with a one-off hit, the 1967 soul classic "Tell It Like It Is." Art (b. December 17, 1938, vocals, piano) had been a member of the Hawketts, known regionally for the perennial turntable hit "Mardi Gras Mambo." Charles (b. December 28, 1939, sax), who served three years for possession of two joints of marijuana, had been a member of Joey Dee and the Starliters and a successful session man, recording with B. B. King and Bobby Blue Bland. Cyril (b. January 10, 1950, vocals, percussion), who had been a member of the Neville Sounds with Aaron, fronted the Soul Machine.

In 1975 the Nevilles got together in a studio backing the Wild Tchoupitoulas, a tribe of Mardi Gras Indians lead by their maternal uncle George "Big Chief Jolly" Landry. The brothers remained together to tour in support of the resultant album. With Jack Nitzsche producing, they recorded their first album as the Neville Brothers. Sales were light and so remained into the late eighties.

In 1989 *Yellow Moon* opened the door to wider notoriety; "Don't Know Much," an extract from the LP showcasing Aaron duetting with Linda Ronstadt, captured two Grammies. Aaron, who has since appeared with Dennis Quaid in the film *Everybody's All American*, was named Best Male Singer by *Rolling Stone* magazine in 1990.

"I call what we're doing happy music," said Art Neville to Jeff Tamarkin in *Goldmine*. "And if you can play happy music you can survive."

KEY RECORDINGS: *Fiyo on the Bayou* (1981), *Neville-ization* (1984), *Yellow Moon* (1989), *Brother's Keeper* (1990); "Don't Know Much" (1990).

NEW YORK DOLLS

During their brief lifetime their status as minor glam-rockers in no way hinted at the tremendous impact their two-album, passion-driven five-year career, devil-may-care attitude, and feminine junkyard fashions would have on the history of rock and roll worldwide. In bouffants, pumps, and lipstick the New York Dolls screeched openly of "Trash," a full-blown "Personality Crisis," and making love to Frankenstein.

Late in 1971, Arthur Kane (bass), Billy Murcia (drums), Rick Rivets (guitar), and Johnny Thunders (a.k.a. Johnny Volume, né John Anthony Genzale, Jr., guitar) began working as Actress at a Manhattan bar called Nobody's. Discovered hanging out and soon a member was street preacher, porno actor, and ex-Electric Jap David Roger Johansen (a.k.a. David Jo Hansen, singer), a pretty version of a big-lipped Mick Jagger. With Rivets's replacement, the Egypt-born, France-raised Sylvain Sylvain (né Ronald Mizrahi, guitar), the Dolls played Beanie's Bike Shop and the Mercer Arts Center in Lower Manhattan, at the latter opening for Eric Emerson's Magic Tramps and the avant-garde Eternal Fire-Eaters.

A glitter rock following rapidly evolved around Doll appearances. Mercury Records took an interest, and demo sessions were arranged. During their first visit to England, in the fall of '72, Murcia, age twenty-one, died; cause, a mixture of alcohol and pills.

With Todd Rundgren producing, Jerry Nolan (drums) appeared with the group on their debut and self-titled album. Although it and its follow-up, *In Too Much Too Soon*—produced by sometime stockcar driver and famed Shangri-las guiding light George "Shadow" Morton—were critically well received, they were commercial disasters; neither album touched *Billboard*'s Hot 100 chart.

After they were dropped from Mercury Records, Malcolm

McLaren—later the svengali behind the Sex Pistols—briefly managed the band. When no further recordings were forthcoming, Nolan and Thunders left the group. Johansen and Sylvain continued to tour as the New York Dolls until 1977.

Nolan and Thunders formed the Heartbreakers with ex-Television Richard Hell; later Thunders fronted various groups, including Gang War with ex-MC5 Wayne Kramer. Kane and Nolan accompanied ex-Sex Pistol Sid Vicious for a few of his solo performances. Johansen started a solo career in 1978; Sylvain accompanied until beginning his own solo efforts in '79. In the eighties Johansen reinvented himself as Buster Poindexter, a decadent lounge lizard.

Thunders died in April 1991, at age thirty-eight, of substance overload. Nolan died of a stroke in February 1992, at age forty-five.

KEY RECORDINGS: *New York Dolls* (1973), *In Too Much Too Soon* (1974); "Trash" b/w "Personality Crisis" (1973), "Stranded in the Jungle" (1974).

MOJO NIXON

He's a humor-spewing anachronism, a self-professed "idiot-phrase generator," unknown for such rock jollies as "Stuffin' Martha's Muffin," "She's Vibrator Dependent," "Debbie Gibson Is Pregnant with My Two-Headed Love Child," and "Elvis Is Everywhere."

"I'm a cult, make no mistake," says gravel-throated Mojo Nixon. "People that like me, like me *real* good. Those that don't understand where I'm comin' from have like these stupid looks on their faces: 'What? What's he's yellin' 'bout? He sings flat and sweats like a hog.' I always tell 'em, 'If you don't like me, you can come over to my house and kiss my hairy ass.'"

Nixon was born Kirby McMillan, Jr. (1957, in Chapel Hill,

North Carolina) and raised in Danville, Virginia. "It was one of those towns where you could do one of two things on a Friday night: Drive 'round and get drunk, or get drunk and drive 'round," explains Nixon. "For most of my life I felt trapped in a Springsteen song, 'Darkness on the Edge of Town.'"

Nixon's father ran a black radio station. "It was a left-wing thing, and he sold ads and was interested in integration. Good music was everywhere," he says. "I decided I wasn't gonna go to law school. I had been in floundering bands when I went on this cross-country bike trip in the fall of '82. It just hit me, this vivid vision. I had this calling. I knew right there that I was really Mojo Nixon, the illegitimate son of Richard Nixon and this voodoo lady, Miss Rudolph. Nixon fucked her good—like the rest of us—during his campaign swing in the fifties. Now it was revealed: I was to be a talkin' blues guy meant to get grandma to take her teeth out and naked butt dance."

To sharpen these skills, Nixon (guitar, wah-wah petal, sonic love jug) and sidekick Skid Roper (né Richard Banke, washboard, bongos, bass, kick-box, bells, jugs), an ex-leader of a surf band, opened for the Beat Farmers and Snuggle Bunnies, dropping tasteless tunes and banging washboards and whatnot.

Restless Records had never heard anything like Mojo and Skid's energized nonsense. Released on the tenth anniversary of Elvis Presley's departure, *Bo-Day-Shus!!!*—with the unforgettable "Elvis Is Everywhere"—caught a large-size audience.

"Elvis" was never issued as a single, and soon Nixon was re-relegated to the fringe zone. "Some power-mongrel buttheads decided that we didn't have the politically correct haircut and attitude and weren't boring enough to be heard by your average listener. They froze us, man."

Before their divorce in '90, Mojo and Skid cut four albums and a hot EP, *Get Out of My Way*. "It's all pitiful shit," says Nixon. "I can't stand to listen to 'em; then again, they never were meant to be. Stuff just falls outta my mouth. I do 'em once and get on my horse and get outta town."

On his cult status, says Nixon: "I never expected much. I mean to call yourself Mojo Nixon, sing like John Lee Hooker, and talk like Richard Pryor, all with some Hunter Thompson and Lou Reed mixed in, you can't expect any success. I'm just lucky enough to have a job at all."

KEY RECORDINGS: *Otis* (1990); **with Skid Roper**—*Mojo Nixon and Skid Roper* (1985), *Frenzy* (1986), *Bo-Day-Shus!!!* (1987), *Root Hog or Die* (1989); **with the Toadliquors**—*Horny Holidays* (1992); **with Dave Alvin and Country Dick as the Pleasure Barons**—*Live in Vegas* (1993); **with Jello Biafra**—*Prairie Home Invasion* (1994); **with New Duncan Imperials**—"I'm Drunk" (1993).

NRBQ

They're underground legends. NRBQ—the New Rhythm and Blues Quartet/Quintet, the Q for short—have been knighted "the ultimate bar band," "the world's most versatile . . . ," "the world's hardest-working band." Their ceaseless proclivity to play anything—well and distinctively—has won the rock band such diverse billings as the Grand Ole Opry, the Berlin Jazz Fest, the New York Folk Festival, as well as a consistent two hundred nights a year of performances in dang near any arena and flea-bitten roadhouse.

The NRBQ sound, what Q likes to call "Omni-pop"—varying nary a mite in its four-decade existence—is a loose, humor-dipped goulash of rockabilly, R&B, jazz, country, pop, and cornball. Audiences have been shaken out of their partying altered states by unexpected otherworldly renditions of the "Bonanza" theme (in simultaneous incompatible keys), Chipmunk tunes, Streisand's "People," the Seven Dwarves' "Whistle While You Work," and a twenty-minute shipwrecking of the "Wreck of the Edmund Fitzgerald," the last while dressed in pajamas.

Anything goes. And such a stance has cost them dearly with America's pigeonholing radio programmers. Consequently, they've gone decades without a mainstream hit recording, despite the obvious talent and the bagload of hook-ridden tunes. The media snubbing hasn't stopped them, and their constant touring, dangerously spontaneous sets, and sporadic releases have built NRBQ a tight line of fanatical believers.

The band first came together in Miami, Florida, when two Kentucky natives, Terry Adams (vocals, keyboards, harmonica) and Steve Ferguson (guitar, vocals), met Joey Spampinato (a.k.a. Jody St. Nicholas, bass, vocals) and Frank Gadler (vocals); the latter two were members of the unsuccessful Seven of Us, a Bronx-based band—incidentally, never seven in number—with a couple of singles issued on a Leiber and Stoller label. Tom Staley (drums) was added. Blues harp giant Slim Harpo spotted them in a New Jersey club and spoke well of them to Steve Paul, owner of the hot New York nightclub the Scene. The press praised the band, and Columbia Records signed them in 1969, changing their name from the Mersey-beats USA. Their debut was hyped as better than the Beatles, panned by critics, and bypassed by the public.

A second album—utilizing rockabilly legend Carl Perkins—was, likewise, a poor seller. Al Anderson, formerly of the Wild-weeds, joined in 1971. Two albums were issued by Kama Sutra. Critics took notice, but sales were disturbingly low. Four years later NRBQ recorded again—*All Hopped Up*—for their own label, Red Rooster. In the interim Ferguson and Gadler had quit, and Tom Ardolino had replaced Staley on drums. The Whole Wheat Horns—Terry Adams's brother Donn (trombone), Keith Spring (sax), Gary Windo (sax)—had become semipermanent members.

The touring and the critically acclaimed albums have continued. Their fanatical following has increased and solidified.

In 1994, Anderson left, replaced by Johnny Spampinato.

KEY RECORDINGS: *NRBQ* (1969), *Boppin' the Blues* (with Carl Perkins, 1970), *Scraps* (1972), *Workshop* (1973), *All Hopped Up* (1977), *At Yankee Stadium* (1978), *Kick Me Hard* (1979), *Tiddlywinks* (1980), *Grooves in Orbit* (1983), *Lou and the Q* (1986), *God Bless Us All* (1987), *Diggin' Uncle Q* (1988), *Wild Weekend* (1989), *Message for the Mess Age* (1994); "C'mon Everybody" (1969), "All Mama's Children" (1970), "Howard Johnson's Got His Ho-Jo Working" (1972), "Got the Gasoline Blues" (1973), "I Got a Rocket in My Pocket" (1977), "Wacky Tobacky" (1979).

OINGO BOINGO

As a kid, red-haired Danny Elfman was into horror, fantasy, and clipping photos from *Famous Monsters of Filmland* magazine. Several decades later he was living the fantasy, scoring music for *Batman* and *Beetlejuice* as an in-demand Hollywood composer. In between was a thing called Oingo Boingo.

Little is known of that eight-piece entity outside Los Angeles and a few odd pockets of underground intelligence. But those on the inside have long hailed Boingo and its manic leader, Elfman, as deft, if not daft, purveyors of progressive rock mixed with dark, addled humor.

In earliest form, the Boingo act—launched by Elfman and his brother Rick in 1973 under the name Mystic Knights of the Oingo Boingo—was an avant-weird theatrical troupe performing "a multimedia cabaret twisted show," as Elfman described it in *Billboard*. There were costumes, backdrops, film clips, and props; gorilla outfits; ten-foot dinosaurs; music from every known style; and story lines, including a show-length history of the world ending in Earth's destruction at the hands of space people.

Elfman, citing boredom, reconfigured the group in 1979 to generate music only, thus giving birth to the Oingo Boingo best remembered today. New members were added to a core of players drawn from the Knights, yielding a horn section plus Steve Bartek on guitar, John Hernandez on drums, keyboardist Richard Gibbs, and bassist Kerry Hatch. Elfman handled lead vocals, guitar, and songwriting.

Amid L.A.'s minimalist new wave of the time, the music of Oingo Boingo was different: complex, precision-played. Others' sounds were stark and monolithic. Boingo's was funhouse-kinetic. Guitars, plunking percussion, and crazed vocals interlocked like something concocted by a rockin' Rube Goldberg.

National top-forty radio proved indifferent; not so, Hollywood. Starting in 1985, sets of Goldbergian variations—written by Elfman—began turning up in soundtracks of "The Simpsons," *Weird Science*, Pee Wee Herman vehicles, *Scrooged*, *The Nightmare Before Christmas*, and other cartoon, puppet, and fantasy fare.

At last glimpse, Elfman was happily ensconced in his home studio composing film scores, while the Mother Unit—now called simply Boingo—was still active, having completed a minitour in late 1993 in which sidemen were seen dressed as clowns.

KEY RECORDINGS: *Oingo Boingo* (EP, 1980), *Only a Lad* (1981), *Nothing to Fear* (1982), *Good for Your Soul* (1983), *Dead Man's Party* (1985), *Boi-ngo* (1987), *Boingo Alive: Celebration of a Decade 1979–1988* (live, 1988), *Dark at the End of the Tunnel* (1990), *Boingo* (as Boingo, 1994); "Wake Up (It's 1984)" (1983).

GRAHAM PARKER

Hippies were still writhing to the euphoric sounds of progressive pop in the early seventies, and sensitive singer-songwriters were wailing about troubled psyches and such. But the purple haze had begun to lift, and patience for lyrical navel-gazing was wearing thin. East London native Graham Parker (b. 1950), who had been pumping out his own brand of folk, blues, and musical psychedelia, sensed that it was time to burn off the mystic fog and reignite the old soul flame—the punchy Otis Redding, Wilson Pickett, R&B sound that had grabbed him as a teen. "I wanted out," he later said to *Musician's* Mark Rowland. "I decided, 'I want short hair again, I want to go against the grain.' "

When next seen, the scrawny Parker was sporting sunglasses, close-cropped curly hair, and a pugnacious attitude, and he was singing self-penned tunes with a voice that suggested an irksome Van Morrison or a cranky early Bob Dylan. It was 1976 when he released his debut album, *Howlin' Wind*, and with its clipped songs and Stax soul backing by a pack of pub-rockers called the Rumour, it offered an earthy answer to the flaky folkiness and spacey experiments that preceded. It also slapped listeners into a state of readiness for more extreme noises, as a battalion of similarly Angry Young Men—the Clash and the Sex Pistols among them—prepared to crash through the walls of musical decency and taste with the screaming sounds of punk rock.

Following close on the heels of Parker was Elvis Costello, whose own first album, *My Aim Is True*, bore a striking similarity to *Howlin' Wind*—the same R&B tinge, lyrical acuity, vitriolic tone, and even the same producer, Nick Lowe. But the paths of the two soon diverged: Costello, heavily promoted for his punkish, Buddy-Holly's-evil-twin image, eventually shed that persona and became a widely hailed musical eclectic and bravura wordsmith—a sort of rock-infused Cole Porter. Parker, on the other hand, never quite seemed to catch the momentum of the new wave that he helped set in motion. He spent the next couple of decades in his own quirky-man, R&B-rock-reggae bag, issuing albums with varied record labels and producers and honing his lyric-writing ability to a fine edge. But he only occasionally gained notice beyond the raves of critics and the continued adherence of a cult audience.

The radio-resistant rasp of his voice may have had something to do with it. The other thing was his roller-coaster career, which took enough sharp twists and turns to unseat even the most tenacious rider. Following his mid-seventies introduction to Dave Robinson (a future cofounder of the indie Stiff Records label) and release of *Howlin' Wind* with the Rumour (comprising members of pub-rock bands Brinsley Schwarz, Ducks Deluxe, and Bontemps Roulez), Parker issued *Heat Treatment* (1976) on Mercury. So far, so good. Then the ride got rocky:

- His third album, *Stick to Me*, had to be rerecorded on a rush schedule after a technical problem made the original tapes unusable.
- Mercury Records released a pink-vinyl EP called *The Pink Parker*—an image-damaging choice of color for a rockin' toughie.

- Newly signed to Arista, Parker issued "Mercury Poisoning," a musical hate letter to his former label. Arista declined to affix its name to the product.
- Parker scored a top-forty album, *Squeezing Out Sparks* (1979), with its notable song about abortion, "You Can't Be Too Strong." He followed it with another hit, *The Up Escalator*—and then stopped working with the Rumour. The next two albums sold poorly; he left Arista.
- Heavy promotion backed the Elektra-issued *Steady Nerves* (1985), recorded with a new band, the Shot (including longtime guitarist Brinsley Schwarz). It yielded the top-forty hit "Wake Up (Next to You)," but album sales were only modest. Parker left Elektra.
- Parker signed with Atlantic, but after a dispute involving creative control, he left without releasing a single record.

Parker returned in the late eighties and early nineties with three well-received albums: the sparsely produced *The Mona Lisa's Sister*, *Human Soul*, and *Struck by Lightning*. At that time, he seemed accepting of his less-than-commercial-blockbusting fate yet still determined to press ahead on his own terms.

KEY RECORDINGS: *Howlin' Wind* (1976), *Heat Treatment* (1976), *Stick to Me* (1977), *Squeezing Out Sparks* (1979), *The Up Escalator* (1980), *Another Grey Area* (1982), *The Real Macaw* (1983), *Steady Nerves* (1985), *The Mona Lisa's Sister* (1988), *Human Soul* (1989), *Struck by Lightning* (1991); "Hold Back the Night" (1977), "You Can't Be Too Strong" (1979), "Discovering Japan" (1979), "Wake Up (Next to You)" (1985), "Don't Let It Break You Down" (1988).

GRAM PARSONS

At death, minutes after midnight on September 19, 1973, Gram Parsons was without a hit record or a major album success. His albums with the Flying Burrito Brothers had barely sold forty thousand. And his only solo work, *GP*, had sold even less.

Twenty years later, Parsons is revered as "the father of country rock," home base for such as the Eagles, Poco, the Byrds, New Riders of the Purple Sage, and Parsons's own Flying Burrito Brothers.

He was born Ingram Cecil Conner III (November 5, 1946, Winter Haven, Florida), son of a citrus- and cattle-farm heiress and "Coon Dog" Conner, a country picker who took his life when Parsons was thirteen. Parsons had a trust fund waiting. With little regard for economics, he ran away at fourteen to hang out in Greenwich Village, played rock and roll with the Legends—then including Lobo and Jim "Spiders and Snakes" Stafford—and folk music with the Shilos, and enrolled briefly in Harvard as a divinity student.

In Cambridge, Massachusetts, in 1966, Parsons formed the International Submarine Band, moved to L.A., and recorded what pundits proclaim the first country-rock album, *Safe at Home*. By album's release, Parsons was a member of the deteriorating Byrds. Though only a member for three months, he left his imprint on the band and their album *Sweetheart of the Rodeo*, the first commercially accepted country-rock fusion.

Soon after taking flight from the Byrds due to their intent to play a segregated South Africa, Parsons joined ex-Byrd Chris Hillman in forming the Flying Burrito Brothers. Parsons can be heard on two of their albums, departing in April '70, prior to their second release, *Burrito Deluxe,* for a solo career.

Early in 1970, he was injured in a motorcycle accident that postponed the recording of his solo debut, *GP*, with newfound protégée Emmylou Harris and members of Elvis Presley's touring band.

One day before earthbound days were done, Parsons completed *Grievous Angel*, considered by many of the pop underground a masterpiece. Upon its release in January 1974 there was no artist to promote, and the album's existence remained a prize captive to Parsons's ever-growing cult of appreciators.

Parsons was found unconscious on the floor of his room at the Yucca Valley High Desert Inn, September 19, 1973. Although rushed to a hospital, he died soon after of a drug overdose. His body was stolen days later by his friend and road manager Phil Kaufman and burned at the Joshua Tree National Monument.

KEY RECORDINGS: with the Byrds—*Sweetheart of the Rodeo* (1968); **with the Flying Burrito Brothers**—*The Gilded Palace of Sin* (1969), *Burrito Deluxe* (1970); **solo**—*GP* (1973), *Grievous Angel* (1974), *Gram Parsons and the Fallen Angels—Live 1973* (1982); "She" (1973), "Brass Buttons" (1974).

PERE UBU

"We're not industrial music—never were," said Pere Ubu leader David Thomas to *Creem*'s John Gatta. "It's just something that got stuck on us because people didn't know how to deal with what we did."

But they weren't spawned in the Mississippi Delta. It happened in Cleveland, Ohio—in the early seventies a hotbed not only of molten steel but of melding rock styles and absorbent musicians regurgitating odd and abrasive new blends. The Pere Ubu alloy—an "avant-garage" amalgam of grinding guitars, art-rock synthesizer, and Thomas's quavery, anxiety-inducing voice—emerged as one of the most effective sonic renderings of modern, urban-addled mental states. "Reality is a scary thing,"

Thomas said in Cleveland's *Plain Dealer*. "What matters is that the listener in some way experiences what was in our minds."

"We used to laugh at the industrial connotations," says long-time bassist Tony Maimone. "But we all lived downtown, we worked down there, we hung out down there. We used to like to cruise down in the valley where the steel mills are and where the coke plant is and where the railroad tracks are on fire to warm up the coal cars before they're used to make coke. That was all a big part of our growing-up experience, of our formative years in music."

Those years led to Rocket from the Tombs, a pre-Ubu entity created in 1974 by Thomas in the days when he went by the name Crocus Behemoth and wrote the occasional column of rock criticism. Apart from originating two songs that became pounding Ubu standards—"30 Seconds over Tokyo" and "Final Solution"—and containing the seeds of the future Dead Boys, Rocket was a vehicle for Peter Laughner, a legendary, one-man combustible catalyst in the local music underground. "He was incredible," recalls Maimone. "You could give him any topic, and he could write a song in ten minutes. He had this unbelievable music collection, and he was a great, great writer, a really good journalist. He and I, we had some fun."

The Rocket imploded in August 1975, but Pere Ubu soon emerged from the rubble in its first of several editions, this one inhabited by Behemoth, guitarist Laughner, bassist Tim Wright, guitarist Tom Herman, synthesist Allen Ravenstine, and drummer Scott Krauss. Named by Thomas after a character in *Ubu Roi*, an 1896 social-satirical play by Frenchman Alfred Jarry ("It sounded good and it doesn't mean anything to most people," Thomas told *Creem*'s John Gatta), the band issued singles of the aforementioned songs on Thomas's own Hearthan label.

Laughner departed (he died of drink and drugs in 1977, age twenty-four). Maimone then joined (in Wright's vacated slot) in time for the band's heyday. There were style-defining albums, travels to hotspots like New York's Max's and CBGB, and linkage (by observers) with the second wave of the original punk movement (Talking Heads, Dead Boys, and others). There was replacement of Tom Herman and Scott Krauss by guitarist Mayo Thompson and drummer Anton Fier. And there was conflict. Members splintered off in 1982, Thomas to pursue a distinctive solo career in various musical guises.

One Thomas project was the Wooden Birds, which in 1985 included ex-Ubus Maimone and Ravenstine. Pere Ubu reformed with Jim Jones on guitar and Chris Cutler on drums, launched its return with the album *The Tenement Year,* and continued from there in a more conventional, perhaps less groundbreaking, vein.

Their dissonant, noise-infused, angst-ridden qualities—along with the Cleveland locale—were what put the band on the receiving end of one inescapable adjective. "Could you imagine giving forty interviews and everybody asks you about 'industrial' music?" Maimone asks. "That's why David might have taken umbrage to that fact. But the fact remains that that's where we were, that's where we were living, and that's where we were spending all our time—of course there had to be an influence."

KEY RECORDINGS: *The Modern Dance* (1978), *Dub Housing* (1978), *New Picnic Time* (1979), *The Art of Walking* (1981), *390 Degrees of Simulated Stereo* (live, 1981), *Song of the Bailing Man* (1982), *The Tenement Year* (1988), *One Man Drives While the Other Man Screams* (live, 1989), *Cloudland* (1989), *Worlds in Collision* (1991), *The Story of My Life* (1993); "30 Seconds over Tokyo" (1975), "Heart of Darkness" (1975), "Final Solution" (1976), "Waiting for Mary" (1989).

PHISH

So attached, so clublike is the Phish following that they urge their favorite band—via computer network and letters to a Phish newsletter—*not* to get bigger and more successful. It might result in a toning down of the band's signature idiosyncrasy and dilute the intensity of the current band-fan relationship. To which bassist Mike Gordon replies: "We hereby officially *refuse* to play for more than a billion people at one untelevised concert."

Phish are big in their own pond. Perhaps taking a tip from the Grateful Dead and its Deadheads, they've cultivated and won over phalanxes of Phish phanatics who stay tuned to gig announcements, converse with each other in cyberspace, tape Phish shows for collecting and trading, and guarantee packed houses in the areas of their concentration.

Mainstream attention has been minimal—but it hasn't really mattered. "Phish has it down to an art form," says John Popper, vocalist for compatriot cult band Blues Traveler. "They have the ability to spend no money on advertising whatsoever, because their fans are so well-organized, and they *know* what's going on. I mean, it's kinda creepy."

The four Phish-men—Gordon, Trey Anastasio (guitar), Page McConnell (keyboards), and Jon Fishman (drums, vacuum cleaner)—floated out of Burlington, Vermont, in the mid-1980s with a sound that was different in an old-wave, back-to-jamming way. With intense study and group practice they've made it even more so. Compositions are complex, eclectic, incorporating anything from jazz to rock to skewed country. Playful ditties mutate into knotty, dissonant extrapolations. Players improvise, with Anastasio's guitar taking the lead in either slinky, stringy jazz tones or soaring, Santana-like riffing.

Attitudes are irreverent; lyrics have an "I am the eggman" loon element. Heated exchanges course through issues of the Phish newsletter as phans offer their decipherings of indecipherable Phish verse. (Was that, "Wash your feet and drive me to Firenze" or "Watch the cheese and drive me to a frenzy"?). On another plane, Phish-heads have been observed debating the relationship of band jams to Nietzschean notions of Apollonian and Dionysian qualities. "The people who see us live are really listening," Anastasio said in a *Rolling Stone* interview. "They understand our music. They *get* it."

KEY RECORDINGS: *Junta* (1988), *Lawn Boy* (1990), *A Picture of Nectar* (1992), *Rift* (1993), *Hoist* (1994); "The Squirming Coil" (1990), "Reba" (1990), "Chalkdust Torture" (1992).

THE POGUES

"A lot of people like our sound because we're up onstage looking so brain-damaged that there's just no way people wouldn't like us," said Spider Stacy, Pogue cofounder, to Todd Avery Shanker in *Pulse* magazine.

They're not a pure Irish band; nor even a folk-punk band. Born of energetic punk inclinations, boarded in traditional Scottish and Irish folk music, and seasoned with opera, country, Spanish flamenco, eastern inflections, and New Orleans Cajun, they are the Pogues, proud proclaimers of "psycho-ceile" music.

The idea of forming a heavily modified Irish traditional band was hatched in the early eighties in the ethnically diverse and economically downsided Kings Cross neighborhood of North London, with the meeting of Shane MacGowan (guitar, vocals)—known as Shane O'Hooligan and referred to as a "toothless moronic pisshead" by the British press when fronting his punkabilly band Nipple Erectors—and Spider Stacy (penny whistle, beer-tray bashing), formerly leader of the punky Millwall Chainsaws.

Combing the squatlands, the pair recruited a motley bunch of runaways, reprobates, and legit musicians—namely James Fearnley (accordion), Jem Finer (banjo), and Andrew Rankin (drums). In fact by 1983, as Pogue Mo Chone (a Gaelic expression translated as "kiss my arse"), they played the backways and pubs of London.

The following year Caitlin O'Riordan (bass) was added and the group printed up some copies of "Dark Streets of London." Radio response was nil, largely due to the group name. Their moniker caused such difficulties that before Stiff Records signed the act, members, had to agree to shorten it to simply the Pogues. *Red Roses for Me* received good reviews; extracted "Boys from the County Hell" failed. The follow-up, *Rum, Sodomy & the Lash* (a title reportedly taken from Winston Churchill's description of life in the Royal Navy), a top-twenty charting album, was produced by Elvis Costello.

In 1986 the Pogues issued the *Poguetry in Motion* EP, toured the U.S. for the first time, lost O'Riordan to marriage to Costello, and headed for Spain's Sierra Nevada to appear as the caffeine-addicted and mightily deranged McMahone family in Alex Cox's mutant spaghetti western, *Straight to Hell*. Pogue appearances also happened in Cox's *Walker*, as well as *Eat the Rich;* Pogue tunes were provided for the Sex Pistol tale, *Sid and Nancy*.

After a celebration concert for the Irish Rovers, the Pogues teamed with the Dublin act for a U.K. top-ten hit, "The Irish

Rovers"—the largest-selling single for either act. Ex-Steeleye Span Terry Woods (cittern, mandolin, concertina) and former Radiators from Space–man Phillip Chevron (guitar) joined the lineup, and the band clicked again in their homeland with "Fairytale of New York."

With the Clash's Joe Strummer (guitar) as a temporary member, the Pogues experienced some mainstream attention with the release of *If I Should Fall from Grace with God.*

The "drunken paddy bullshit," as Chevron refers to the charges, is inappropriate. "That all comes from the early days when, to be fair, we were playing in bars and we got paid by being allowed to drink as much as we wanted."

While *Peace and Love* and *Hell's Ditch* solidified the group's eclectic popularity, MacGowan was knocked down by a taxi and suffered bouts with pneumonia, permanently being replaced by roadie Darryl Hunt (bass) in 1991.

"Pogue music is good music to dance to, drink to—it's also good music to dance to and listen to," says Chevron. "You can celebrate with the Pogues, but you can also cry in your beer with us as well."

KEY RECORDINGS: *Red Roses for Me* (1984), *Rum Sodomy & the Lash* (1985), *If I Should Fall from Grace with God* (1987), *Peace and Love* (1989), *Yeah Yeah Yeah Yeah* (EP, 1990), *Hell's Ditch* (1990); "Boys from the County Hell" (1984), "Fairytale of New York" (1987).

IGGY POP AND THE STOOGES

Ripped flesh and shattered glass. Torso contortions. Displayed privates. If those were Iggy Pop's only contributions to the fine art of rock, his permanent place in the cult pantheon would be assured. But there was more. Much more.

Way before punk rock; years before hardcore; decades prior

to the advent of slam-dancing, stage diving, and crowd surfing, Iggy set a new standard for extremism on stage, on disc, and in life.

When he first popped into view with the Ann Arbor, Michigan–based Stooges, flower power was slow-fading into the post-hippie seventies and sleek corporate rock was oiling up its lumbering engines. The Stooges were different. hard, aggressive, and bent on dispensing with frills to get to rock's nasty core.

Their rowdy first platter—served in 1969—shoveled up a not-too-nice mess of garage-rock noise. Two, maybe three chords per song. A set of moronic, blockhead grooves. Sawtooth distortion, blunt eruptions of fuzz guitar, and tinges of bad-acid psychedelia. And it had Iggy, singing with punk pushiness such torpor-addled, pre-slacker tales as "1969" ("another year with nothin' to do"), "No Fun" ("to hang aroun', freaked *out* fo' anotha day"), and other verse that reduced life to its basic, dumb teen urges.

That disc was not a Grammy Award nominee. Nor was the

song "I Wanna Be Your Dog" on any known mainstream radio playlist.

Iggy's live act was notorious. The band would Igg-nite him, and as crowds watched in shock, a half-nude Iggy would go ballistic. "The music drives me into a peak freak," he told *Rolling Stone*'s Eric Ehrmann in 1970. Reports had him writhing around on broken glass, smearing himself with peanut butter, diving into crowds, and having sex with a fan—during a show.

He sliced himself with broken bottles. He got into fights. "I became carried away, obsessed with this chick," he said of one incident, "and I scooped her from her seat. She screamed and scratched me, so I bit her and dropped her to the floor. I still have scars from her."

"This guy will stop at nothing," observed rock manager John Sinclair in Clinton Heylin's *From the Velvets to the Voidoids*. "This isn't just a show—he's out of his mind!"

"I can't feel any pain or realize what goes on around me," claimed Iggy at the time. "When I dive into a sea of people, it is the feeling of the music, the mood. Nobody ever knows how it's going to end up." "Nobody" included guitarist Ron Asheton, drummer Scott Asheton, and bassist Dave Alexander—the three dutiful Stooges who jammed along night after night as it all went down.

What witnesses saw seemed to be actual psychodrama, real catharsis—not an act. And it inspired them. Alan Vega and Stiv Bators (of Suicide and the Dead Boys, respectively) were among those in the early seventies who absorbed Stoogecraft into their acts—like a virus—and spread it throughout rock's nether regions and outer zones. In years since, the Stooges have been widely credited—along with the Velvet Underground, MC5, and a couple of others—with setting the stage for the aggro-oriented mutation of rock into the 1990s. And David Bowie, Don Was, Blondie's Chris Stein, and members of the Sex Pistols are just a few who've made a point of working with Iggy on record.

Pop was born James Osterberg on April 21, 1947, and grew

up around Ann Arbor, Michigan, where he played drums in local bands the Iguanas (whence came the name Iggy) and the Prime Movers. He migrated to Chicago after high school, "apprenticed" there with the Butterfield Blues Band's Sam Lay, and then returned home to put together the Psychedelic Stooges—as a singer—with his former high school friends the Ashetons and Alexander.

Called Iggy Stooge at that point, he and his band attracted notice mostly around Detroit as that town's distinctive scene sprouted. Elektra Records' Danny Fields, in town to check out the similarly raucous MC5, caught a Stooges show on the side and enthusiastically signed them on. They issued two albums, broke up, and then returned in slightly altered form as Iggy and the Stooges. With the encouragement and backing of fan David Bowie they recorded *Raw Power*, a work now oft-cited as a precursor of punk and grunge. In January of 1974 the band played its last gig.

On an occasion when Pop deemed it necessary to get a grip, he checked into an institution. "I didn't need to go through therapy or anything else," he told *Creem*'s Vicki Arkoff. "I went to the Neuro-Psychiatric Institute and I said, 'Look, I'm a young guy and I've lost control. I'd like a little help while I get it back.'"

He got it back enough to carry on—Stooge-less, as it happened, though initially aided and abetted by Bowie. The albums *The Idiot* and *Lust for Life* were the first indicators of Pop's still-active vital functions. Those discs remain centerpieces of his catalog to this day.

In the early eighties, he said, he was "living hand-to-mouth, flophouse to flophouse, hotel to basement to some society mansion with some girl," while making records that he later found wanting. Yet his career—or "rehabilitation," as it's been called—continued to gain momentum. By the early 1990s he was grinding out discs, like *American Caesar*, that longtime Pop boosters heard as ample justification for continued adherence.

More than two decades after the Stooges' debut, Pop's once decidedly antisocial acrobatics have, paradoxically, become socially acceptable—at least to a broad-based rock crowd no longer fazed by scenes of onstage mayhem, bodies being passed overhead, or dead animals used as props. "I believe there's pressure on Iggy Pop," comments Bill Laswell, producer of Pop's *Instinct* album. "It turned into entertainment. Twenty years ago a radical idea was [just] that, and now twenty years later it can be fairly conservative without actually changing at all. Part of him is really an artist who would love to experiment, and another part of him has the responsibility of an ongoing relationship with an audience."

The Godfather of Punk, while still noted for undiminished stage power, has been seen engaged in amiable chat on no less a mainline show-biz showcase than *The Tonight Show*. "I live easily with my adulation," a mellowing Pop once admitted. "I'm very comfortable with it."

KEY RECORDINGS: The Stooges—*The Stooges* (1969), *Funhouse* (1970); "I Wanna Be Your Dog" (1969); **Iggy and the Stooges**—*Raw Power* (1973); "Search and Destroy" (1973); **Iggy Pop**—*The Idiot* (1977), *Lust for Life* (1977), *New Values* (1979), *Soldier* (1980), *Party* (1981), *Zombie Birdhouse* (1982), *Blah-Blah-Blah* (1986), *Instinct* (1988), *Brick by Brick* (1990), *American Caesar* (1993); "Nightclubbing" (1977), "Candy" (1990).

THE PRETTY THINGS

"Most of the time we called ourselves Little Boy Blue and the Blue Boys," says Dick Taylor of the Rolling Stones' formation in 1962. Taylor was the original bass player with the Stones. "Mick Jagger was Little Boy Blue. Charlie [Watts] did a lot of the drumming. Keith [Richard] and I had met at Sidcup Art College and liked the same music—Chuck Berry, Bo Diddley. It was there that we actually rehearsed—much more than we ever played any place."

Taylor and the rest of his own group, the Pretty Things—formed the following year and named after an influential Bo Diddley tune—created the first "rock opera," *S.F. Sorrow,* but lost the acclaim to the Who and Pete Townshend's *Tommy.*

"Our British label made a deal [in 1968] with Motown to issue *S.F. Sorrow* in America on their new Rare Earth label," explains Taylor. "Bad luck, it was. They had no experience with the rock market, waited a year or so until after *Tommy* was out, and then got this progressive idea to put our disc in a package with rounded corners. Imagine that. It looked nice, but record buyers' fingers would miss it when they flipped though the racks."

The Pretties were anything but. They were loud, aggressive, and crude. They had that look—the dirtiest long hair, or so it seemed, and scruffy street clothes. "The songs weren't merely played," wrote critic Greg Shaw, "they were attacked, as by a tribe of wild-eyed barbarians."

The Stones were shocking and morally upsetting, but the Pretties were a mother's nightmare. "Would you let your daughter date a Pretty Thing?" asked the British media.

Despite their critically acclaimed repertoire for Fontana Records—arguably the raunchiest rock 'n' blues records of the sixties beat-group era—Taylor's band, initially comprising Taylor (guitar), Phil May (vocals), John Stax (bass), Brian Pendleton (guitar), and Viv Prince (drums), never had a hit recording in America.

Those who noticed have stuck with the band through the bad and the worse times—thirty years. Fifteen albums were issued by the Pretties, in Europe. Nothing has been issued in the States since *Cross Talk,* in 1980. Hardcore fans have been living off of Pretty Thing imports almost from the get-go.

On life's paths not taken, Taylor is philosophical. "I'm certainly not the same person I would've been if I had stayed with the Stones, but I have no regrets."

As for the fame that eclipsed the Pretties, Taylor is self-effacing.

"We were actually all quite clean, at the time," he says, with a laugh. "We were all just being ourselves. People wrote of us as crazed, and our manager just played on it. We got painted as too over-the-top to ever be acceptable to a big audience. We gotta be your classic cult band."

When not gigging with original Pretty Phil May and the Yardbirds' Jim McCarty as the Pretty Thing–Yardbirds Blues Band, Taylor—who lives on the Isle of Wight off the southern coast of England—works the pubs as an accompanist for Angelina Glamshaw or as a member of local favorites the Jukes. By day, he works at a sweet-corn packing factory.

"Hopefully, I won't have to do that forever," says Taylor.

KEY RECORDINGS: *The Pretty Things* (1965), *S.F. Sorrow* (1969), *Parachute* (1970), *Silk Torpedo* (1974), *Savage Eye* (1975); "Rosalyn" (1964), "Don't Bring Me Down" (1964), "Honey I Need" (1965), "Midnight to Six Man" (1965).

PROFESSOR LONGHAIR

He was "the Picasso of Keyboard Funk," "the Bach of Rock," "the King of the Crescent City Keyboard," an icon. Professor Longhair (né Henry Roeland Byrd), or Fess, for decades was the spirit of Mardi Gras, and his joyously eccentric vocalizing and distinctive "rumba boogie" style—comprising an infinite spray of sophisticated syncopation and piano kicking—influenced a generation of piano players from Fats Domino, Huey "Piano" Smith, and Dr. John through Allen Toussaint, James Booker, and Art Neville.

Legend has it that Fess played as he did out of necessity. "When he was a child they didn't have no piano in his house," explained historian Stevenson Palfi. "He and his friends went out in the alley and got an old piano that only had a certain number of keys. Most of the keys were broken; some didn't have hammers or strings."

Fess (b. Bogalusa, Louisiana, December 19, 1918) started his career as a street tap dancer, boxer, and card shark. In the late forties he graduated to playing the piano in New Orleans clubs disguised in bizarre costumes and under various monikers— the Four Hairs, Blues Scholars, the Shuffling Hungarians, and Roy Byrd and His Blues Jumpers.

From the forties through the early fifties he worked for a succession of labels, collecting a major R&B hit with "Bald Head" in 1950 and cult status with "Tipitina" in 1954. Due to a musicians union dispute and a slight stroke, Fess turned to hustling to make do in the early sixties.

National minor-league recognition eluded him until his reemergence at the Second Annual New Orleans Jazz and Heritage Festival in 1971 and Dr. John's early-seventies recording of his "Tipitina."

Live on the Queen Mary, a tape of Fess's performance at a 1975 party for Paul and Linda McCartney, was issued. Things were looking up. In 1979 he filed his first income tax return ever and bought a home. A tour opening for the Clash was scheduled to take Fess to an entirely different realm.

Months later, Fess died in his sleep, at age sixty-one.

KEY RECORDINGS: *New Orleans Piano* (1972), *Rock 'n' Roll Gumbo* (1974), *Live on the Queen Mary* (1978), *Crawfish Fiesta* (1980), *Mardi Gras in New Orleans* (1982), *The Last Mardi Gras* (1982), *Houseparty, New Orleans Style* (1987); "Bald Head" (1950), "Tipitina" (1954), "Go to the Mardi Gras" (1959), "Big Chief, Part 2" (1972).

PUBLIC IMAGE LTD.

In the 1978 song "Public Image," Johnny Rotten reclaimed the person behind his hyped-up star Sex Pistol identity. With reference to "my grand finale" and "my goodbye," the tune marked the end of Rotten, his reversion to his legal name of John Lydon, and the launch of his new musical vehicle, Public Image Ltd.

It didn't mark the end of his abrasiveness and anger. Still bugging him were human apathy, conformity, deception, man-induced worldwide decay—the usual annoyances. But a new, improved Lydon—older and wiser from bruising battles with corporate musicdom—had apparently moved to take control of his output and career. "I steer the ship of fools," he told *Creem*'s Toby Goldstein. "When there's a storm, I'm heading straight for it."

Since then, Public Image Ltd.—often called PiL—has essentially been Lydon's one-man show. "[It's] my little gem, my artistic vehicle," he said. Musicians have come and gone. Key members have included guitarist Keith Levene and bassist Jah Wobble in the early years and guitarist John McGeoch starting in 1987.

The sound, unlike that of the punkoid Pistols, has been largely groove-driven. "Death Disco," a song issued in 1979 and included under the title "Swan Lake" on the acclaimed album *Metal Box* (which was actually packaged in a metal container), offered an early sample. On that track and others, chest-pummeling funk rhythms and metal-toned guitar support the trademark Lydon howl—still crazy, though more variably so, after all these years. "My possibilities are literally limitless," he bragged to *Creem* writer Jeff Hays. "I play with my voice. They said I couldn't sing. Now they know I can't. And they're right."

Lydon has tended toward flexibility, trying to keep the music unconventional and free of cliché. Helping to make it so have been efforts like the generically titled *Album* of 1986, in which cult producer Bill Laswell matched Lydon with jazzmen Tony Williams and Malachi Favors, violinist L. Shankar, funkster Bernie Worrell, and former Cream drummer Ginger Baker.

The mainstream, at least in the U.S., has remained at a distance. Lydon's been dismissive. "It's very hard for me to tell the difference between all of that kind of MOR stuff," he said. "While they're being so bland, I, of course, stand out like a diamond in a mud stack. Which is fine. There's a place for all of us."

KEY RECORDINGS: *Public Image* (1978), *Metal Box* (1979), *The Flowers of Romance* (1981), *This Is What You Want . . . This Is What You Get* (1984), *Album* (1986), *Happy?* (1987), *9* (1989), *That What Is Not* (1992); "Death Disco" (1979), "(This Is Not a) Love Song" (1983), "Rise" (1986).

THE RAMONES

"We were like aliens to most listeners; still are. Some people never got it, but there was no such thing as punk music until the Ramones," proclaims Joey Ramone. "There was the Count Five and Shadows of Knight—garage bands—but no punk rock. We created it."

After two years of talk of forming a band, in the fall of 1973 Johnny Cummings (guitar), Douglas "Dee Dee" Colvin (bass), Jeffrey "Joey" Hyman (vocals, drums) and Thomas Erdelyi (drums)—preteen friends who lived within blocks of each other in Forest Hills, New York—decided to get serious and pick up some instruments.

The name Ramones came from a Paul McCartney pseudonym (Paul Ramone); their identifiable Ramones sound just happened. "For the first year we saw ourselves as a bubblegum

Roberta Bayley

band, like the Bay City Rollers," says Johnny Ramone. "We were warped and were just figuring out our instruments, so it just didn't come off that way."

After a stay in 1974 as the house band at the protopunk club CBGB, the band was picked up by Danny Fields, formerly affiliated with the Stooges, MC5, and Lou Reed. With Fields as their manager, the Ramones were soon in the studios cutting their genre-defining self-titled debut. Neither it nor their first 45, "Blitzkrieg Bop," charted. But that minimalist wall-of-noise sound, that high school dropout look, and those trademark countdowns ("one, two, three, four!") and "gabba gabba, hey" chants were there as if the band's career plans had been finely figured out in advance.

"We were rock 'n' roll fans—into Buddy Holly, the Stooges, Beach Boys—and wanted to play pure rock 'n' roll," Joey says.

"We never wanted to do anything that would be heavy and have to be analyzed. And image was never something we thought about," explained Johnny. "We were just street kids, rockers. The ripped jeans and leather jackets are timeless signs of teenage rebellion."

The punk scene was just forging when they toured England in 1977. Ironically, many of the bands the Ramones influenced—such as the Clash and Sex Pistols—overshadowed them in popularity. That year *Leave Home* and *Rocket to Russia* charted modestly, and "Sheena Is a Punk Rocker" came the closest to being a stateside hit, peaking at 81 on the *Billboard* Hot 100.

In 1979, they starred in Roger Corman's commercial-flop flick *Rock 'n' Roll High School*. Phil Spector produced their turn-of-the-decade album *End of the Century*. With some minor re-touches on the Ramones style tried, the group plowed on through the eighties and into the nineties.

"We're typecast—there's no getting free," says Johnny, "but I feel fortunate that twenty years later I still can do it. I can play whatever when I'm home in my room.

"At this point, we take it one year at a time. We got maybe two, three years. When we can't maintain the visual or it's not any fun anymore, we'll walk away."

KEY RECORDINGS: *Ramones* (1976), *Leave Home* (1977), *Rocket to Russia* (1977), *Road to Ruin* (1978), *End of the Century* (1980), *Too Tough to Die* (1984); "Blitzkrieg Bop" (1976), "Sheena Is a Punk Rocker" (1977), "Rockaway Beach" (1977), "I Wanna Be Sedated" (1978), "Do You Wanna Dance?" (1978), "Needles and Pins" (1978), "Rock 'n' Roll High School" (1979), "Do You Remember Rock 'n' Roll Radio?" (1980), "Time Has Come Today" (1983), "Pet Sematary" (1989).

REDD KROSS

The brothers McDonald—singer-guitarist Jeffrey and bassist-singer Steven—were but tiny tykes when they were swallowed up into the L.A. club scene as Red Cross. It was 1978, their ages were fourteen and eleven respectively, and the sound du jour was punk-crude. As show openers for Black Flag and such, the Cross kids were initially aligned with the harder-core segment of the scene (their first drummer and guitarist later eased into the slamming Black Flag and Circle Jerks). That didn't last for long; soon the McDonalds were exhibiting a taste for ear-candy songcraft and pop hooks that led, with a legally required name adjustment, to the cult-acclaimed Redd Kross of today.

Consumers of Kross confections cite two interacting layers of pleasure. On one, there's the sheer catchiness of the tunes, with Beatles-ish melody, lots of rich backup harmony, and tastes of late-sixties psychedelia, power pop, and sugary bubblegum (for which Jeff McDonald's clean-toned lead vocal has proved a perfect match). On another are the references to seventies pop culture that have led some to dig Kross mainly as a parody-leaning-toward-tribute band.

Seems that what others gladly dumped from that denigrated decade Jeff and Steve saw fit to retrieve—and then glorify. Songs offer bemused but reverent nods to mainstreamers like the Archies, ABBA, Bachman-Turner Overdrive. Present in the act are bits of T. Rex glitter, Bowie androgyny, glam-band spandex, swirling paisley. They've professed affection for schlock TV and B movies: They named *Born Innocent* after the 1974 Linda Blair girls-in-prison flick and covered a song from Russ Meyer's *Beyond the Valley of the Dolls*.

The campy McDonalds—the only constant Kross members over the years—haven't always been understood. They've been mistaken for female, due to Rapunzel-length hair and gaudy garb. Slam-dancing denizens of their former scene have had occasion to catcall and pummel them with bottles. The Krosses have struck back with parodies like "Old Punks" and have otherwise continued to spread their message.

"Americana: There's so much to love," Jeffrey purred to *Melody Maker's* Everett True. "It's our contribution to world culture: hot fudge cake and fake toilet seat covers. We're very proud of it and like to bring our own interpretation of it to other countries . . . so people can better understand their brothers."

KEY RECORDINGS: *Born Innocent* (1982), *Teen Babes from Monsanto* (1984), *Neurotica* (1987), *Third Eye* (1990), *Phaseshifter* (1994); "Bubblegum Factory" (1990), "1976" (1990).

LOU REED

He's the much-emulated "apostle of rock nihilism," "the Homer of the Underground," "the King of Decadence," and cofounder with John Cale of the genre-twisting Velvet Underground. Lou Reed is a noisy iconoclastic rock and roll animal. One of the most enigmatic and significant rock performers of the last three decades, he has left an ever-deviating trail of masterworks and cherished rubbish.

Reed was born Louis "Butch" Firbank, March 2, 1942, to a Long Island, New York, upper-middle-class family. He studied the clarinet; early on there were indications that he had the potential to be a concert pianist. By fourteen, Reed was leaning toward rock and roll rebellion. Garage bands like Pasha and the Prophets, the Jades, the Shades, and the Eldorados had him on guitar. His parents disapproved and allegedly admitted him to a hospital for electroshock therapy.

Reed attended Syracuse University, scratched around as a journalist, dabbled in acting, and worked for a number of years as a staff songwriter and artist for Pickwick Records. He wrote hot-rod and surfing songs, recorded as the Beach Nuts, and almost scored a hit with a dance tune called "The Ostrich" under the name the Primitives.

In 1964 Reed merged with John Cale and Sterling Morrison and came under the guiding force of artist Andy Warhol. As a group they worked under various guises until the addition, the following year, of Maureen Tucker. They were now the mind-altering Velvet Underground, a dark band with tales of urban decay and perversity. Their albums sold only marginally, initially, and their time as a band was short—but their influence is unshakable.

By 1970 and the release of the group's *Loaded*, Reed had experienced enough. For a year he walked out on music and worked at his father's accountancy firm in Long Island. But he was back the following year with the issuance of his first of now thirty-plus albums. Each one, prodding fans proclaim, has its distinctive direction, style frames, and Reedian personas, with his unmistakable talk-sung utterances serving as the common sound and key anti-pop ingredient.

KEY RECORDINGS: *Transformer* (1972), *Berlin* (1973), *Rock 'n' Roll Animal* (1974), *Sally Can't Dance* (1974), *Coney Island Baby* (1975), *Street Hassle* (1978), *The Bells* (1979), *The Blue Mask* (1982), *New Sensations* (1984), *New York* (1989), *Magic and Loss* (1992); "Walk on the Wild Side" (1972), "Dirty Boulevard" (1989), "Romeo Had Juliette" (1989).

THE REPLACEMENTS

While mainstreamers were selling records by the millions in the mid-eighties, a gang of four Minneapolis rowdies touted as "the greatest rock and roll band in the world" were lurching around the underground playing for pocket change.

They never did get much, recognition-wise, from the broad

listening public. But the four Replacements—Westerberg (guitar, vocals), Tommy Stinson (bass), Bob Stinson (guitar), and Chris Mars (drums)—won the die-hard loyalty of those in the know and, especially, the acclaim of rock critics, with a mix of punk rawness, "classic rock" range, and hell-raising abandon. Sounding too good to be true for seekers of passion and power without show-biz artifice, the Replacements proved real—and then near-ideal, as leader Westerberg grew from rough-edged thrasher to a songwriter of sensitivity and depth.

Years after folding, they were hailed by *The New Yorker* as "the best raunchy rock band of the eighties." Cult followers were still tallying their artifacts. And music alternativists were on the airwaves with the 'Mats' brand of grungy retro-rock.

Why were the 'Mats (short for Placemats) forever stuck in the margins of musicdom? "We were pioneers," Westerberg told *Pulse*'s Ira Robbins, "and the pioneers—Iggy, Johnny Thunders, the Dolls—don't get it. Somebody's got to pick it up—maybe water it down, crank it up, do something to make it work."

They had an against-the-grain scrappiness that attracted fans but deterred mainline masses. The 'Mats embodied "all of the funky quirks of the classic rock bands—the Who, the Rolling Stones, the Ramones—that critics found endearing," said Westerberg to Robbins. "We didn't have the things that made those bands huge, we had the thing that made them infamous and decadent and, perhaps, great."

From the beginning they flaunted their amateurism and lived the punk ethos "success is bad." A self-described misfit and loner, Westerberg was an aspiring singer who took up guitar, he claimed, so that he could drown out people who might be laughing at his voice. The other three, as he described them, were beer-drinking hoods. Tommy Stinson was twelve at the time; none of them graduated from high school. When the band first got together, sometime in 1979, they'd practice in the Stinsons' basement, drink, and then pick up guitars almost as an afterthought—to work on songs dashed off by Westerberg.

Ultimately they penetrated the Minneapolis club scene—a setting that would spawn fellow post-punk acts Soul Asylum and Hüsker Dü. By 1981 the 'Mats had wangled a recording contract with the independent Twin/Tone label, debuted with punklike speed and blast-level volume, and followed up with the hardcore thrash EP *The Replacements Stink*. In no time they were members of a neopunk movement populated by such fellow fringe dwellers as Black Flag, the Minutemen, and the Meat Puppets.

'Mats club dates were notoriously drunken, unpredictable affairs. There were missed notes, dropped chords, and hapless cover versions of seventies schlock-rock classics. Bob Stinson—the band maniac—was quite likely to appear on stage in skivvies or diapers.

"We have fun at all costs," Westerberg once said to *Musician's* John Leland. "Attitude and humor are our strong suits. The people that like us are wise enough not to pay their money to see us hit the right chords. They come to see something exciting and fun." .

Musically, the four stretched out some on 1983's *Hootenanny* album, merging the sounds of punk, pop, rock and roll, and blues ("without really having a feel for any of them," as Westerberg pointed out to *Rolling Stone*'s David Fricke).

The classic 'Mats discs—the three issued between 1984 and '87—brought wider attention to Westerberg's songwriting. Singled out were "Answering Machine" (from 1984's *Let It Be*), linking loneliness and the technological world in one skillful shot, and "Left of the Dial" (from the band's major-label debut, *Tim*). *Pleased to Meet Me*—a 'Mats masterwork—offers a fully varied menu of bashing blues-punk ("I.O.U."), cocktail swing ("Nightclub Jitters"), an arena-scale anthem ("Never Mind"), glistening acoustic folk ("Skyway"), and a hip reference to alternative rock's most-sung unsung hero ("Alex Chilton").

But, with Westerberg high-rolling and dissension rising, the 'Mats began going the way of all things perishable. Fans noted the absence of Bob Stinson on *Pleased to Meet Me*—he'd been ousted for overkill in the debauchery department. Slim Dunlap joined for the next LP. By the last, *All Shook Down,* the Replacements were essentially Paul Westerberg plus some studio musicians—Mars and Tom Stinson among them. Mars quit and was replaced by Steve Foley in time for a tour, a fizzle, and the final curtain.

Chris Mars put out two solo albums. Tommy Stinson created his own group, Bash & Pop. Westerberg issued a well-received solo disc and entered the next phase of the rock and roll life cycle: no longer an upstart, and not yet a veteran awaiting the next batch of replacements.

KEY RECORDINGS: *Sorry Ma, Forgot to Take Out the Trash* (1981), *The Replacements Stink* (EP, 1982), *Hootenanny* (1983), *Let It Be* (1984), *Tim* (1985), *Pleased to Meet Me* (1987), *Don't Tell a Soul* (1989), *All Shook Down* (1990); "God Damn Job" (1982), "Left of the Dial" (1985), "Alex Chilton" (1987), "I'll Be You" (1989).

THE RESIDENTS

Behind an unmarked door in an unfamiliar universe reside the Residents, the best-known bunch of unknown performers ever to saturate the cult underground with audio and video exotica.

Anonymity has been their signature. Members' identities have been kept hidden under giant eyeball masks, top hats, white ties, and tails, or such other disguises as death masks, black hoods, mummy wraps, and radioactivity-protection suits. Two "spokesmen," Homer Flynn and Hardy Fox, describe themselves only as the Cryptic Corporation. "What we are," said Flynn in a *Melody Maker* interview, "is the group that officially interfaces reality for the Residents . . . The only way the Residents interface reality through themselves is through what they do, through their recorded work, their live shows, and their videos."

They began "interfacing reality" in 1970, around the time the founders abandoned Shreveport, Louisiana, in favor of northern California and ultimately San Francisco. Their maiden vinyl voyage, the twin-45 *Santa Dog,* signaled a satirical, pop convention–bashing ethic. On the subsequent *Meet the Residents* and *The Residents Present the Third Reich 'n' Roll* (in which they parody/reinterpret the Beatles, Doors, Box Tops, Iron Butterfly, and other pop figureheads), along with *The Residents Commercial Album* (forty minute-long ditties) and such epic originals as *Eskimo* (evoking an arctic ambience) and the Mole Trilogy (creating a fantasy world of underground dwellers), the Residents emerged as a cross between Frank Zappa, experimental performance artists, and a ranting, seriously addled C. W. McCall.

Live shows are elaborately staged (within cult-budget limits). Eyeball heads have been present, as have otherworldly sets, eerie lighting, body-stockinged dancers, Devo-like robot/mime movement, and hooded Residents standing at a bank of sci-fi synthesizers.

These orb-head enigmas have built a small industry around an obscure, hard-to-peg product: themselves. Through their own Ralph Records they issue Residents merchandise (from trinkets to T-shirts) and their vast sonic catalog. Ambition has increased: 1990's music/theatrical work *Cube-E* recounts the "History of American Music in 3 E-Z Pieces"; the American Composer series is planned as a sixteen-disc Residential interpretation of such band faves as John Philip Sousa and James Brown; and 1993's *Freak Show* is an interactive CD-ROM—one of the first music-group efforts in the digital multimedia realm.

KEY RECORDINGS: *Santa Dog* (double 45, 1972), *Meet the Residents* (1974), *The Residents Present the Third Reich 'n' Roll* (1975), *Fingerprince* (1976), *Not Available* (1978), *Duck Stab* (EP, 1978), *Eskimo* (1979), *The Residents Commercial Album* (1980), *Mark of the Mole* (1981), *The Tunes of Two Cities* (1982), *The Residents' Mole Show* (live, 1983), *George & James* (1984), *Whatever Happened to Vileness Fats?* (1984), *The Census Taker* (1985), *The Big Bubble* (1985), *Stars & Hank Forever* (1986), *God in Three Persons* (1988), *The King and Eye* (1989), *Cube-E Live in Holland* (1990), *Freak Show* (1991).

JONATHAN RICHMAN AND THE MODERN LOVERS

As leader of the rough and primitive-sounding Modern Lovers, Jonathan Richman made music that prefigured punk rock. Yet for most of his near quarter century in show business he's been an adult-child spinner of such winky-dink whimsy as "I'm a Little Aeroplane," "Ice Cream Man," and "I'm a Little Dinosaur." The Richman hardcore have stayed the course. Mainstream musicdom's been oblivious.

"I make so-called adult songs for adults who can't grasp the regular stuff," he explained to *Creem*'s Bill Holdship in 1984—

thirteen years after his debut. "The turning point may have been playing for and entertaining children. It made a difference, and changed the way I saw entertainment."

The writer who at thirty-two recorded "Not Yet Three"—a view of life from a tot's perspective—began with a streak of grown-up angst. A Boston-born (in May 1951) baby boomer, Richman saw his late-sixties entertainment idealized in the droning gloom of Lou Reed, John Cale, and their Velvet Underground bandmates. "I followed them around as much as I could," he said. "I saw them perform over and over again. I watched them rehearse, and I became a big pain in the neck."

Inspired, he assembled a quartet—dubbed the Modern Lovers—in 1971. Keyboardist-guitarist Jerry Harrison (later a Talking Head) was there, as were drummer David Robinson (later of the Cars), and bassist Ernie Brooks. They matched hard, distorted sonics to songs that oozed Richman's simple romanticism ("Roadrunner"), teen frustration, and out-of-step wholesomeness ("I'm Straight") and rejection of drugs ("She Cracked"). It could have been cloying but came off as intriguing and offbeat.

Boston club dwellers took note. And awareness traveled to points south, where New York pundits perked at the sound of something blasting from Bean Town that differed markedly from the day's Osmonds–Carpenters–Tony Orlando top-forty coalition.

Major record labels made moves and backed the recording of song demos in 1972, with former Velvet Underground member John Cale producing. But nothing committed to tape—including some other stuff overseen by pop-cult producer Kim Fowley—reached public ears at the time.

The Richman star stab stiffed, apparently, because of his creeping desire to pare down the sound and move away from the preapproved grit and grime. "It was gradual," he told Holdship. "I started playing quieter and making up stuff like 'Hey Little Insect' as early as '72. Every year was a little different from the year before. I was already enough of a nuisance to turn off my original band by 1973." Their differences were irreconcilable, and the Lovers separated.

In 1975, Northern California's Beserkley Records stepped in, first releasing a smattering of Richman tracks on a compilation album and then, in 1976, issuing *The Modern Lovers,* partly made up of those demo tracks that Cale had overseen in 1972. The cut "Roadrunner"—today a key piece of rock history—hit the charts in England, and with potent punk impact. Ironically, the band that waxed it was no more, and Richman was already well into a new, punk-free phase.

Wide-eyed innocence—with a touch of the ridiculous— erupted on *Jonathan Richman & the Modern Lovers* and its follow-up, *Rock 'n' Roll.* Titles like "Hey There Little Insect" and "Rockin' Rockin' Leprechaun" were indicative of their tyke-friendly tone. Punk patronage desisted. Lovers of quirkiness signed on.

There was puzzlement in the press. Was this a case of arrested development? Of tongue in cheek? Of appropriating cheeriness as others mope and slack? Was his charming naïveté a sign of eccentricity? Oddity? The questions themselves stoked the JoJo mystique. "Most of the rock press and audience still don't know me and have mistaken ideas about me," he complained to *Rolling Stone's* Kristine McKenna. "All my songs come from being in love with life. It's something I've felt since I was a kid, and I think it's a gift I was born with."

The grooves of 1983's *Jonathan Sings!*—a disc clutched tightly by Richmanites—are clogged with the kinds of cozy themes, quaint humor, and antique rock sounds oft cited as signature. The classic "That Summer Feeling" has Richman, in a Lou Reed talk-singing voice against minimal electric backing, taking a witty, wistful look at youthful times that will "haunt you the rest of your life"—it's a kind of "Walk on the Child Side." There's a nutty paean to an instrument—"Those Conga Drums"—that shakes and rattles in "Stranded in the Jungle" style. A ditty glorifies the simple act of walking, while another, "Stop the Car," puts JoJo at odds with reckless drivers stoned on pot. Throughout, Richman's forced rhymes (matching "because you oughta" with "no reason notta," for example) keep the tone a tad cartoon-loony.

Time hasn't stilled the Richman pen. The albums have flowed steadily, with nary a nod to the "Roadrunner"-era tastes of old punks still on the bandwagon. He's dipped into country, delved into foreign-language songs, doled out spoken words. He's become firmly fixed as the family singer who once said he wanted to play where "there's popcorn, and there's six-year-old kids running around." As for that first Modern Lovers album—judged by many to be among the seventies' finest—it's "past history to me now," he said. "I'm younger than I was when I made that early stuff."

KEY RECORDINGS: The Modern Lovers—*The Modern Lovers* (recorded 1972, released 1976); "Roadrunner" (1976); **Jonathan Richman and the Modern Lovers**—*Jonathan Richman & the Modern Lovers* (1977), *Rock 'n' Roll with the Modern Lovers* (1977), *Back in Your Life* (1979), *Jonathan Sings!* (1983), *Rockin' and Romance* (1985), *It's Time for Jonathan Richman and the Modern Lovers* (1986), *Modern Lovers 88* (1987); "Hey There Little Insect" (1977), "Rockin' Rockin' Leprechaun" (1977), "That Summer Feeling" (1983); **Jonathan Richman**—*Jonathan Richman* (1989), *Jonathan Goes Country* (1990), *I, Jonathan* (1992).

ROXY MUSIC/BRIAN FERRY

They were distinctively cool and surely decadent. Roxy Music's mutant art-rock was without precedent—a seamless mix of fifties sleaze, modal jazz, avant-garde noise, and melancholic forties crooning, all to decidedly nihilistic effect.

With David Bowie, they helped redefine rock as a visual medium. Front man Brian Ferry preened and pranced in lounge-lizard drag. Keyboardist and androgynous "treatment" artist Brian Eno issued dense walls of auditory distortion with glam-rock poise. Visually, Roxy Music was freak chic—a decked-out display of leather, glitter, feathers, mascara 'n' rouge, and Cadillac-finned hairstyles.

"We were terrified to go on stage, in the early days," Ferry told Mark Rowland in *Musician* magazine. "Dressing up and becoming other people made it possible for us to perform."

The son of a coal miner, Ferry (b. September 26, 1945, Washington, Tyne and Wear, England, vocals) had attended the University of Newcastle. For three years, he studied art with pop visual artist Richard Hamilton, a student of Dadaist Marcel Duchamp. While at school he sang with the Banshees, later the R&B-oriented Gas Board, which also included Graham Simpson (bass).

By 1970, Simpson and Ferry—then a schoolteacher—were looking to start something musically experimental. Andy Mackay (sax, oboe), who had played the oboe with the London School's Symphony Orchestra and the sax at Reading University, was the first to join. Mackay introduced them to Brian Eno (synthesizer, keyboards). Fleshing out the earliest lineup were classical percussionist Dexter Lloyd and Roger Bunn (guitar). Both left after a few months; ex-Smokestack drummer Paul Thompson and Davy O'List (guitar), formerly of the Nice, were added. O'List was soon gone; Phil Manzanera (né Phillip Targett-Adams Manzanera, guitar) took his place.

Roxy Music was an immediate success in England. Their self-titled debut album and first single, "Virginia Plain," went top ten. Critics loved their campy, post-psychedelic, artsy doodlings. "Pyjamarama" and *For Your Pleasure* likewise stopped at the top of the charts.

Ferry and Eno argued over the group's direction; Eno departed for the avant-garde regions of sound. With ex-Curved

Air member Eddie Jobson replacing him and Ferry in charge, Roxy Music moved toward—though never touching—a more streamlined, mainline pop sound. Further success followed in the U.K. By the time they finally broke a semi-hit in the States in 1975, "Love Is the Drug," members began solo projects, and Roxy Music disbanded for the first time in 1976.

Two years later, Ferry, Mackay, Manzanera, and Thompson reunited for *Manifesto* and *Flesh + Blood;* their last studio effort, *Avalon,* appeared in 1982. Their fanatical fan base has never diminished.

KEY RECORDINGS: Roxy Music—*Roxy Music* (1972), *For Your Pleasure . . .* (1974), *Stranded* (1973), *Country Life* (1974), *Siren* (1975), *Viva!* (1976), *Manifesto* (1979), *Flesh + Blood* (1980), *Avalon* (1982), *Heart Still Beating* (1990); "Virginia Plain" (1972), "Do the Strand" (1973), "The Thrill of It All" (1974), "Love Is the Drug" (1975), "Jealous Guy" (1981); **Brian Ferry**—*These Foolish Things* (1973), *Another Time, Another Place* (1974); "A Hard Rain's A-Gonna Fall" (1973), "Heart on My Sleeve" (1976).

TODD RUNDGREN

He's had his share of visits to the pop mainstream. Mass audiences have had their ears pleasured by such top-forty memorables as 1970's "We Gotta Get You a Woman," 1972's "I Saw the Light," and 1978's "Can We Still Be Friends."

Yet Todd Rundgren has been most revered by underground dwellers: a crowd of fanatical followers who've idolized him for years, closely monitoring disc and concert doings and nowadays spending lots of time in cyberspace exchanging information bits about him. To them, he's not Todd Rundgren or the founder of the band Utopia or the leader of the Nazz—he's just "Todd."

He's tailor-made for cultdom: Both extraordinarily talented (a

singer, multi-instrumentalist, composer, engineer) and unusually accomplished (soloist, producer, band member), he's made the kinds of intriguing, against-the-grain records pounced on by the faithful—those who secretly "get it," identify with his quirkiness, and then like to share the thrill with others. His prodigious output has more than satisfied aficionados' hunger for artifacts to scrutinize, pick apart, and stash away.

As a guitar-wielding, vocalizing, and songwriting team player, the lanky, long-haired Todd—born on June 22, 1948, and raised in Upper Darby, Pennsylvania—has been a member of two revered bands. Following a 1966 warmup in the blues-bashing outfit Woody's Truckstop, he launched the Nazz, a now-legendary power-pop quartet whose Rundgren-penned track "Hello, It's Me" became a minor hit in 1969. When he departed that year, Rundgren left a trail of three treasured and now hard-to-find Nazz albums.

Todd's other major group effort, Utopia, came together as his "dream band" in 1973—an outlet for his artier, more progressive musical musings and flashy guitar work. The group coalesced, by 1976, into a permanent membership of Roger Powell on keyboards, Kasim Sultan on bass, John Wilcox on drums, and Rundgren; all sang. They would record ten albums over the next seventeen years, issuing a superbly played, often fusion-like, Mountain-meets-Chick-Corea sound.

The solo Rundgren has been waxing discs since 1970, after leaving the Nazz and signing with manager Albert Grossman. The first platter, *Runt,* revealed him as a one-man band and hit-making entity. But instead of following up with formula radio "product," he's since tended to turn where his eclectic interests have led. There've been sprawling double-album sets (one, 1972's acclaimed *Something/Anything?,* yielding a blockbuster remake of "Hello, It's Me"), mixtures of potential hits with sonic novelties and synth space-outs, and tributes to favored rock and soul classics (on *Faithful* and *A Wizard, a True Star*).

Todd first toyed with synthesizers on the *Wizard* album. A long-term interest in technology would place him on the leading edge in the early 1990s when, in the midst of the San Francisco Bay Area's burgeoning "multimedia" movement, he produced the interactive CD *No World Order* that allows users to manipulate various elements of the tracks he recorded for it.

That fit the wizard/hermit/tortured-artist image he's long lampooned with his album titles, even while making noted spotlight-dodging moves. "I found having to be on the road and promoting yourself to radio stations sort of distasteful," he said (quoted by Steve Roeser in *DISCoveries*), "so I wanted to do something that had more to do strictly with the music. That's why I quit the band [the Nazz]—I looked at production as a way to remain in the record business without having the responsibilities of 'pop stardom.'"

Todd's behind-the-scenes credits are wide-ranging in musical style. Among his productions are protopunk and punk rock (the seminal first New York Dolls album and a Patti Smith disc), midwestern hard rock (a number-one hit with Grand Funk Railroad's "We're an American Band"), and blue-eyed soul (Hall and Oates).

But the varied career bells, whistles, and sidelines have tended to drown out what many consider the main Rundgren attraction: his gospel-tinged, R&B-laced vocal style and his ability to write both stirring pop vocal anthems and songs in the smooth, sophisticated Philadelphia soul tradition—songs that can induce chills.

Yet in 1985 he recorded an album, *A Cappella*, in which he used multiple overdubs of his own voice as stand-ins for nearly all band instruments, in one case replicating a complete Mo-town/Philly-soul style of arrangement on the irresistibly catchy "Something to Fall Back On." And four years later he crowded a studio with a boisterous chorus to back his own voice on *Nearly Human*, an album of heart-rending, wailing R&B that *Rolling Stone* called "the record that Todd Rundgren has refused to make for over fifteen years—simple, superb, white pop soul."

KEY RECORDINGS: *Runt* (1970); *The Ballad of Todd Rundgren* (1971), *Something/Anything?* (1972), *A Wizard, a True Star* (1973), *Todd* (1974), *Initiation* (1975), *Faithful* (1976), *Hermit of Mink Hollow* (1978), *Back to the Bars* (live, 1978), *Healing* (1981), *The Ever Popular Tortured Artist Effect* (1983), *A Cappella* (1985), *Nearly Human* (1989), *2nd Wind* (1991), *No World Order* (1993), "We Gotta Get You a Woman" (1970), "I Saw the Light" (1972), "Hello, It's Me" (1973), "Can We Still Be Friends" (1978).

RUSH

Rush resisters dismissed them as pretentious and overblown. Detractors batched them with a clutch of rejected arena rock-ers—slingers of sonic bombast and mystic-fog lyrics worthy only of parody, punk revolt, or psychotic reaction.

Yet the Canadian trio of Geddy Lee (vocals, bass, keyboards), Alex Lifeson (guitar), and Neil Peart (drums, lyrics) has, over the years, survived the harsh judgments and more than a few musical revolutions. They bask today in a revisionist light, as aging critics grow mellow and banner-carriers of the grunge generation accord the band new respect. More to the point: not only has Rush succeeded on the mainstream level (nine platinum-selling albums between 1976 and 1990) but they've retained and even expanded an underground, hardcore following—a Rush-crazed cult whose number and activities put them in the Deadhead and Jimmy Buffett Parrothead league.

Cyberspace networks of "Rush Fanatics" maintain a computer fanzine/bulletin board, trade bootleg recordings, swap discographies, and share arcane bits of trivia. They analyze lyrics, claim hidden meanings, hypothesize about band members, and keep close tabs on upcoming tour dates. Their fanaticism at times puzzles even the band. "Every once in a while you get the overly intense Rush fan who has come to know you, and it's a little scary," said Geddy Lee to *Request*'s Jim DeRogatis. "But," he qualified, "for the most part, they're pretty considerate, polite, and introspective."

Why the loyal following—and the longevity? "They're some of the most highly regarded musicians in rock," according to a radio programmer quoted in the San Francisco *Chronicle*. Their compositions, often complex and grand in scale, inspire awe among the receptive. Neil Peart's lyrics—which over the years have touched on mythological, philosophical, and fantasy themes (J.R.R. Tolkien, Ayn Rand, and Carl Jung among their inspirations)—are treated by many as Rorschach-like invitations to interpretation. Band members are viewed as heroes. "Rush fans perceive Rush as these real godlike figures: Neil the superintellectual lyricist and master of the drum kit," said band assistant Andrew MacNaughtan.

At first—back in the late-sixties days when grade-school friends Lee (b. Gary Lee Weinrib) and Lifeson (b. Alex Zivojinovic) were bashing around in Toronto basements—they were emulating English blues-rockers like Cream, pretending they were Jack Bruce and Eric Clapton, respectively. Through three years of club gigs with first drummer John Rutsey and into their 1973 self-released eponymous debut album, they kept motors revved to metallic, power-blast levels. Then the U.S. Midwest took notice, Chicago's Mercury Records signed the troupe (rereleasing their disc), and on the verge of a maiden stateside voyage, Peart took over the drum chair; at that point the group moved into an artier phase, building on Peart's lyrics to create epic-proportioned albums and live shows.

Then came the punk backlash and new-wave movement of the late seventies, along with calls for simplicity, and Rush responded. "For us it was time to come out of the fog for a while and put down something concrete," Lee told *Guitar World*'s John Swenson. Doing so with shorter pop tunes, they racked up two of their most successful albums, *Permanent Waves* and *Moving Pictures*.

In the techno eighties, the Rush sound underwent a sleekening, digitizing process that left it glistening with multiple synth tones. Then in the nineties, noting yet another back-to-basics surge—especially coming out of Seattle—the band moved again, this time away from overly mechanical production. They put out *Counterparts*, an album that proved as popular as much of the concurrently trendy grunge and so-called alternative rock.

KEY RECORDINGS: *Rush* (1973), *Fly by Night* (1975), *Caress of Steel* (1975), *2112* (1976), *All the World's a Stage* (live, 1976), *A Farewell to Kings* (1977), *Hemispheres* (1978), *Permanent Waves* (1980), *Moving Pictures* (1981), *Exit . . . Stage Left* (live, 1981), *Signals* (1982), *Grace Under Pressure* (1984), *Power Windows* (1985), *Hold Your Fire* (1987), *A Show of Hands* (live, 1989), *Presto* (1989), *Roll the Bones* (1991), *Counterparts* (1993).

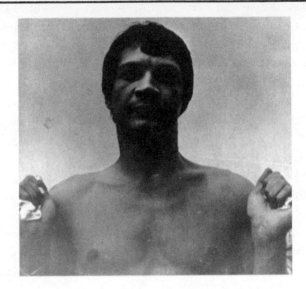

MITCH RYDER

"I'm not dead. Let's get that straight," says Mitch Ryder, sixties-ruler of the hardest working little R&B cover band from out of the Motor City. "That's a misconception some [top-forty] people seem to have about me."

The White Soul King's not inactive, either. The touring is nearly nonstop, and numerous recordings have been issued in the last decade throughout Europe.

The hits and the mainstream attention, however, did stop—more than twenty-five years ago.

Then the airwaves were filled with "Jenny Take a Ride," "Little Latin Lupe Lu," "Devil with the Blue Dress On/Good Golly Miss Molly" and "Sock It to Me, Baby!" to name a few. Now, the same sounds are heard exclusively on oldies radio and in the households of his hardcore followers.

At the top of his form in mid-'67, the raucous Ryder made a major move and dismissed John Badanjek, Jim McCarty, Earl

Elliot, and Joe Kubert—the Detroit Wheels, his fusion-packed backup—and prepared for what he was told would be a film career and the lucrative easy-listening audiences of Las Vegas. For a moment, such atypical and placid pop as "What Now My Love" and "You Are My Sunshine" charted moderately for Ryder, the solo crooner. In a flash all was gone.

Ryder quickly recharted his course, returning to his roots and reforming the Detroit Wheels. As "Detroit," they issued one critically acclaimed album. Bitterness and drugs were taking their toll; members dropped away, and the mass audience never looked back.

"I was burnt up," he says. "I did too much of everything. I needed to get away." After a suicide attempt, Ryder and his wife moved to Denver, where he worked in manual labor jobs for five years. All the while he wrote songs; planning his return, he formed his own label and in 1978 recorded two limited-edition albums, *How I Spent My Vacation* and *Naked But Not Dead*. Ryder had not left that blue-eyed soul music he was singular at producing. Devotees eagerly sought out copies and small-club appearances.

In his teens he sang R&B with a black group called the Peps. One single was issued on a small gospel label under his God-given name, Billy Levise, Jr. While performing at Detroit's Village club—immortalized in '62 by Nathaniel Mayer's top-forty hit, "Village of Love"—Ryder struck up a relationship with a visiting band, the Rivieras.

"There was already a group in Chicago using that name," he says. "So, we had to change it. I found my name in a telephone book. Mitch Ryder seemed popular. I mean, there was more than one guy in there with that name.

"We met Bob [Crewe, record company owner and producer for the Four Seasons and Freddy Cannon] just by way of some demos we were sending around."

With their second single, "Jenny Take a Ride," a compiled

cover of the standard "C. C. Rider" and Little Richard's "Jenny Jenny" for Crewe's company, their two-year string of hard-rockin' blue-eyed soul was initiated.

Says Ryder, "It's still a complete joy to perform. I can't get enough of that applause. The travel—the getting from point A to point B—wears me. Other than that I'm quite happy singing for my supper."

KEY RECORDINGS: *Take a Ride* (1966), *Breakout . . !!!* (1966), *Sock It to Me!* (1967), *Detroit* (1971), *How I Spent My Vacation* (1979), *Naked But Not Dead* (1980), *Never Kick a Sleeping Dog* (1983); "Jenny Take a Ride" (1965), "Little Latin Lupe Lu" (1966), "Devil with the Blue Dress On/Good Golly Miss Molly" (1966), "Sock It to Me, Baby!" (1967).

DOUG SAHM

"Whatever I sound like, it's 'cause-a my blood," says Doug Sahm, Tex-Mex legend and sometime leader of the Sir Douglas Quintet. "See, I'm from Texas and saw T-Bone Walker live and heard Webb Pierce. And then I got this Chicano thing in me, too. It's all jumbled up in me."

For forty-plus years, Doug Wayne Sahm (b. November 6, 1942, San Antonio, Texas) has been freely dabbling in every genre from fifties R&B, swamp-pop, and Tex-Mex border music to honky-tonk, cornball country, and psychedelic hippie-dippy.

Sahm could play anything with strings. Locals knew him as "the hottest steel-guitar kid in San Antonio." At age twenty, he was recording as Little Doug. Parents made him turn down a spot on the Grand Ole Opry to complete his schooling.

"Hank Williams sat me on his knee, in '53, at his last performance. I had my first [local] hit in '60," Sahm quickly adds, "with 'Why, Why, Why' as Doug Sahm and the Markays; then 'Two Hearts in Love' and 'Crazy, Crazy Feelin'" went local.

"When the British Invasion started, I bugged Huey [Meaux, noted record producer]. He said, 'You need a gimmick, boy,' so me and Augie [Meyers] and the guys [Jack Barber, Johnny Perez, Frank Morin] grew our hair, became the Sir Douglas Quintet, and everybody thought we were British. Man, that was before the Byrds. Us and the Beau Brummels were the first American long-haired groups."

After a few top-forty hits—notably "She's About a Mover" and "Mendocino"—and hometown drug busts, Sahm and an evolving band of hippies moved to San Francisco, then toured the land with Bob Dylan's Rolling Thunder Revue. Numerous solo and Sir Doug reunion albums have kept fans intrigued.

In 1990 Sahm, Augie Meyers, Flaco Jimenez, and Freddy "Wasted Days and Wasted Nights" Fender formed the Texas Tornados. "We're sort of a Tex-Mex Traveling Wilburys," says Sahm in a rapid drawl. The band has been successful on the country charts.

"I'm proud—nobody in the world does it like me," says Sahm. "B. B. [King] does the blues, Dylan has his folk thing, but I got fans that let me do whatever I want. I got the Tornadoes, and me and Augie got the Sir Douglas thing, and then when I want I can go off and do solo stuff. It keeps me on my toes and fresh."

KEY RECORDINGS: Sir Douglas Quintet—*Best of Sir Douglas Quintet* (1966), *Honkey Blues* (1968), *Mendocino* (1969), *1+1+1=4* (1970), *Border Wave* (1981), *Sir Douglas Quintet* (1993); "She's About a Mover" (1965), "The Rains Came" (1966), "Mendocino" (1969). **Doug Sahm**—*Doug Sahm and Band* (1973), *Groover's Paradise* (1975), *Texas Rock for Country Rollers* (1976), *Hell of a Spell* (1980), *Juke Box Music* (1989).

SAM THE SHAM

Decades have passed, but to hardcore appreciators the poorly recorded but mystifying Tex-Mex ode "Wooly Bully" and its creators, the two-time Grammy-winning Sam the Sham and the Pharoahs, are the stuff cult legends are made of.

Domingo Samudio was born in 1937 in the farmlands outside of Dallas, Texas. His parents were of Mexican descent and Spanish-speaking. "We lived in what they called shotgun shacks, just three rooms in a straight row," Samudio told the authors of *Where Have They Gone?* "Someone was always singing. My father was part of a trio and played Mexican folk music."

Samudio won a school contest while in second grade and made his radio debut singing "I'm Always Chasing Rainbows." In his teens, he formed a music group with Trini Lopez, later of "If I Had a Hammer" fame. With graduation Sam joined the Navy. Once out of the service, he became a floorwalker at

Smitty's, a club in Jacksonville Beach, Texas, and later a carny selling french fries.

The Charlton Heston flick *The Ten Commandments* was in reissue when Samudio had the itch to return to wiggling—"shamming"—and making musical noise in front of people. "We thought Ramses, the king of the Pharoahs, looked pretty cool, so we became the Pharoahs." Samudio, a self-taught musician, was not much of a keyboardist. "That's how I got my nickname, the Sham," he said.

After a few failed efforts in the early sixties, Sam and group were approached by the tiny XL label for whom they recorded a peculiar dittie about some weirdie named Hattie Mattie and Sam's cat, Wooly Bully.

Before the dance disc charted, all the members of the group heard on what would become a classic three-million-plus seller had left. Not to be deterred, Samudio found a combo at the Metropole in New York City, Tony G. and the Gypsies. Dressed in their garish, pseudo-Arabic costumes, they became the next Pharoahs, the ones responsible for "Li'l Red Riding Hood," "Red Hot," and the rest.

"We went out on tours all over the country, Europe, and the Far East," Samudio explained. "But it was getting to me. I was primarily a blues singer, and the company still wouldn't let us record what we wanted, so I decided to hang it up. When you're not happy, you can't do it right."

After studying at the Herbert Berghof Drama Studio in Greenwich Village, in 1970 Samudio did get to record one album's worth of what he considered the real thing, the blues. Even with backup provided by Duane Allman and the Memphis Horns, *Sam, Hard and Heavy* slipped into obscurity. "People still want to remember me for that other stuff," Samudio added.

In 1982, Samudio supplied two tunes sung in Spanish to Ry Cooder's soundtrack for the flick *The Border.* Reportedly, after a long spell of drug abuse, the Memphis-based Sam Samudio has created a book of unpublished poetry and turned to a life of street preaching and hands-on work with transients and prisoners.

KEY RECORDINGS: *Wooly Bully* (1965), *On Tour* (1966), *Li'l Red Riding Hood* (1966); "Wooly Bully" (1965), "Ju Ju Hand" (1965), "Ring Dang Do" (1965), "Red Hot" (1966), "Li'l Red Riding Hood" (1966).

THE SEEDS/SKY SAXON

Rock critics dismissed them as amateurish oddballs. Their musical abilities, pundits charged, were limited to two irksome chords and mystical meanderings on sex and drugs. Never did they have a national top-twenty record; their official lifespan barely touched twenty-four months. Given the establishment assessment, Sky Saxon and the Seeds should have long ago been but a mere epitaph in a deserted Southern California graveyard.

Although this primal seedy-looking outfit of hypno-fuzzies ceased to exist in its original incarnation a quarter of a century ago, the Seeds cult continues to sprout new and quite unfathomed adherents. The Damned, Violent Femmes, and the Jesus and Mary Chain have acknowledged a heavy-duty Seeds debt. Belinda Carlisle of the Go-Go's, Duran Duran's Andy Taylor, Vicki and Debbi Peterson of the Bangles, Box Tops/Big Star vocalist Alex Chilton, and a virtual who's who of punks/new wavers/music alternativists have not only chanted praises but gone out of their way to appear—even if for a moment—in one of Saxon's ever-reforming ragtag bands; among others, members of the Droogs, Fuzztones, Pandoras, Iron Butterfly, Dream Syndicate, Fraternity of Man, Redd Kross, Steppenwolf, and the Plimsouls. Seed tributes have been recorded by the Hoodoo Gurus, Nightmares, Golden Horde, and the Unclaimed.

All such adoring accolades have largely passed without

mainstream notice. Their continuing peripheral popularity has not, however, gone without adequate attention by GNP Crescendo, the Seeds' original label. Sales are still steady and, as astonishing as it may seem, none of the Seeds' six peak-period albums has ever gone out of print. Gene Norman, the company's president, freely admits that his label owes its very existence to those classic Seeds LPs, cut between 1966 and 1968.

In the seventies, Saxon moved to Hawaii, became a guru, and issued numerous packages of spiritual and cosmological chants and universal whatnots. Back in North America, Saxon's aggregates—with monikers that range from the Stars New Seeds to Ya Ho Wa 13 and Universal Stars Peace Band—have recorded an ever-flowing underground stream of left-field LPs.

"I'll tell you why I'm so important," says lead Seed Sky Saxon, now known to himself and close followers as "Sky Sunlight." "We had no competition back then and still don't. We were from L.A. like the Doors, but opposites. We didn't play rock and roll; never did. That's why we're not credited in rock histories. We were seeds planted underground, flower children, and played flower-power music."

Saxon (b. Richard Marsh, in Salt Lake City, Utah, 1945) made his first record ("Baby, Baby, Baby, Baby") as Little Richie Marsh and the Hoodwinks. Darla Hood, a member of the short-lived act, was a former member of the moviemaking Little Rascals. After more failed 45s and the advent of the British Invasion, Saxon placed an advertisement in a local paper and acquired keyboardist Daryl Hooper and drummer Rick Andridge. With the addition of guitarist Jan Savage, the famed Seeds lineup was intact.

"We were the Vikings [in 1964] and wore fur vests," Saxon explains. "This is long before Sonny and Cher. We couldn't afford full Viking costumes, so we became the Seeds. A deejay had suggested the name to us. The name was without harm. Hippies were getting a bad rap and I wanted to change things. I created flower power and—I'm told—was the first to use the peace sign. We wanted to represent growth and vegetables and such. We wanted to get back to nature and dressed like this new age of farmers. We definitely were in touch with the stars or a different time."

The Seeds took up an extended residence at the Bido Lito, on Los Angeles' teen-hot Sunset Strip. They were signed to the L.A.-based GNP Crescendo label—known for Billy Strange guitar instrumentals and assorted polka and ethnic folderol—and with the simultaneous release of "Pushin' Too Hard," their second single, and their self-titled debut album, the Seeds became nationally noticed.

"They called me 'America's answer to Mick Jagger,'" says Saxon. "We got noticed fast 'cause of that [first album] cover. We were the first band with *real* long hair. I'd get into fistfights about my hair all the time; three times this one day that I wrote 'Evil Hoodoo' about these small-headed, square people. The Stones had just started happenin' and everyone was talking about how long their hair was. They just had pageboy cuts. We hadn't done a thing with our hair in two years."

"Pushin' Too Hard" went top thirty; it's an "oldies" staple and the tune most associated with the cult act. "I wrote it in ten minutes in this supermarket parking lot," Saxon says. "I wrote it 'cause they tore down Pandora's Box. It was this pink building on Sunset Strip where we'd all hang out and drink coffee. You could bring your dog there and meet and it was groovy. Some ass tore it down and there's still a parking lot there. The establishment did it!

"I'll tell ya, paranoia was around. People were afraid and thought that we were anarchy, 'cause of our hair and the way we dressed. I sang of drugs, but Nixon didn't understand. He tried to ban my songs. I wasn't into drinking alcohol, or anything. I was into drinking water, pure water."

"People come to me everyday telling me that I'm great," says Saxon, "and that we're protopunk, or this, or that. We're still hip now, man, 'cause we're something new. The West Coast bands know that. My 'Mr. Farmer' says it best. Listen. We play flower music. Our message is: Love, man; get back and grow what you need, whether it's fruits or sacred herbs. Dress and live as you need; the earth will take care of you. Peace."

Key Recordings: *The Seeds* (1966); "Pushin' Too Hard" (1966), "Can't Seem to Make You Mine" (1966), "Mr. Farmer" (1966), "A Thousand Shadows" (1967).

SEX PISTOLS

"The Sex Pistols were a total failure," wrote Glen Matlock, the band's bassist, in *I Was a Teenage Sex Pistol*. "It was like a case of premature ejaculation; over in a flash and deeply unsatisfactory."

Spin magazine has labeled them one of the "Seven Greatest Bands of All Time." Though they were not the first punk band, their relentless energy and stance of rage and despair connected with a sizable segment of Britain's youth underclass. Their brief outspoken rampage liberated thousands from what they perceived as the shackles of the rock and roll dinosaurs, the Zeppelins and Floyds.

The Pistols were the brainchild of Malcolm McLaren, owner of Sex, a London boutique specializing in "anti-fashion." McLaren had the notion that rock and roll had gotten dry and complacent. During their final months, in the mid-seventies, McLaren had the chance to manage the New York Dolls.

In 1975 electrician Paul Cook (drums), housepainter Glen Matlock (bass), and professed burglar Steve Jones (guitar) were a band-in-the-making without a singer. Matlock worked part-time at the Sex shop and let McLaren know of his band's need. McLaren had noticed a rude-looking, orange-haired, green-eyed character hanging about his store's jukebox and approached him about joining the band.

Sex Pistols

259

Roberta Bayley

John Christopher Lydon had never sung before. "They had me bopping up and down madly in a pub, miming to an Alice Cooper song," Lydon told Ralph Heibutzki of *DISCoveries*. Lydon was dubbed Johnny Rotten by Jones, allegedly due to his poor personal hygiene.

November 6, 1975: Their first performance, at St. Martin's College of Art, lasted ten minutes. Their amplifiers were unplugged by the program's organizer. Utilizing a word-of-mouth approach, the Pistols got known on the streets. By October of '76 EMI Records signed them up—handing over $80,000, the largest advance ever given by the label—and prepared their debut disc, "Anarchy in the U.K."

The word "fucker" used by band members during a nationally televised program brought the group front-page notice. Kids loved it, and the punk revolution was under way. All but five dates of their national concert tour were canceled.

EMI dropped the band, reportedly even giving the Pistols an extra $20,000 to get lost. A&M had them signed for a few days, losing $150,000 in advance money; then Virgin bravely stepped in. Matlock left to form the Rich Kids, and Lydon's school buddy and hooligan Sid Vicious (ne John Ritchie, or Beverly) was enlisted to play bass. "God Save the Queen," their second 45, was issued in time for Queen Elizabeth II's Silver Jubilee. The disc was banned, though it became the top-selling single that summer.

Never Mind the Bollocks, issued in November '77, would prove to be their lone studio album. With virtually no place to play in England, the Pistols toured the Continent in July and in late '77 came to America. The stateside response was largely curious bewilderment. After their appearance in San Francisco in January 1978, Lydon announced the band's breakup.

Cook and Jones continued as the Professionals. Vicious started a solo career that ended when he was incarcerated for the death of his girlfriend, Nancy Spungen. He died of a heroin overdose before his trial. Lydon denounced the Sex Pistols and formed Public Image Ltd.

Reflecting nearly two decades later, Lydon said, "The Pistols weren't nihilistic. We certainly weren't on a death trip. Maybe it was wreck-and-destroy stupidity, but I'd hardly think that was nihilistic."

KEY RECORDINGS: *Never Mind the Bollocks, Here's the Sex Pistols* (1977), *The Great Rock 'n' Roll Swindle* (1979); "Anarchy in the U.K." (1976), "God Save the Queen" (1977), "Holidays in the Sun" (1977).

SHADOWS OF KNIGHT

"People know you when you're hot," says Jimy Sohns, front man for a realigned but still-together Shadows of Knight. "It's the only part they remember." For four months they were "hot," but now thirty years later their stable fanatic following still awaits the release of remaining audio scraps from the proto-garage band's heyday.

Within a year of learning how to tune their respective instruments, they were the Shadows of Knight—Sohns (vocals, keyboards), Joe Kelley (lead guitar, bass), Warren Rogers (lead guitar, bass), Tom Schiffour (drums), and ex-Saturday's Children/future H. P. Lovecraft member Jerry McGeorge (rhythm guitar)—a high school surf band from Prospect Heights, Illinois, and soon creators of "Gloria," one of rock's timeless anthems—the "Louie Louie" of '66—and the catalyst behind the short-lived "Chicago Sound."

At teen hops and as regulars at the area's famed Cellar club, the Shadows performed "Gloria"—which they'd heard on a Them record—for nearly a year before the fledgling Dunwich company took the band into Universal Studios. Recorded in thirty-five minutes on January 31, 1966, "Gloria" and the Shadows of Knight became an overnight sensation. Waiting in the wings for such a hit to happen to focus attention on the area and what was to become the Chicago Sound were the Mauds, Flock, Trolls, Buckinghams, Cryan' Shames, New Colony Six—nearly all destined for national hits.

The Shadows made the listings twice more; nothing major. "We were put on a salary and were to get lump sums every now and then," explains Sohns of the group's initial deterioration. "The lumps never came." And then there was a lack of direction. "We were the first happening band from out of Chicago," he explains. "They didn't know what to do with us." Dunwich never taped their burning renditions of Them's "I Can Only

Give You Everything" and "Baby Please Don't Go," nor was their early cut of "Hey Joe" issued as a single.

"There was so many missed opportunities that could have put us over the top," Sohns adds. "It just tore the band apart." Late in '67 the group broke up, only to reassemble as the studio group behind the Jerry Kasenetz–Jeff Katz "bubblegum" explosion, becoming—of all unimaginable things—the unbilled band heard on countless pimples-and-preteen hits for the Ohio Express, Lemon Pipers, and 1910 Fruitgum Co.

"We were the studio band that made all those songs. We would go in there and sing all the parts, whether it was 'Indian Giver' or 'Yummy, Yummy, Yummy.' It was always my voice on the cut and then they'd take my voice off for each particular group. It was always done that way; backups on all those songs are me."

Sohns and Van Morrison, the original "Gloria" vocalist, met. Says Sohns: "He was a hard guy to talk with, strange accent . . . he was very hard to understand. He took another drink and said, 'I like my version better.' I said, 'So do I.'"

KEY RECORDINGS: *Gloria* (1966), *Back Door Men* (1967); "Gloria" (1966), "Oh Yeah" (1966), "Bad Little Woman" (1966), "I'm Gonna Make You Mine" (1966).

SHONEN KNIFE

Grungy punk-rock emulations with a happy twist, played by two "office ladies" and a clothing designer from Osaka, Japan— the concept was strange, its appeal not obvious. Yet Shonen Knife (*shonen* translation: "young boy") became a hip discovery of the U.S. musical underground. Soon after, they were smattering cultish corners of the entire planet with discs of catchy, kitschy charm.

Shonen Knife began in 1981 when bored receptionist Naoko

Yamano—a fan of seventies punk rock and other blasts of Western sound—opted to indulge her singing and writing "hobby." Sporting a cheapo yellow guitar and flanked by her sister Atsuko (drums, voice) and their friend Michie Nakatani (bass, voice), she began infusing the night nooks of Japan with her colorful, innocent paeans. There were ditties about "chocobars," snacks, Barbie, animals, and such.

The homeland response to initial waxings was minimal. But licensing agreements with foreign labels spread the sounds, surreptitiously, to distant shores.

There they caught ears. Time passed. Word traveled. There were nudges, whisperings, "check this outs." And it erupted. The trio's 1989 U.S. debut—at L.A.'s Second Coming club—drew a crush crowd of subterranean Shonen Knife cherishers. Meanwhile, record racks rocked with an album of Shonen Knife obscurities played by Redd Kross, L7, Sonic Youth, and other knowing cultsters.

In an additional blink, the Osaka three turned up as guests on an album by Tater Totz (a Redd Kross spinoff) and were tapped by Seattle grunge kings Nirvana to join them on tour—all leading *Billboard,* the mainline show-biz sheet, to note their pose "on the edge of a breakthrough."

To some, the initial Knife attraction was along "so bad it's good" lines. "The three women's success is a result of their inability to mimic their heroes accurately," declared *The New York Times.* Pundits pleasurably pointed out Knife's signature English mispronunciations.

As fame spread—and Knife skills sharpened—"endearing" became the favored adjective to describe them, along with "unjaded," "guileless," "genuine," and "optimistic." "We get many letters from fans," said Naoko. "They say, 'I wake up in the morning and I am not happy. I play Shonen Knife and I am happy.'"

The girls' innocence bore fruit. They quit their day jobs. There were new options. New hopes. New dreams. "I don't want to become only famous," Naoko told the *Village Voice*. "I want much money."

KEY RECORDINGS: *Shonen Knife* (1990), *Pretty Little Baka Guy + Live in Japan* (1990), *712* (1991), *Let's Knife* (1992), *Rock Animals* (1993); "Flying Jelly Attack" (1990), "Twist Barbie" (1990), "Space Christmas" (1991), "My Little Tree" (1993).

SIOUXSIE AND THE BANSHEES

Wild dominatrix garb, heavy eye shadow, and exploding hair didn't hinder the rise of Siouxsie Sioux, post-punk diva and main wailer for the gloom-infused Banshees. Attention was instantly riveted. And she held it—through many years, many costumes, and many changes of band personnel.

Rashers of Banshee records rocked the British charts during the 1980s, shooting these howlers to the forefront of the few surviving punk bands. Their main achievement is that they got there with a sound cited as exceedingly grim, abrasive, and dark. They experimented. They scrounged for musical oddity. They professed to be uncompromising. Devotees flocked to them.

Pundits were divided. The *Village Voice* called their debut "one of the 10 Best Records of the whole 1975–80 epoch" and Siouxsie "the most influential female Brit pop star of the decade." *Rolling Stone*, in its *New Record Guide,* dismissed their discs as "uniformly ghoulish, self-indulgent, and monotonous." The two views were not incompatible.

Shock value and indulgence were major pluses at the beginning. The operative word was anarchy, Sex Pistols–style, and Sioux was a member of the notably fevered Bromley Contingent of Pistols followers. Siouxsie (b. Susan Janet Dallion, May 27, 1957, London) debuted in September 1976 at London's 100 Club Punk Festival, where she performed a lengthy, chaotic interpretation of the Lord's Prayer, supported by future Sex Pistol Sid Vicious on drums, future Adam Ant member Marco Pirroni on guitar, and bassist Steve Severin.

Some two years later, with a band of Banshees comprising Severin, drummer Kenny Morris, and guitarist John McKay, Siouxsie issued the primal *Scream,* a disc—recorded in but seven days—against which later Banshee howlings have often been measured. Not for the squeamish, its standout ditties include "Carcass," detailing a butcher's close relations with a piece of meat and his attempts to carve himself into compatible form. "It's a love song, really," Siouxsie explained to a writer for *Melody Maker.*

By 1984's *Hyaena*—with a different Banshee batch, now including Budgie (drummer Peter Clarke) and Robert Smith (guitarist from the Cure)—the band's mood, lyrically at least, was no less sour. Writers Sioux and Severin were now on a nightmare ride through lusting spawn, sucking leeches, drooling vultures, and frenzied vipers, worms, and jackals on a landscape of corrosion and rot. "Bring Me the Head of the Preacher Man," "Pointing Bone," and "Belladonna" are among the apt titles on a disc considered one of the Banshees' friendlier listens.

But friendliness wasn't the attraction. It was Siouxsie's onstage icy decadence and Brechtian distance, her otherworldly sexuality, and her invulnerability that struck chords in both male and female fans and made her influential. Many a female rocker—and fan—would aspire to a Siouxsie-like spikiness and alien appeal.

When the unthinkable happened and the surface world finally phoned underground for the Banshees, the man on the line was film director Tim Burton with a call for help. In 1992 he needed sonics for the eerie visuals of *Batman Returns.* The sounds of the Banshees were heard in the final film.

It was one of the few instances of stateside audibility for the 'Shees, whose overall U.S. presence, despite fame in Britain, has been that of a fleeting apparition, intangible and ghostlike.

Many know the name—and have even caught a gig or two. Yet airplay, apart from the hits "Peek-a-Boo" in 1988 and "Kiss Them for Me" in 1991, has been negligible.

In the mid-nineties, Sioux and her crew—unchanged since the 1988 addition of guitarist Jon Klein and keyboardist Martin McCarrick—were still comfortably floating in their own chosen purgatory.

KEY RECORDINGS: *The Scream* (1978), *Join Hands* (1979), *Kaleidoscope* (1980), *Juju* (1981), *A Kiss in the Dreamhouse* (1982), *Nocturne* (live, 1983), *Hyaena* (1984), *Tinderbox* (1986), *Through the Looking Glass* (1987), *Peepshow* (1988), *Superstition* (1991), *The Rapture* (1994); "Hong Kong Garden" (1978), "Happy House" (1980), "Spellbound" (1981).

SLADE

U.S. radio stations wouldn't play them; critics didn't like them; stores don't stock them. They were the hottest band in all of England from 1972 to '74. As Slademania spread, foreigners hailed Slade as heirs to the Beatles' emptied throne. Mainstream American youth missed out. And Britain still can't get their fill; "Coz I Love You," a twenty-year-old disc, topped the homeland charts in 1991.

Before Noddy Holder (né Neville Holder, vocals, guitar), Dave Hill (guitar), Jim Lea (bass, violin, keyboards), and Don Powell (drums) got together in 1966 as the 'N Betweens, each had labored long in local bar bands in the industrial reaches of Wolverhampton, England. When their first disc, cut under the supervision of Hollywood jack-of-all-trades Kim Fowley, bombed, they became Ambrose Slade for an album. With something missing, the disc refused to sell.

Enter Ex-Animal bassist and Jimi Hendrix manager Chas Chandler. Eyeing an *en vogue* craze, Chandler shaved their heads, put them in suspenders and construction boots, shortened their name, and promoted Slade as Britain's first skinhead group. Their cut "The Shapes of Things to Come" was not to pass; horrified promoters feared the group would incite havoc and violence.

When their hair had grown out, Slade charted—the first of twelve consecutive top-five singles, six reaching number one, three of which debuted at number one—with a remake of Little Richard's "Get Down and Get With It." They were now gaudy but working-class glam-rockers with sci-fi outfits and four-inch platform shoes. "Take Me Back 'Ome," "Mama Weer All Crazee Now," "Cum On Feel the Noize" defined the Slade sound: melodic, hoarse-throat bursts, usually with clever phonetic (mis)spellings.

Slademania raged through the Continent, Australia, and the Far East. Fans stomped and yelled themselves into frenzies. Yet stateside, they were hardly noticed.

Slade in Flames, their lone film, failed to live up to the hype proclaiming it another *Hard Day's Night*. Their string of consecutive hits stopped in 1976 with "Let's Call It Quits."

Slade has persisted, playing smaller clubs, recording in spurts, and to the amazement of all but the Slademanians, they have repeatedly returned to the top of the British charts, where their total number of hits now exceeds those gathered by the Beatles.

KEY RECORDINGS: *Slade Alive* (1972), *Slayed* (1972), *Old, New, Borrowed and Blue* (1974); "Coz I Love You" (1971), "Take Me Back 'Ome" (1972), "Mama Weer All Crazee Now" (1972), "Gudbuy T'Jane" (1973), "Cum On Feel the Noize" (1973), "We'll Bring the House Down" (1981), "Run Runaway" (1984).

PATTI SMITH

The British media proclaimed her "America's biggest cult phenomenon"; Dave Marsh called her "one of the greatest figures of seventies rock 'n' roll." For too few years, Patti Smith employed what few women prior had even considered: guitar bashing, Keith Richard stances, and screaming, raw rock-and-roll poetry. The skinny, androgynous street kid shocked many with her unorthodox persona. She was one of the first to be labeled a punk-rocker, and without her the movement might have been a mere flash in the pan.

Patti Lee Smith (b. Chicago, December 30, 1946, guitar), was raised in Pitman, New Jersey, and grew up "shy, sickly and creepy lookin'," per an early, self-penned press bio. Dad was a tap dancer and factory worker, mom a waitress. By age seven, Smith was struck with tuberculosis, scarlet fever, and an eye infection that left her wearing an eye patch. With such traumatic experiences combined with shyness, Smith withdrew into a fantasy world. "When I was young," Smith told *DISCoveries's* Mary Ann Cassata, "we read the Bible and UFO magazines. I'd say I'm equal parts of Balenciaga and Brando."

In the sixties, she attended Glassboro State Teachers College in New Jersey for some months. With savings earned while doing assembly work in a toy factory, Patti and sister Linda tripped to Paris, where Patti waitressed and recited verse with a street troupe of poets, singers, and fire-eaters. Back in New York she befriended photographer Robert Mapplethorpe, who took her in for a stay in his Chelsea Hotel apartment.

The next several years were productive. With Sam Shepard, Smith cowrote a book, *Mad Dog Blues*, and performed in their one-act play, *Cowboy Mouth;* had her first book of poetry (*Seventh Heaven*) published; and wrote articles and reviews for *Creem, Crawdaddy,* and *Rolling Stone.* Her poetry readings at St. Mark's Church in lower Manhattan began attracting a sizable following. On February 10, 1971, Smith invited Lenny Kaye (guitar) to accompany her readings; by 1973, Richard Sohl (keyboards) had been added, and the Patti Smith Group was born. This avant-garde aggregation recorded "Piss Factory" b/w "Hey Joe," a one-off, limited release single for Mer Records.

Ivan Kral (bass, guitar) and Jay Dee Daugherty (drums) soon climbed aboard. An engagement at New York's CBGB caught the attention of Arista Records head Clive Davis, who signed the act in 1975. *Horses*, their debut album—produced by former Velvet Underground member John Cale—sold well beyond expectations. "Gloria" and "Pumping (My Heart)" (from the follow-up album, *Radio Ethiopia*) received heavy underground airplay.

On January 23, 1977, Smith suffered a near-fatal accident when she fell fourteen feet off a stage in Tampa, Florida. Two vertebrae were broken in her neck. "I know the finger of God pushed me off the stage," she told the press. After a year's recuperation, Smith and group returned with *Easter* and "Because the Night," a single written with Bruce Springsteen. In 1979, after the *Wave* album and two further 45s, the Patti Smith Group dissappeared.

Smith married Fred "Sonic" Smith (d. 1994), founder of the militant MC5 and the Sonic Rendezvous Band.

In 1986, Smith started work on a comeback album. Three years later, a full nine years after her "retirement," her *Dream of Life* disc appeared. The sound was strikingly calm and peaceful, compared to her previous work; critics differed in their assessments. "People Have the Power," the only single extracted, was not widely noticed.

KEY RECORDINGS: *Horses* (1975), *Radio Ethiopia* (1976), *Easter* (1978), *Wave* (1979), *Dream of Life* (1988); "Gloria" (1975), "Pumping (My Heart)" (1976), "Because the Night" (1978), "Frederick" (1979), "So You Wanna Be (A Rock 'n' Roll Star)" (1979).

THE SMITHS/MORRISSEY

Morrissey's vocal drone and gloomy lyrics led some Smiths listeners to dismiss the band. Others turned ears only to melodist Johnny Marr's elegant, crystal-toned guitar.

That left the rest: the Morrissey hardcore, one of the most devoted cults in the annals of popular music.

Morrissey's songs have made him "a hero to the lonely, the disenfranchised, the outsider," said *Spin* magazine. The attraction? He wrote "You're the One for Me, Fatty," "Accept Yourself," "Heaven Knows I'm Miserable Now," and more.

Claimed a fan, he's "the only one who understands."

The Smiths emerged from Manchester, England, and were based around the songwriting team of onetime music reviewer Morrissey (b. Stephen Morrissey, May 22, 1959) and Marr (b. John Maher, Oct. 31, 1963). With the propulsive support of bassist Andy Rourke and drummer Mike Joyce, they began issuing singles in 1983 and were shortly riding up the U.K. charts and prompting critical raves.

They were different—clean in look, clean in sound. Marr's guitar jangled colorfully. Morrissey's minimal croon added grays. His lyrics—with weight plus wit—were both catchy and haunting. Such early stage habits as wearing hearing aids (for show) and throwing fresh-cut flowers into the audience struck some as endearing. The songs' sexual ambiguity added touches of mystery and controversy.

But it lasted only five years and four main albums. Marr went on to back the Pretenders, Talking Heads, and more. Rourke and Joyce dove into Adult Net, the band led by the Fall's Brix Smith, and rocked with Sinead O'Connor. Morrissey, meanwhile, meandered toward a solo career. After a tentative start—replacing the Marr guitar was hard—he found footing with substantial discs like *Kill Uncle* (1991) and *Your Arsenal* (1992).

Morrissey has described the hysteria of his crowd as baffling. And dangerous, as he told *Spin*'s David Thomas, "when I'm in a car that cannot move and all I can see is flesh pressed against every surrounding window. It's very unnerving, and suddenly, the temperature in the car rises and you can't breathe and whoever has sat next to you starts to panic, and . . . it's wonderful!"

KEY RECORDINGS: *The Smiths* (1984), *Hatful of Hollow* (compilation, 1984), *Meat Is Murder* (1985), *The Queen Is Dead* (1986), *Louder Than Bombs* (compilation, 1987), *Strangeways, Here We Come* (1987); "Hand in Glove" (1984), "What Difference Does It Make?" (1984), "This Charming Man" (1984), "Please Please Please Let Me Get What I Want" (1984).

SOFT MACHINE/ROBERT WYATT

Soft Machine was on the far-out edge of sixties avant-jazz-rock and arty, progressive pop. But they weren't overbearing about it. A dash of whimsical, Dadaist humor kept things down to earth. It came mostly from Robert Wyatt, the puckish drummer who later plunged from a fourth-story window, became permanently wheelchair-bound, yet continued to make records. In years since, he's been overlooked by the mass market but cherished by admirers for his intimate, childlike singing and compositional experiments—often with lyrics reflecting his political and social concerns.

The strange trip began in Canterbury, England, where Wyatt (born on January 28, 1945, in Bristol) was among like-minded musical fringe floaters who coalesced in a group called the Wilde Flowers. Fellow Flowers Mike Ratledge (organ), Kevin Ayers (bass, vocals), Daevid Allen (guitar), and Wyatt formed Soft Machine in 1966, naming it after a William Burroughs novel.

The Softs geared up for the big city, where a young Pink Floyd and a psychedelic scene were in action. "London wasn't ready for us yet," Ratledge said in *Down Beat*. "Then we found we could play the way we wanted, call it 'pop,' and have a chance to be heard."

A rapid series of events moved the Machine forward. They issued a single—containing the guitar plinkings of a not-yet-celebrated Jimi Hendrix. Then they descended on the French Riviera, concocting after-show cacophonies for a Pablo Picasso play, *Desire Caught by the Tail*. Later, reduced to a trio with the departure of Daevid Allen, the Softs reentered the orbit of the by-now-famous Hendrix and opened for the Purple Hazemaker on his 1968 U.S. tour. Their debut disc appeared in the same year.

Soft Machine's emissions—at first psychedelic—became jazzy with rock volume. Solos were Coltrane-modal, blurting from fuzz organ and later from sax. There were repeating riffs, in odd meters. Songs were long—twenty minutes, in some cases. Live, the Softs wore hippie garb, long hair, sunglasses, beads; Wyatt sometimes only a bikini bottom. Light projections swirled, courtesy of an artist whose earlier work "Bodily Fluids and Functions" had pictured human liquids blending with electrocardiograms of people making love.

All this—and acclaim came for leading the way in the burgeoning new movement labeled jazz-rock.

Ayers departed, and Hugh Hopper replaced him. Albums *Volume Two* and *Third* arrived. Saxist Elton Dean joined. The *Fourth* album emerged. All were critically embraced, but not widely sold.

Wyatt's expanding talent needed release. "I had my own ideas," he said in a *Musician* interview, "and I didn't know anybody except me who was interested in them. [In Soft Machine] they wanted a drummer who could play in any time signature for very long solos. They didn't want a drummer who kept showing alarming tendencies toward turning into something else."

Those "alarming tendencies" became the basis of Wyatt's solo career. It began with his singing, playing keyboards, and drumming on an album, *The End of an Ear,* in 1971. Wyatt then quit the Softs entirely to form Matching Mole, the name a phonetic spelling of the French term for "soft machine." The Softs went on without him for several more years, with varying musicians (guitarist Allan Holdsworth a notable one)—though the sound wasn't up to par, many say.

Two Matching Mole albums poked up, but a third was not in the offing. For it was while planning it—in 1973—that Wyatt had his accident. It happened at a party. "Here's how the accident went," he said, "in order: wine, whiskey, Southern Comfort, then the window."

From that point on, drumming and walking were no longer options. Ironically, not playing drums freed him to conceptualize. After recovering, he recorded *Rock Bottom,* a disc that some place among the seventies' best, his frail, charming voice permeating it. He then had a minor, surprising hit with the Monkees song "I'm a Believer." Following the 1975 album *Ruth Is Stranger Than Richard,* Wyatt retreated from solo work, occasionally collaborating with such musical progressives as Mike Mantler and Carla Bley, Brian Eno, and Phil Manzanera.

In the eighties Wyatt reemerged with a series of singles. At their heart were political views that he'd been simmering during the layoff. He'd noted the punk movement's so-called rebellion—and been reminded that rock's longtime image as dangerous, rebel music was but a pose. In the Wyatt worldview, rock was both the cultural establishment and—in its history of white musicians usurping black innovations—part of a larger Western cultural imperialism. "I became interested in retrieving the idea of a sort of, if you like, *disobedient* music," he said.

He chose nonoriginal material like Chic's "At Last I Am Free," Billie Holiday's "Strange Fruit," and Elvis Costello and Clive Langer's antiwar comment, "Shipbuilding" (all compiled on a 1986 disc, *Nothing Can Stop Us*). He then capped the period with a politically infused album, *Old Rottenhat,* and disappeared again until 1992's spare and haunting *Dondestan.*

Melody Maker once called Wyatt "one of the great abiding presences of the English rock scene." Yet in show-biz terms, he appears destined to remain on the commercial periphery. "In my case," Wyatt acknowledged, "I don't think [industry] people are saying, 'Well, we've got Diana Ross, I know what we need now . . . Robert Wyatt!'"

KEY RECORDINGS: Soft Machine—*The Soft Machine* (1968), *Volume Two* (1969), *Third* (1970), *Fourth* (1971); "Moon in June" (1970); **Matching Mole**—*Matching Mole* (1972), *Matching Mole's Little Red Record* (1973); **Robert Wyatt**—*The*

End of an Ear (1971), *Rock Bottom* (1974), *Ruth Is Stranger Than Richard* (1975), *Old Rottenhat* (1985), *Dondestan* (1992); "At Last I Am Free" (1980).

SONIC YOUTH

"I used to be afraid of playing in a band where everything we did was an alternative to the norm," said Thurston Moore, Sonic Youth leader, to *Goldmine*'s Steve Roeser. "But we created this whole totally weird indigenous language for ourselves. I was afraid that maybe it was all too exclusive and we'd just be this elitist venture. I'm finally enlightened and thankful."

Normal musicians just don't work their stringed instruments quite like Moore's Sonic Youth. Searching for the sound, the Big Apple–based band has been experimenting with extra frets and taking sharpened screwdrivers, sticks, and broken bottles to their guitars. To add to the cauldron of noise, these sonic rejuvenators don't tune their axes to A=440, E–A–D–G–B–E.

Why such an abusive attack on sound? "Because the guitars we used were so bad," explained Moore to *Only Music*'s Michael Azarrad. "If we had played them in standard tuning, we would have sounded like a really cool garage band, but we weren't into that."

As a consequence, Sonic Youth has been lovingly labeled the Godfathers of Grunge.

Performing in the post-punk environment, Sonic Youth was first influenced by Manhattan composers Glenn Branca, Rhys Chatham, and Steve Reich and the No Wave noise of the Contortions, DNA, and Teenage Jesus and the Jerks.

In the late seventies Thurston Moore (guitar) met Kim Gordon (bass) on New York's Lower East Side. They became lovers and bandmates and were joined in later maneuvers by Lee Ranaldo (guitar). After a succession of drummers, Steve Shelley became the group's permanent pounder.

A self-titled EP and a debut album, *Confusion Is Sex,* both issued on Neutral and later reissued on Black Flag's SST label, started the onslaught of hard-to-finds heavily sought by hardcore Sonic hounds. Only since 1990 has the group's output been mass-issued by David Geffen's major DGC label.

"Our ambition has been to go as far as the Butthole Surfers, or maybe Black Flag, that's the zenith," Moore told Alan Di Perna in *Guitar Player.* "You just can't go any further. Who would want to?"

KEY RECORDINGS: *Confusion Is Sex* (1983), *Bad Moon Rising* (1985), *EVOL* (1986), *Sister* (1987), *Daydream Nation* (1988), *Goo* (1990), *Dirty* (1991), *Experimental Jet Set, Trash and No Star* (1994).

SPECIALS

They were the main movers behind England's 2-Tone movement of 1978–81. The Specials were "rude boys," sporting shaved heads, short-brimmed pork-pie hats, flat-heeled wingtip shoes. Musically they fused the skifflin', skankin' ska—a Jamaican prereggae, dance-oriented sound, also known as rock steady or bluebeat—with three-chord punk. Madness, Selecter, Bad Manners, the English Beat soon followed.

The Specials preached an obliteration of the inequalities of the world via their infectious island shuffle and their rallying lyrical cries—"Dawning of a New Era," "Doesn't Make It Alright." For a moment, they brought black and white youth together; ergo the name 2-Tone. All this, however, remained largely an alien happenstance to North Americans.

The seven biracial Specials—John Bradbury (drums); Roddy "Radiation" Byers (guitar), Jerry Dammers (né Gerald Dankin, keyboards), Lynval Golding (guitar), Terry Hall (vocals), Sir Horace "Gentleman" Panter (bass), Neville Staples (vocals)—

came together as the Automatics in the working-class area of Coventry, England, in the fall of 1977. Dammers wrote all of their original material, and in order to maintain their creative freedom, organized 2-Tone, the band's own record company, for some months the hottest independent label in all of England.

Elvis Costello produced their self-titled debut album. Gigantic British hits followed—"Gangsters," "A Message to You Rudy," "Too Much Too Young." A Dammer-dominated second album, light on the ska rhythms and heavy on Muzak, confused 2-Tone devotees.

Discontent flared, and concurrent with the release of "Ghost Town," the act's lone chart-topper, Golding, Hall, and Staples left to form Fun Boy Three. Several successful singles followed—"The Lunatics Have Taken Over the Asylum" and "It Ain't What You Do It's the Way That You Do It," the latter with Bananarama. The three separated in 1984. Hall formed Colour Field.

Dammers and the three remaining members, plus Rico (trombone) and Dick Cluthell (flugelhorn), recorded some singles as Special A.K.A., notably "Free Nelson Mandela" and the BBC-banned "Boiler," a monologue from a rape victim.

Becoming increasingly political, Dammers aided in the formation of Artists Against Apartheid in 1986, organizing a free concert attended by over 200,000, and he was the prime mover behind the 1988 Nelson Mandela birthday tribute broadcast worldwide.

KEY RECORDINGS: *The Specials* (1979), *More Specials* (1980); "Gangsters" (1978), "A Message to You Rudy" (1979), "Ghost Town" (1981).

SPIRIT

A seventeen-year-old Hendrix acolyte on lead guitar; his bald, black-clad, sunglassed stepfather on drums—those were no minor fan-attracting factors when Spirit materialized in 1967. But the band, in early stages, proved something more—a distinctive fusion of rock and jazz with an outstanding guitar player.

As ear candy in varied flavors clogged sixties airwaves, Spirit played music that was darker, denser, more cerebral. Its sound— matched with a collection of catchy and quirky songs—took them to the edges of mass acceptance before placing them permanently in the pantheon of classic cult rockers.

Spirit's first incarnation was in 1965 as an L.A.-based blues-rock band called the Red Roosters, whose members included guitarist Randy California (born Randy Wolfe), his stepdad Ed Cassidy (drums), Jay Ferguson (vocals), and Mark Andes (bass).

Thirty-four-year-old Cassidy had played with Dexter Gordon, Zoot Sims, and a few other name jazz acts. "My story," he told *Melody Maker*'s Richard Williams, "was nearly like hundreds of other jazz musicians, who can play great but who remain and die unknown. They're all afraid to move forward. But I try to be a leader and not a follower."

When the Roosters dispersed, California and Cassidy migrated briefly to New York—the teenaged California to work with Jimmy James (Jimi Hendrix) and the Blue Flames—before reconvening with Andes and Ferguson in L.A. "We got back together into a group," said Cassidy, "which we decided wouldn't be restricted by any one style." They enlisted the jazz-trained fingers of keyboardist John Locke and named their new entity Spirits Rebellious, soon shortened to Spirit.

At the beginning they mixed rock-tinged originals with tunes by John Coltrane and Thelonious Monk, to "get the group into playing a certain kind of music that people weren't used to hearing," claimed Cassidy. Later, they dropped the jazz covers and began to focus on their own music, mostly penned by Ferguson. It impressed Lou Adler, producer of the Mamas and the Papas, and he took on the band as producees.

"Fresh Garbage," the opening track of Spirit's 1968 debut album, modeled the offbeat, idiosyncratic emanations to come. Its vaguely Latin rhythm, jagged guitar/keyboard riff, and strange, world-as-a-garbage-can metaphor—not to mention its jazzy break in a different meter—hooked a select sect of the counterculturally inclined. So did "Straight Arrow," a ditty that poked fun at a brain-police establishment type while meshing pleasant pop with chaotic free jazz.

Spirit followers came to embrace Randy California as head guru. Likened to a rock John Coltrane by one pundit, California enhanced his signature rich tone with echo, enhanced sustain, and studio overdubs. There were thick, fuzzy chords, and there were solos in two- and three-part harmony—common enough in later days but fresh and exciting at the time.

Spirit enjoyed a four-album heyday. It produced one hit single—"I Got a Line on You" from the 1969 disc *The Family That*

Plays Together—and culminated in what some view as their masterwork, the suitelike *Twelve Dreams of Dr. Sardonicus*, released in 1971.

After that, the "classic" Spirit lineup dematerialized. Jay Ferguson left to form Jo Jo Gunne with Mark Andes. Randy California went on to pursue a solo career, putting out an album, *Captain Kopter and the Fabulous Twirlybirds*, in 1972. John Locke led a revamped Spirit for the disc *Feedback* but failed to reignite the original spark.

A number of Spirit albums were released with varying personnel in later years (including the five founders on 1984's *Spirit of '84*), none adding much to the band's legend. But by the late eighties and early nineties, Randy California and Ed Cassidy were back together, performing vintage material for the smattering of Spirit-ualists still roaming the material world in search of transcendent musical moments.

KEY RECORDINGS: *Spirit* (1968), *The Family That Plays Together* (1969), *Clear* (1969), *Twelve Dreams of Dr. Sardonicus* (1971), *Feedback* (1972), *Spirit of '76* (1975); "Fresh Garbage" (1968), "Uncle Jack" (1968), "I Got a Line on You" (1969), "1984" (1970).

STEELY DAN

Some people never did get it. Rock and roll, they charged, was supposed to be rough and ragged. It was meant to be simple—three, four, or five chords, tops. And if a band's name was printed on a record, then dammit, it should be a real group, not a batch of faceless hired musicians. And the act had to play *live* occasionally.

Donald Fagen and Walter Becker—together as Steely Dan in a seven-album streak from 1972's *Can't Buy a Thrill* to 1980's *Gaucho*—broke those rules. Their famously painstaking recording methods yielded a sound that was pristine, crisp, perfect in its interlacing of vocals, horn parts, guitar fills, keyboard chords, synth colors, bass melodies, and drum accents. Their songs were complex, a style-setting fusion of jazz and rock with vocals, at radio-ready lengths. And Steely Dan, for years, was no performing band—just those two composer-producer-players, a recording studio, and an ever-changing cast of jazz-tainted studio musicians.

"We were aware of the high degree of incompatibility between jazz and rock music," admitted Walter Becker to *Musician's* Tom Moon. "And that it didn't take very much jazz to offend a rock listener pretty badly in a way they would never, ever forgive."

The offended tuned out. But decidedly unoffended have been packs of ardent Dan-ophiles—their numbers including active players and music theory buffs—who have long championed Steely Dan and tracked its passage from early years through 1980 shutdown to reactivation in the 1990s.

Fagen and Becker's careful constructions pushed the sonic envelope, claim the Dan-crazed, and set a standard for studio craft. "They are as meticulous as everyone says," notes session guitarist Hiram Bullock, one of the players on *Gaucho*. "I think we worked a week on one song. At one point we worked nine hours on one four-bar insert. You know, you just do it. They wanted perfection."

Dan tracks are noted for incredible individual performances—especially by guitarists. "Soloists are challenged by the complexity of the chords," Donald Fagen told Tom Moon.

"With Steely Dan and Donald's solo stuff," says Bullock, "they have these sort of crystalline compositions, like little jewels. They don't want you to imprint your personality over their music; they want you to get inside their music and use your talent to bring their song to life."

Those songs, in turn, brought the guest players wider recognition—making a Dan session a career picker's peak. "I'm a fan of Steely Dan," admits Bullock, "so I was thrilled and flattered that they called me."

Topped with Fagen's acidic vocals and Bob Dylan–influenced lyrics—ironic, oblique, sometimes cryptic—Steely Dan's songs mix spikiness with the sheen. It made them instantly recognizable on the FM radio airwaves they rode with high frequency in the fusion- and disco-drenched seventies.

Friends from their days at Bard College in upstate New York, singer-pianist Fagen (b. January 10, 1948) and guitarist-bassist Becker (b. February 20, 1950) formed Steely Dan in 1972 at the suggestion of Gary Katz, an A&R man at ABC-Dunhill who had brought the two in as staff writers. (Katz would become SD's longtime producer.) Before that, they'd written a soundtrack for the Richard Pryor movie *You've Got to Walk It Like You Talk It or You'll Lose That Beat*, played in the backup band for Jay and the Americans, and worked with guitarist Denny Dias in the obscure group Demian.

"[Steely Dan] was put together very quickly," Fagen said. "It was while we were making the first album, and we'd never played together before." The lineup comprised Dias, Jeff Baxter (guitarist, ex-Ultimate Spinach), Jim Hodder (drums, ex-Bead Game), and vocalist David Palmer. The name came from a reference to a dildo in the William Burroughs novel *Naked Lunch*.

There was a successful single, "Do It Again." Then "Reeling in the Years," the shuffling follow-up, attracted notice for its catchy chord cycle, sleek vocal harmony, acerbic words, and a lead guitar part—by hired hand Elliott Randall—that added some Hendrixy grit.

Successive discs were issued (minus Palmer, and augmenting the band with session players), and Steely Dan took to the road. Strangely, they found their thinking-man's pop billed with such fist pumpers as the hard-rocking Slade and Humble Pie. "Often, the audience didn't quite know what to think of us," Becker told the *San Francisco Chronicle*'s Graham Rayman. "It had never been my ambition or Donald's to be entertainers. We wanted to write songs and make records and suddenly we were thrust into this concert context . . . It just was never really satisfying for us, and at a certain point we figured, 'Fuck it. People are buying our records anyway.' "

They retired from the stage in 1974. The other Steely Dan members departed (though Dias would turn up on later discs), and Becker and Fagen holed up in studios for the next six years.

Their output during that period added up to a catalog-full of body-grabbing brain pleasers—groove-based numbers, like "Josie" and "Hey Nineteen," joyriding through odd yet logical harmonic twists.

Fagen's keyboards and the slinky, distinctive guitar of Becker anchored many a tune, joined by such studio mainstays as drummers Bernard Purdie and Steve Gadd, bassist Chuck Rainey, guitarists Larry Carlton and Steve Khan, vocalist Michael McDonald (later a Doobie Brothers hit maker), and jazz sax player Wayne Shorter.

Virtually all of Steely Dan's albums proved the kind that the faithful cherish and champion, with *Aja,* from 1977, probably garnering the most praise (its "Deacon Blues" and "Peg" are Dan classics). But numerous vinyl moments have been singled out over the years as special evidence of Steely Dan worthiness. Such highlights include:

- The multitracked guitar solo in "Reeling in the Years"—plus the song-opening figure.
- The drumming of Steve Gadd at the end of "Aja"—and the song's exotic tone colors and chords.
- Larry Carlton's guitar solo on "Third World Man" from the album *Gaucho.*
- On 1980's "Time out of Mind," that weird little end-of-phrase chord turnaround in the instrumental interlude.

- The panoramic sound and elegant soul-plus-
gospel-plus-Keith-Jarrett flavor of the track "Gaucho"—and the climactic, sky-high guitar melody at
song's end.

That climax marked the end of Steely Dan's legend-making
period. With the languid fadeout of *Gaucho*'s "Third World Man,"
Fagen and Becker stopped recording and parted ways—right
around the time that punk rock's anti-gloss, anyone-can-do-it
ethic was spawning a new generation of raucous "alternative"
rockers.

Separate, sporadic post-Dan activity filled the next ten years.
Fagen issued his solo *The Nightfly*, wrote a music column for
Premiere magazine, and contributed the song "Century's End" to
the film *Bright Lights, Big City*. Becker (based in Hawaii) pro-
duced albums for others, including China Crisis and Rickie Lee
Jones.

When the nineties dawned, the two reappeared in the Fagen-
organized New York Rock and Soul Revue. They noted that of
the rock and soul classics in the Revue, the few Steely Dan songs
seemed to generate the greatest frenzy. Following a 1993 collaboration on Fagen's Steely Dan–like solo album *Kamakiriad*, the
never-expected happened, and Steely Dan announced a return
to touring.

Faint punk and grunge grumblings were heard when the sophisticated sounds filled halls for the first time in nearly two
decades (some for the first time, period). But the heavy turnout
of fortyish fans, plus major-event press coverage, suggested that
Dan music would be around a long time—at least until the next
pack of raunch-rock rebels began trying out a few slick harmonic tricks of their own.

KEY RECORDINGS: *Can't Buy a Thrill* (1972); *Countdown to
Ecstasy* (1973), *Pretzel Logic* (1974), *Katy Lied* (1975), *The Royal
Scam* (1976), *Aja* (1977), *Gaucho* (1980); "Do It Again" (1972),
"Reeling in the Years" (1972), "Rikki Don't Lose That Number"

(1974), "Aja" (1977), "Josie" (1977), "Deacon Blues" (1977), "Babylon Sisters" (1980), "Hey Nineteen" (1980), "Time out of Mind" (1980).

THE STRANGLERS

They were four loud lads in the right place at the right time. Science teacher–guitarist Hugh Cornwell had chucked his chalk to answer the call of the wild. He and bassist Jean-Jacques Burnel, keyboardist Dave Greenfield, and drummer Jet Black (b. Brian Duffy) had been scuffling around England as the Guildford Stranglers in the mid-1970s. Then punk rock became the national rage. The ragged foursome seemed to fit its back-to-basics mold. In a wink the Stranglers were opening shows for punk queen Patti Smith and making swell-selling records for the leather-and-chains set.

Some thirteen years later they were aging but still active, having outlasted most punkers ("we're Punkasaurus Rex, this dinosaur that's still around," Cornwell told writer Ian Gittins). By then it was clear they'd not been punks—in the self-consciously arty or rebellious sense—so much as journeymen rockers ("commercial artists" in their words) with a distinctively pugnacious but durable style.

Their music—more melodic and moody than punk's fast-loud assaults—harkened back to late-sixties garage rock, with, some say, a touch of the Doors. Compact, tight, and punchy, with caustic and bitter vocals by Cornwell and swirling, Halloween/carnival organ, the sound saturated the entire Stranglers output—which was prodigious. Till Cornwell's departure in 1991, it arched from early records like "(Get a) Grip (on Yourself)" and the defining album *No More Heroes* to their weird, sped-up cover of Burt Bacharach's "Walk on By" (1978), the midcareer plateau of *Aural Sculpture*, and a 1990 rehash of the garage classic "96 Tears."

The Stranglers were no strangers to controversy. The press blasted them for misogyny in song titles like "Bitching" and "Bring on the Nubiles" and the use of onstage strippers. Some of England's local councils banned them, for a time. The BBC rejected the song "Peaches" for its lyrics.

Yet hardcore Stranglophiles have remained devout. "We've always had the nuttiest people being attracted to us," Cornwell told *Creem's* Toby Goldstein. "We always get the nutters, the completely abnormal types, the sociopaths." There've been enough of them to keep the Stranglers active into the post-digital nineties, when the group's brand of raw-toned rock was in style yet again.

KEY RECORDINGS: *IV Rattus Norvegicus* (1977), *No More Heroes* (1977), *Black and White* (1978), *Live (X Cert)* (1979), *The Raven* (1979), *The Meninblack* (1981), *Feline* (1982), *Aural Sculpture* (1984), *Dreamtime* (1987), *10* (1990), *Stranglers in the Night* (1993); "(Get a) Grip (on Yourself)" (1977), "Something Better Change" (1977), "Golden Brown" (1981).

SUICIDE

Alan Vega and Martin Rev were outcasts—two psycho-sonic extremists amid New York's punk-rock rabble. Many were repulsed; few wanted to hire them. Yet in years since their 1977 debut album they've been called art-rock innovators, pioneers, and unsung heroes.

Suicide was crudely futuristic, proto-technoid. They combined Alan Vega's raving stage act and his Elvis-influenced vocals (croons, mumbles, hiccups, shrieks) with Martin Rev's stark electronic keyboard riffs and machine-generated rhythms.

The two merged in 1970. Brooklyn-born Vega had done sculpture. Bronx native Rev was a formally trained piano player who'd been fronting a free-jazz band. The Suicide idea was simple: Replace rock guitar with spacey electronics. The two—and their idea—found receptive ears in the rock underground. They played at Mercer Arts Center during the New York Dolls glam period. Later "events" were at Max's during the punk boom. European tours with Elvis Costello and the Clash came in 1978.

There was controversy. Some rejected Suicide as impersonal, hostile. Others hailed them as founders of a new synthesizer music. The battle became real when Suicide performed. Onstage, they were abrasive. In black leather and chains, Vega beat himself with a microphone, confronted audience members, tried to block the exits. Listeners fled, or attacked, throwing bottles. At their first show, half the crowd ran out screaming. On later tours there were riots, beatings, tear gas eruptions.

Gigs were infrequent. Records sold poorly. Suicide was not commercially successful. But the act's impact was pervasive. Suicide's minimalism and droning dissonance fueled the shock-rocking New York No Wave scene, and its electro-keyboard sound powered the rise of some later technopop figureheads. Yet Suicide remains virtually unknown to the mass public.

"It was rough," Vega later told *Musician*'s Michael Hill. "Suicide took a lot out of me. It wasn't even the bottles. It was what was coming from inside me. Suicide was like a living work of art, abstract expressionism onstage, a very physical, emotional thing. We never were a bar band, yet we had to play a bar-band circuit to make bucks. And that took a lot of the spiritual quality out of it."

Rev and Vega went separate ways in 1981. They've since periodically reconvened, shocked to discover batches of new disciples awaiting their resurrection.

KEY RECORDINGS: *Suicide* (1977), *Suicide* (Alan Vega and Martin Rev, 1980), *Half-Alive* (1981), *Ghost Riders* (live, recorded 1981, released 1986), *A Way of Life* (1988); "Ghost Rider" (1977), "Rocket USA" (1977), "Cheree" (1977), "Dream Baby Dream" (1980).

T. REX/MARC BOLAN

Marc Bolan (a.k.a. T. Rex) never gathered a mainline following in the States. Most rock and roll fans—even those Americans with a historic bent—have little idea of just how big a star this fey glam-rocker was through Britain and parts of Europe.

At the peak of his heyday, in the early seventies, T. Rex was the top teen idol, and his concerts could generate the kind of hysteria that greeted the Beatles. Before his decline and death, Bolan sold thirty-seven million records, outselling the combined sales of all product issued by Jimi Hendrix and the Who in his homeland.

For a moment, it was Bolanmania in Britain. Ringo Starr was so impressed, so taken with T. Rex's manic fan reaction that he set out to document the phenomenon on film. *Born to Boogie*, he called it. It flopped, but that's another tale.

Mark Bolan (né Marc Feld, September 30, 1947, London, guitar) had gone to the same primary school as Procol Harum's Keith Reid. Father was a lorry driver; Mother ran a stall in a street market. Early on Bolan was determined to make something of himself. By fifteen he was a male model, an experience that left him with a hunger for the spotlight.

British Decca signed him on for a few solo singles as "Toby Tyler," then "Marc Bowland." Briefly, in 1967, he was a member of the proto-glam-rock band John's Children. The following year, Bolan was off to hippieland. With percussionist Steve Peregrine-Took and some imagination and some borrowed images from Tolkien's hobbit trilogy *Lord of the Rings,* Bolan assembled a bag of catchy, quirky poetic pieces and his vehicle, Tyrannosaurus Rex.

For a few albums (their British debut: *My People Were Fair and Had Sky in Their Hair But Now They're Content to Wear Stars on Their Brows*—what a title!) they were an acoustic duo dressed in "flower-power" threads, love beads, and headbands. Bolan's lyrics told tales of unicorns, gnomes, impish forrest folk, and fairies. Tyrannosaurus Rex—one of the largest beasts to walk the earth—was an underground happening; Bolan an impish elf.

More electricity was seeping into Bolan's recordings: Nineteen sixty-nine's *Unicorn* was half acoustic and half electric. By the following year and album number four, *A Beard of Stars*, Took was gone. His replacement was Mickey Finn—a former member of the obscurity Hapsash and the Coloured Coat—that Bolan had met in a macrobiotic restaurant in Notting Hill. Added also were bassist Steve Currie and drummer Bill Legend (né Bill Fifield). Subtracted were a number of letters from the group's name—now they were simply T. Rex. A single, "Ride a White Swan," took them to number two on the British chart.

"With a few exceptions I've never had a good review for anything," Bolan told *Rock*'s Alan Betrock, here speaking primarily of the British press. "All their reviews ever say is, 'Sounds just like the same piece of shit, must be number one . . .' Now what does that mean?"

While Bolan in all of his various incarnations only had one hit, "Bang a Gong," in the States, the act had gathered album attention for *Electric Warrior* and *The Slider*.

Back in Great Britain, Bolan and the boys could do little wrong through the mid-seventies. Twenty-five of their singles made the charts. Times changed, however, and new teen idols appeared.

A comeback tour was arranged for late '76. Of his declining days, Bolan lucidly told *Rolling Stone*, "I was living in a twilight world of drugs, booze, and kinky sex."

Bolan died, on September 17, 1977, in a car crash, near Putney Common, England. Peregrine-Took died in 1980. Currie died in 1981.

KEY RECORDINGS: *Unicorn* (1969), *A Beard of Stars* (1970), *Electric Warrior* (1971), *The Slider* (1972), *Tanx* (1973); "Ride a White Swan" (1970), "Hot Love" (1971), "Bang a Gong (Get It On)" (1971), "Telegram Sam" (1972), "Metal Guru" (1973).

Roberta Bayley

TALKING HEADS

At first they were three people on a stage, playing three-minute songs. But in every other way, Talking Heads broke the standard rock-band mold.

Live at the dingy Bowery club CBGB in 1975, the Heads—David Byrne (guitar, vocals), Tina Weymouth (bass), and Chris Frantz (drums)—were straight arrows with a jittery edge. No glam or glitter. Just a sound that was minimal, acoustic-sparse. And a singer with twitches and quirks. And a signature song that probed the thoughts of a psycho killer.

How did this trio of head-trippers become one of the most successful, if always offbeat, acts to emerge from the Lower East Side punk-rock underground?

It happened in two main phases. First came the small, high-strung trio with the Norman Bates–like Byrne in front. Later emerged an expanded Heads, in which the Bates boy became a

291

stiff-backed James Brown to an arty dance-groove ensemble with a wild world-music tinge.

"At the beginning I had no idea I appeared like a psychotic lunatic," Byrne told *Musician*'s Scott Isler. "I *still* don't think I look like Tony Perkins. I just wasn't at all aware that was the impression I was giving."

Little else about the act escaped members' scrutiny. Talking Heads was one of the more thought-out, purposefully conceived bands of the punk era. They were different by design.

It was at Rhode Island School of Design in 1973–74 that students Byrne and Frantz met and played in a cacophanous cover band called the Artistics. The two reunited the following year in New York amid a developing rock scene, centered at CBGB, that counted the bands Television and the Stilettos (later called Blondie) among its early arrivals. Preferring the immediacy of rock to what he saw as the art scene's elitism, Byrne—with Frantz—launched the notion of Talking Heads. RISD schoolmate and Frantz girlfriend (later wife) Tina Weymouth joined on bass, her lack of ability perceived as a plus by these clean-slate conceptualizers.

Noting a "hole" in the rock scene—that the day's bands weren't adequately ministering to the musical needs of a thinking crowd—they set out to fill it. Needed was an angle that would both set them apart and allow them to function without competing with bands better able to churn out mainstream rock and roll. The result? A rock act devoid of guitar solos and grand gestures, pared down to the musical minimum, and fronted by a herky-jerky man.

The pieces were in place in time for a spring '75 CBGB debut, although witnesses didn't quite get it at first. "A lot of people either laughed at us or shook their heads," said Chris Frantz, quoted in Clinton Heylin's *From the Velvet to the Voidoids*.

But while appearing at the CBGB festival of unsigned bands in summer of 1975, the Heads began attracting notice both from the press—as subjects of a *Village Voice* cover story—and from record labels. They eventually signed with Seymour Stein of Sire Records.

In early 1977, before recording the first album, they brought in Jerry Harrison on guitar and keyboards. He had been a Harvard architecture student and, in the early seventies, a member of Boston's influential Jonathan Richman and the Modern Lovers.

The fleshed-out Heads began building a following among downtown artsies who were drawn to the band's small scale, its catchy case of urban jitters, and its conservative, unsleazy look.

Record one was issued, with a pack of appropriately spare, arch songs. It caught ears, one set belonging to British ambient-rock meister Brian Eno. He and Byrne, they found, shared an affinity for pulsating sounds of African origin. Eno also liked what he called Talking Heads' "genuine disorientation" created by its mix of powerful rhythm with hesitant, disturbed vocals. He signed on to produce the second Heads album, and an increase in percussion was applied. It became more pronounced on the third disc, *Fear of Music*. By the next one, *Remain in Light*, the formerly four-piece oddball act was fully into a new phase. Dance grooves were dominant, sometimes taking an itchy-twitchy funk turn that copied Byrne's nervous energy. Songs were long, built on simple melodies but without complex harmony. The sound was bigger than before, helped by such added musicians as animal-sound guitarist Adrian Belew.

The expanded edition of Talking Heads, which continued with changing support musicians through three more albums (including the live *The Name of This Band Is Talking Heads* and the soundtrack for the acclaimed 1984 concert film *Stop Making Sense*), held to its rhythm-heavy, African tribal sound. The now-many Talking Heads aficionados—*not,* to anyone's knowledge, called Head-heads—could either groove to the beat or spin out to David Byrnes's still-addled image and weirdo lyrics. A broader base of listeners could turn to the band for a rock-accessible entry into world music. While some naysayers complained about their seeming coldness and overcalculation, the Heads' popularity was not affected. They were the most commercially accomplished of the CBGB graduates, after the hit-making Blondie.

The 1984 *Stop Making Sense* tour was the band's last. But they continued recording. A pair of albums, *True Stories* (with songs from Byrne's film of the same name) and *Little Creatures,* amounted to a departure. They explored indigenous American styles like Tex-Mex, Cajun, and country. The last official Talking Heads album, *Naked,* brought them back to the large-band, world-music approach, delving into West African rhythm, Caribbean zouk music, and Afro-Cuban horn arrangements.

Outside the Talking Heads, David Byrne has established a presence as a respected art-music conceptualist, multimedia star, and avid world-music aficionado. Following an experimental disc with Brian Eno in 1980, *My Life in the Bush of Ghosts,* he wrote the music for Twyla Tharp's dance piece *The Catherine Wheel* and for part of avant-garde dramatist Robert Wilson's play *The CIVIL WarS.* He contributed to, and shared an Oscar for, the music for Bernardo Bertolucci's film *The Last Emperor.* He recorded albums under his own name—discs that drew from Latin-American and other influences. The 1986 film *True Stories* (satirizing everyday life in the Lone Star State), yielded a soundtrack along with the Talking Heads disc. And as a Latin-American music fan, he produced a series of artist compilations—*Brazil Classics* and *Cuba Classics.* By 1994, Earth appeared to have beckoned, and Byrne was back with a stripped-down rock quartet on the disc *David Byrne* and in clubs.

Jerry Harrison, meanwhile, has recorded albums of groove-heavy music under his own name and that of Casual Gods.

In 1981 Weymouth and Frantz launched their own spinoff entity, Tom Tom Club, initially employing Weymouth's three sisters on vocals. The unit attracted enough Tom Tom heads to succeed independently of Talking Heads, thanks largely to a popular 1982 dance single, "Genius of Love."

KEY RECORDINGS: *Talking Heads '77* (1977), *More Songs About Buildings and Food* (1978), *Fear of Music* (1979), *Remain in Light* (1980), *The Name of This Band Is Talking Heads* (live, 1982), *Speaking in Tongues* (1983), *Stop Making Sense* (soundtrack, 1984), *Little Creatures* (1985), *True Stories* (1986), *Naked* (1988); "Psycho Killer" (1977), "Once in a Lifetime" (1980), "Burning Down the House" (1983).

TANGERINE DREAM

The chemically treated brain, confused, addled, and deprived of outside stimulus, might find itself throbbing, blobbing, and pulsing to imagined sounds identical to those generated electronically by Tangerine Dream.

Simulated psychedelic states—at swirling-paisley and total zone-out levels—were the intended effects of the Dreamers' earliest "space music." That was back in the late sixties, when West Berlin–based founder Edgar Froese (keyboard, guitar) and a growing movement of German bands like Can and Amon Düül found themselves cosmos-bound and emulating U.S. acid rock. "Everyone was into psychedelics then," Froese told *Down Beat's* John Diliberto.

"Over in Germany, we have no roots in rock and roll," said Froese. "As a rock band, we could not compare our talent with American musicians. So what we had to do was step away from that and move through the back door into different ways of expressing ourselves."

The result: electronic atmospheric music, rendered without vocals, pop melodies, or screaming solos. Tangerine Dream in its best-known lineup—Froese and synthesists Christophe Franke and Peter Baumann—oozed an otherworldly, steadily morphing mélange of texture, color, and pitch in a vast audio space. Onstage they stood immobile, studiously tinkering with sound modules as disembodied drones, bleeps, and blips issued from distant speakers.

Well over twenty albums have been released. Space and time have worked their changes: The music has become more composed, less improvised, and more computer-based. New Age and synth-rock have evolved, their adherents acknowledging the group's influence. Hollywood has tasted Tangerine and ordered more (*Sorcerer, Legend,* and *Risky Business* among TD's scores). And many members have come and gone, notably synthesist Klaus Schulze (playing drums on the first album), Johannes Schmoelling (replacing Baumann in 1980), Paul Haslinger (replacing Schmoelling in 1986), and Ralf Wadephal (replacing long-termer Franke in 1988).

Now, as always, the Dreamers' dream is to transport listeners far from the cramped confines of earthbound reality. "There is a desire all men on their planet have—and ever will have—and they can't reach it," Froese told *Creem*'s Dave DiMartino. "We transformed it into music."

KEY RECORDINGS: *Electronic Meditation* (1970), *Alpha Centauri* (1971), *Zeit* (1972), *Atem* (1972), *Phaedra* (1974), *Rubycon* (1975), *Ricochet* (1976), *Stratosfear* (1976), *Cyclone* (1978), *Force Majeure* (1978), *Tangram* (1980), *Exit* (1981), *White Eagle* (1982), *Hyperborea* (1983), *Le Parc* (1985), *Underwater Sunlight* (1986), *Tyger* (1987), *Optical Race* (1988), *Rockoon* (1992).

Roberta Bayley

TELEVISION

They're known for a guitar sound that's clean and sleek. For dual guitars that work together with watchlike precision. For lyrics that are coy, oblique, spoken-sung with icy-cool detachment. And for a group history that some deem legendary.

Television is the band that, on March 31, 1974, inaugurated regular live rock at the New York nightspot CBGB. Soon thereafter, the club opened up as a steady performance venue for a parade of new acts: the Patti Smith Group, Blondie, the Ramones, and others. The result was the birth of the vastly influential punk-rock and new-wave movements of the mid-seventies.

Tom Verlaine, the lanky, bohemian guitarist, singer, and writer who fronts the group, points out that there was no great master plan. When they started out, they were just looking for a place to play. "It was just an accident that I was walking down the Bowery with a friend of mine . . . He said, 'Well, what's that bar over there? It says Live Music.' It happened to be CBGB's, and we just happened to walk in." Television played there on

Sundays for a while. "I think the first band we shared bills with was Debbie Harry's three-girl-singer band, the Stilettos," Verlaine recollects. "Then they sort of broke up, and Chris [Stein] and Fred [Smith] and Debbie formed [Blondie], and they started playing. And then the Ramones showed up about a month after that." Patti Smith debuted at CBGB in 1975, completing the first wave of punk bands.

The Television tale dates back to the late sixties, when one-time Delaware high school mates Richard Meyers and Tom Miller descended on the Big Apple. Meyers was a literary type, a fan of nineteenth-century poets Rimbaud and Baudelaire. Miller was a recent convert to guitar, an ex-student of saxophone who dug jazzmen John Coltrane and Albert Ayler along with the European symphonic sound. The two collaborated on underground publishing ventures and then decided that rock and roll might be more noticeable. Impressed by such pre-punkers as the Velvet Underground and the New York Dolls, they briefly formed the Neon Boys, a trio with Miller on guitar, Meyers on bass, and Billy Ficca on drums. Some months later, they added blues-influenced guitarist Richard Lloyd, came up with the name Television, and redubbed the founding members: Meyers became Richard Hell; Miller named himself Verlaine, after the French symbolist poet.

They attracted attention. Onstage, Hell's wild-man act bounced off Verlaine's angular intensity. Songs—like "Blank Generation" (later a punk anthem as sung by a solo Hell) and the odd "Venus" (by Verlaine)—defied or twisted convention. The band's early, ragged-but-right performances devalued technical competence—a gate-opening notion for a flood of musicians-to-be. And their look was anti-glitz, a ripped T-shirt expression of soon-to-be-pervasive rock angst.

Hell left in 1975—soon joining Johnny Thunders in the Heartbreakers and later to form the Voidoids—and Fred Smith of Blondie replaced him on bass. Verlaine manned the Television controls, and the sound gradually became more polished, the songs longer, the music more improvisational—setting the band apart from the day's faster-and-louder punk brethren. An independently released single, "Little Johnny Jewel," drew major-label interest, and in 1977 Television released its album debut, *Marquee Moon*, now regarded as one of the key recordings of the punk era.

Sales failed to match the critical assessment, however, and the band broke up following the release of a second album, *Adventure*, in 1978. Verlaine embarked on a solo career, Lloyd did the same, and Ficca later showed up in the Waitresses.

Television's reputation didn't dim, and the band's sound—with its trademark interlocking guitars—returned in 1992 on an eponymous album that received near-unanimous acclaim. When asked whether he thought it retained the character of the two earlier Television discs, Verlaine laughed sardonically. "Yeah," he said. "It's as uncommercial in its day as the others were in theirs." In the early days of 1994, no plans were in place for a follow-up.

KEY RECORDINGS: *Marquee Moon* (1977), *Adventure* (1978), *Television* (1992); "Little Johnny Jewel" (1975), "Venus" (1977), "Call Mr. Lee" (1992), "In World" (1992).

THE THE

Spinning a disc by the The means entering the dark, Fritz Langian world of Matt Johnson, the act's songwriter, vocalist, guitarist, and—for some time—sole creative force.

In sound, the Johnson universe is not uninviting. Dance-pop substructures have been used, overlaid with Johnson's funky voice, soulful female backup singers, bluesy horns, and touches of musical theater and electro-collage sound effects. The The's signature disjunction begins at the intersection of appealing sonics and nightmare lyrics. In words, Johnson depicts a world gone to seed. Panoramas of broad-scale human suffering (AIDS, war, decay) alternate with close-ups of one-person bouts with lost hope, frustration, hunger, anger. "It's important to juxtapose conflicting elements," Johnson told *Musician's* Robin Schwartz. "Placing musical ideas out of their usual context sets up new kinds of moods. I create an atmosphere to shatter it."

Visual images have been used to bolster the impact. An album-length video for the 1986 *Infected* disc shows a Bolivian prison, a New York brothel, and Johnson holding the barrel of a loaded pistol—a real one—in his mouth.

Religious references abound, sometimes to illustrate man's use of religion as "a tool for suppressing humanity." "God didn't commit these evil acts," said Johnson to John Wilde in *Melody Maker*. "They're mankind's doing. All this wickedness is the animal nature of man being expressed. There is no Satan. The Devil lies in the human heart."

Johnson (born c. 1960) started playing in bands at age eleven and learned sixties hits by listening to the jukebox at his father's London pub. In 1977 he went to work at a recording studio and began making what he called "little cassette albums." In 1979 he formed the The—that is, Matt Johnson with a changing parade of supporting players—and began his odyssey of music plus sociopolitical depth-plumbing.

The journey has been followed with interest by Johnson's not-too-large core constituency. "The cult thing suits me fine, you know," he told writer Wilde. "I'm not even aware of what people think of me. At least it's good that I'm not perceived as an oddball artist, an English eccentric."

KEY RECORDINGS: *Soul Mining* (1983), *Infected* (1986), *Mind Bomb* (1989), *Dusk* (1993); "Uncertain Smile" (1983), "Perfect" (1984), "Slow Train to Dawn" (1986), "Armageddon Days Are Here (Again)" (1989).

THEM

They were named after a fifties sci-fi flick about giant ants and barely lasted a year, but fronted by young Van Morrison, Them recorded some of the grittiest, most cherished of all mid-sixties British Invasion music. Like a man possessed, Morrison wailed; rough and ragtag Them fleshed it out; and thirty years later thousands swear Van Morrison never sounded so good.

Belfast-born Morrison (b. George Ivan, August 31, 1945) was surrounded by music. His mother was a respected jazz singer, his father a blues record collector with thousands of discs by Muddy Waters, Bobby "Blue" Bland, Ray Charles. "Some people are brought up on jam," Morrison has said. "I was brought up on Leadbelly and heads like that. I was nervous, but y'see man, I got these depressions and I had to sing about them."

In his preteen years Morrison put aside his poetry writings and took lessons on the sax, guitar, and harmonica. By thirteen, he was a window washer and playing in skiffle bands; school was done by fifteen. By 1960 Morrison was a professional musician with a rock and roll cover band, the Monarchs. They toured Europe and landed in Germany for a year of seven hours a night, seven days a week, blasting armed-forces clubs and hothouses in Hamburg, Frankfurt, Heidelberg. Worn to the brink, Morrison returned to Belfast.

With two Monarchs—Billy Harrison (guitar), Alan Henderson (bass)—and friends Ronnie Millings (drums) and Eric Wiksen (piano), Morrison (vocals, harmonica, sax) formed Them, an outfit more fitting with his R&B and blues passions. They became Ireland's first punk band, the house band at a newly opened club in the Maritime Hotel in Belfast.

In the summer of '64, Morrison and group entered a London recording studio. In quick succession a take on Slim Harpo's

"Don't Start Crying Now," Big Joe Williams's "Baby Please Don't Go," producer Bert Berns's "Here Comes the Night," and a debut album were issued.

Morrison was bothered. His band's presence was minimized; session musicians—including Jimmy Page—were used to fill in the spaces. And a "dirty ruffian" image akin to that affixed to the Rolling Stones and the Animals was constructed by the label. Nothing much charted in the States, and by summer '65, when the second album was cut, the group existed largely in name only.

KEY RECORDINGS: *Them, with Here Comes the Night* (1965), *Them Again* (1966); "Gloria" b/w "Baby Please Don't Go" (1965), "Here Comes the Night" (1965), "Mystic Eyes" (1965), "Richard Cory" (1966), "I Can Only Give You Everything" (1966).

THIN LIZZY

Thin Lizzy was known for its macho themes, poetic lyrics, tough sound, and raised fists. "The aggression is what I love," said Phil Lynott, lyricist and bass anchor of Thin Lizzy. "I'm sure I'd be locked up for doin' something if I didn't have rock and roll."

Lynott died, January 4, 1986, of pneumonia and heart failure. He was thirty-four. While on a solo outing just prior, he claimed, "There's no way, no way at all that I'll let Thin Lizzy die. It's just on hold. The popularity of Lizzy in Europe is so great that I couldn't stop it, even if I tried."

In the States, Thin Lizzy sold albums but outside its ever-growing pack of fans is remembered for only one song, "The Boys Are Back in Town."

Lizzy's history was marred by constant lineup changes. Aside from Lynott (vocals, bass), Brian Downey (drums), with whom

Lynott had gone to school and performed in the Black Hawks, was the only member from start to finish.

For a while they separated. Lynott joined guitarist extraordinaire Gary Moore—later with Ginger Baker and Jack Bruce in BBM—in Skid Row. Downey joined Sugar Shack. By 1969, Downey and Lynott had formed Orphanage with guitarist Eric Bell, a onetime member of Van Morrison's Them. Orphanage scored a homeland success with "Morning Dew."

Word of these Irish rowdies reached Decca Records. One of their A&R men scouted them out, signed them, and by 1972 had them moved to London for what would eventually prove a most successful worldwide, but America-free, career.

As Thin Lizzy, Lynott and Downey saw a number of fine musicians come and go, including John Cann (ex-Atomic Rooster), Andy Gee (ex-Ellis), Gary Moore (later with Colosseum), Brian Robertson, Snowy White (ex-Pink Floyd, Peter Green Band), and later Ultravox member and ex-Rich Kid, Midge Ure.

Before their intended-to-be-brief separation in the mid-eighties, Thin Lizzy had gathered nearly twenty charted singles in Great Britain—"Whiskey," "Waiting for an Alibi," "Killer on the Loose," and "The Boys Are Back in Town" among them. In the States, nine of their albums made the listings.

During their eighties hiatus, Lynott recorded a pair of solo albums and for a while fronted an act called the Greedy Bastards with Gary Moore, Jimmy Bain (ex-Rainbow), and Gary Holton (ex-Heavy Metal Kids).

Said Lynott: "Lizzy will be back. If I thought Thin Lizzy was so old-fashioned or so bad or something and that we shouldn't be around I'd be the first one to leave the sinking ship." Thin Lizzy never reunited. Today all of their product is considered contemporary, is still in print, and sells at rates equal to an active band's.

KEY RECORDINGS: *Night Life* (1974), *Fighting* (1975), *Jailbreak* (1976), *Johnny the Fox* (1976), *Bad Reputation* (1977), *Live* *and Dangerous* (1978), *Black Rose* (1979); "The Boys Are Back in Town" (1976), "Cowboy Song" (1975).

13TH FLOOR ELEVATORS/ROKY ERICKSON

They are the very stuff of which legends are made. Said Bill Bentley, producer of the 1990 tribute album *Where the Pyramid Meets the Eye: A Tribute to Roky Erickson,* to *Rolling Stone,* "The Elevators took their music further than anybody and clearly paid the price for doing that."

Together for barely two years, the 13th Floor Elevators discovered psycho-space and became the trans-generation-inspiring original psychedelic band—a cosmo-clearing collective of audio-teens driven with a divine purpose: altering mankind's mind.

"They'd take a tab of acid a day," said country crooner Kenny Rogers's brother Leland, owner of International Artists, the Elevators' label. "They were stoned out of their heads all the time," Rogers told *Goldmine's* Jack Ortman and Norm Silverman.

Formed in 1965 from the merger of two Texas garage bands—the Lingsmen and the Spades—the 13th Floor Elevators (so named for the thirteenth letter of the alphabet, M for marijuana) were Roky Erickson and Stacy Sutherland on over-amplified psycho-spiritualized guitars; Benny Thurman, bass; John Ike Walton, drums; and Tommy Hall, the unit's guru, a University of Texas psychology major and blower of the holy electrified jug—a $1^1/_2$ gallon galvanized aluminum kerosene jug.

The release of *The Psychedelic Sounds of the 13th Floor Elevators* early in '66 marked the first time the term "psychedelic" ever appeared on an album cover. The liner notes preached of the "quest for pure sanity," clearly advocating a better life through chemistry. The local sheriff and the Texas Rangers, too,

were immediately alerted and on their trail. *Easter Everywhere* altered the group's philosophy slightly; chemical substances were now declared only one of the multiple means of finding "the Ultimate."

Harassed by authorities, Thurman and Walton got off the ride. In 1968, Erickson was busted again and given the option to attend state prison or rest in a state mental facility. Claiming that he heard "voices," Erickson chose the latter and was assigned to the Rusk State Hospital for the Criminally Insane, in Rusk, Texas. Cashing in on the swelling underground status, two further LPs were assembled by the label—substandard material comprised of out-takes and faked "live" performances.

The Elevators were grounded and dispersed. There were reunions in '72 and '77, but things weren't the same. After his three year stay at Rusk, Erickson was calling himself the Rev. Roger Roky Kynard Erickson and announcing that he was a Martian hounded by earth-bound doctors who were constantly administering shock therapy to him via the power lines. Despite very real emotional difficulties that have repeatedly returned the icon to mental wards—an eight month stay in '89 due to a mail theft misunderstanding—Roky Erickson continues to perform and record tales of two-headed dogs, bloody hammers, and baby ghosts.

Sutherland died of a gunshot wound suffered in a domestic squabble.

KEY RECORDINGS: *The Psychedelic Sounds of the 13th Floor Elevators* (1966), *Easter Everywhere* (1967), *All That May Do My Rhyme* (1995); "You're Gonna Miss Me" (1966), "Reverberation" (1966).

RICHARD THOMPSON

The broad listening public doesn't follow him. His songs aren't heard on mainline, top-forty radio airwaves. Though his records sell in bulk, they've never neared platinum levels. Yet Richard Thompson—master guitarist, songcraftsman, singer, soloist, band member, and pioneering British folk-rocker—is revered by clutches of committed fans and tuned-in professional musicians.

Thompson's influence has crossed most known stylistic bounds. Those who've covered Thompson's songs, employed him as producer or guitarist, collaborated with him, or simply sung praise include Elvis Costello, the Pointer Sisters, Graham Parker, R.E.M., John Cale, David Thomas of Pere Ubu, Bob Mould of Hüsker Dü, Syd Straw, Shawn Colvin, Dinosaur Jr., and scads of other proto-punk, post-punk, avant-punk, new wave, old wave, hardcore, softcore, straight pop, folk-pop, and pop-rock music-making entities.

Newcomers, unlikely to hear Thompson's dark and intricate matter on the fast lanes of the sonic superhighway, have had to stumble across him in other ways: personal referral, accident, or exposure to the printed utterings of pundits—many of the latter remaining puzzled by Thompson's perennial consignment to the back roads of recognition.

His records have been described as gloom-infused, bleak, melancholy, angst-ridden, mordant. "The musical traditions I come out of aren't exactly buoyant and joyous," he admitted in *Frets*.

In a voice dry and unaffected and in instrumental settings that augment his rock-band bash with the rustic tones of mandolin, fiddle, Northumbrian bagpipes, and varied antiques, Thompson often evokes ancient English, Irish, and Scottish folk ballads and dance tunes—with lyrics updating old themes of lost love or tragicomic misadventure. His songs can be complete short stories, with narrative flow, dramatic tension, and vivid characters—characters usually heading for some kind of a fall. "It deals with serious subjects sometimes," he said. "But I don't find it depressing. And I think, really, people who find it depressing should look to their own paranoid schizophrenia, and not mine."

The only schizoid aspect of Thompson has been his matching of carefully rendered, often unusually constructed songs with searing, firebrand rock-guitar soloing. Cited for its cliché avoidance, Thompson's picking echoes the human voice and traditional Celtic instruments rather than the chattering note volleys of standard rock guitar heroes. "I'm glad there are a lot of guitar players pursuing technique as diligently as they possibly can," Thompson said to *Guitar Player*'s Joe Gore, "because it leaves this whole other area open for people like me. There are millions of guitarists—the competition is terrible. I'm happy to think that lots of them are doing something I think is worthless. That's great—it narrows down the field."

Thompson's also noteworthy for longevity and musical rejuvenation in a field crowded with twenty-five-year-old burnouts. Nineties albums *Rumor and Sigh* and *Mirror Blue* are cited as being among his best. Yet Thompson was noted as far back as the late sixties. At that time Thompson (who was born in London on April 3, 1949) was a founding member of Fairport Convention, a collection of players and singers developing an alternative to white blues-rock.

"We were looking for a style that would be uniquely ours," Thompson recounted to Joe Gore. "We didn't want to sound like bad imitations of bad imitations of Blind Blake or Muddy Waters. The thing to do was to revive British traditional music and wed it with the popular style of the day, namely rock." The resulting sound spearheaded the British folk-rock movement, of which Thompson then went on to serve as the leading purveyor in a duo with his wife, Linda, after leaving Fairport in 1971. Their ten-year run ended in divorce in the early eighties, at which point Thompson launched his ever-evolving and improving solo career—or "careen," as he calls it.

"I've tried to survive by being flexible," he said. Collaborations with a cast of other nonmainstreamers—among them David Thomas, the Golden Palominos, and avant-guitarists Fred Frith and Henry Kaiser—have kept him in exploration mode. "It takes some discipline and a willingness to forgo the usual trappings of the music business," he pointed out. "Never having been too successful helps."

KEY RECORDINGS: with Fairport Convention—*Unhalfbricking* (1969), *Liege & Lief* (1969); **solo**—*Henry the Human Fly* (1972), *Strict Tempo* (1981), *Shoot Out the Lights* (with Linda Thompson, 1982), *Hand of Kindness* (1984), *Across a Crowded Room* (1985), *Daring Adventures* (1986), *Amnesia* (1988), *Rumor and Sigh* (1991), *Watching the Dark* (compilation, 1993), *Mirror Blue* (1994); "Old Man Inside a Young Man" (1974), "She Twists the Knife Again" (1985), "King of Bohemia" (1994).

JOHNNY THUNDERS

"The rock 'n' roll Dean Martin of heroin" was how Richard Hell described him. After leaving the glam-trash New York Dolls in 1975, guitarist Johnny Thunders (b. John Anthony Genzale, Jr., 1952) became a fixed figure in the darker crannies of the rock underground, both with his band the Heartbreakers (off and on till 1984) and as a solo act. But as much as for Dolls pedigree and his own erratic output, he was known for high-profile drug intake and debauched excess at self-destruction levels. It was said that for the last ten years of his life fans were just waiting for him to die.

He milked his strung-out image, using the junkie angle as concert shtick. An early Heartbreakers poster blared, "Catch 'em while they're still alive!" "I don't have to tell you who's [Junkie] Number One," he mumbled onstage during between-song patter. At another gig, according to writer Nina Antonia, he announced, "OK. You got it. I'm gonna die tonight," to a cheering audience. "It had become his act," wrote onetime Heartbreaker Richard Hell in *Spin*. "I'd see him be completely alert before a concert and then begin to stagger the moment he hit the stage. He knew that's what they were paying for. He was a professional junkie."

His songs reflected the lowlife fascination, although there were never enough of the dark ditties to jack his career to a stage of sustained mutation. One of his anthems, the heroin tale "Chinese Rocks," was reportedly penned for the Heartbreakers by Hell with Dee Dee Ramone; Thunders later tacked his and other band members' names onto the credits.

Johnny had his boosters—those who saw his dirty-toned, slashing guitar and trashy decadence as having injected vital fuel into punk rock and heavy metal. "Everywhere I look I see Johnny clones," said Dolls drummer Jerry Nolan in the *Village*

Voice. "Poison. Mötley Crüe. I could name a hundred bands that had a Johnny clone in them."

Few were surprised when Johnny finally kicked the bucket, found slumped in a New Orleans rooming house on April 23, 1991, at the age of thirty-eight. The coroner's office cited toxic levels of methadone and cocaine as the cause of death.

KEY RECORDINGS: The Heartbreakers—*Live at Mothers* (import, recorded 1975, released 1991), *Live at Max's Kansas City* (1979); "Chinese Rocks" (1975); **Johnny Thunders**—*So Alone* (1978), *In Cold Blood* (1983), *New Too Much Junkie Business* (1983), *Que Sera, Sera* (1985), *Stations of the Cross* (live, 1987), *Bootlegging the Bootleggers* (live, 1990), *Copy Cats* (with Patti Palladin, 1988), *Gang War* (with Wayne Kramer, 1990); "Too Much Junkie Business" (1982), "Sad Vacation" (1983).

THE TROGGS

They're recognized as the archetypal punk band, precursors of a movement. The Trogg approach was primitive, abrasive; their "singer" snarled, ogled, half-spoke lyrics begging for salacious interpretations. Tame by present-day rap/hiphop standards, the Troggs sang of a "Night of the Long Grass," "Anyway You Want Me," "Give It to Me," and that perennial punk-lust paean, "Wild Thing."

A dirty little band of preprimate intellect, thought the executive powers at top-forty radio. Most of their garage greats were either banned or given little airplay, only to be discovered years later by gender-bending glam-rockers and punks.

"I never sang a dirty line in my life," said head Trogg Reg Presley to author Fred Deller. "I had a line in 'I Can't Control Myself' that went, 'Her slacks were low and her hips were showing.' Everybody took that to mean that the girl's slacks were undone—and that's not what I meant. I was just talking about hipster trousers [hip-huggers]!"

In 1964, Presley (né Reg Ball) and Ronnie Bond (drums) formed the Troglodytes—cave dwellers, workers of the dirty, dark beer joints and dank village halls of Andover, Hampshire, population 18,900. Chris Britton (guitar) and Pete Staples (bass) were brought in to replace earlier members.

It was a couple of hitchhiking female schoolteachers who suggested they call themselves the Grotty Troglodytes. "That name kind of stuck in the back of my mind," explained Presley to *Goldmine*'s Mike Richard. "It was between the Croaks, Ten Feet Five, and the Grotty Troglodytes. We dropped the Grotty part; it means grotesque."

Noting their country-bumpkin image and raw sound, Kinks manager and seasoned press manipulator Larry Page got them a recording contract and a splash in the papers. Page dressed the small-town mods in cheap, striped pajama suits and planted stories of youths reverting to cave dwelling.

"Wild Thing" and "With a Girl Like You" were cut in a total of twenty minutes. "We sat outside the studio waiting for [Page's] orchestra to finish," Presley explained to Joseph Tortelli. "At the end of their session there was three quarters of an hour left. We had to get our gear in, set up, get a sound check, record, and get out within those forty-five minutes."

The Troggs toured America, and over the next twenty-four months the hits happened. During 1968 they experienced their last stateside notice when rebilled a "flower power" band and charted with "Love Is All Around," a toned-down, pop-string thing. Unwilling to adapt to the changing sounds, they disbanded.

In the late seventies, the Troggs became almost fashionable again. Punk found an affinity with their minimalism, rough-raw sound, and nasty-adolescent stance.

With no further hits, critical acclaim, or attention, the

Troggs—who reformed in the mid-seventies—still trudge on. No performance is complete without snarling that infamous "Wild Thing" number, complete with ocarina break.

"I still get lumbered with that 'dirty songwriter' classification," said Presley to Deller. "Any single I put out now has to be super-clean and gleaming white." For that reason, possibly, Troggs recordings—though sporadic—seldom sell.

KEY RECORDINGS: *Wild Thing* (1966), *Love Is All Around* (1968); "Wild Thing" (1966), "I Want You" (1966), "I Can't Control Myself" b/w "Gonna Make You Mine" (1966), "Give It to Me" (1967), "Anyway You Want Me" (1968), "Good Vibrations" (1975).

THE TUBES

They were known for presenting one of the wildest stage shows in all of rock and roll. The Tubes mixed rock, theater, satire. There were shock-inducing antics, onstage nudity, destruction, and obscenity—something for everyone with a bent but discerning taste, particularly their select pot-appreciating, college-bound clique. It was lavish and deliciously tasteless, B-grade softcore porn with a beat. Critics loved it. Record buyers missed out.

The group was formed at the University of Arizona in the late sixties as the Beans. Bill "Sputnik" Spooner and his art-school friends moved their experimental rock theater to San Francisco in 1972, where the show went on for three years before their cult status was noted by A&M Records.

"Sputnik" Spooner (guitar), Fee Waybill (né John Waldo, a.k.a. "Quay Lewd," vocals), Rick Anderson (bass), Michael Cotten (synthesizer), Prairie Prince (percussion), Roger Steen (guitar), Re Styles (vocals), and Vince Welnick (keyboards) remained together ten years without a personnel change.

A&M issued five albums—highly appreciated by their inner circle of fans, but box-office bombs. "Don't Touch Me There" and "White Punks on Dope" smelled like hits, said pundits. They weren't.

"Never having made it big kept us hungry for years and years," explained Waybill to *Rock Magazine*'s Angela Herd. "If we had been Boston and had a triple-platinum on the first album, I'd guarantee that today there would be no Tubes, because we would have all gone off the deep end."

Being hitless wonders kept them hungry and together but lost them their label. With no money to pay for their props, the Tubes mothballed their stage act and appeared as a straight-ahead rock band. They tried their hardest to be pop-radio–friendly, to make hits. Finally, hits (and some money) came with "Don't Want to Wait Anymore" and "She's a Beauty."

Explained Waybill: "'She's a Beauty' is severely cynical. It's about those places where you can pay a dollar and talk to a naked girl. It's a parody of that disgusting situation."

The hits stopped.

"We have got a solid foundation of people who have seen the Tubes, heard the Tubes, have something with the Tubes that they can relate to their own life," said Waybill.

As such, the following continues; the Tubes appear sporadically.

KEY RECORDINGS: *The Tubes* (1975), *Young and Rich* (1976), *Now* (1977), *Remote Control* (1979), *Outside Inside* (1983); "White Punks on Dope" (1975), "What Do You Want from Life" (1975), "She's a Beauty" (1983).

VELVET UNDERGROUND

"We were the original alternative band," Sterling Morrison told the Chicago *Tribune*'s Greg Kot. "Not because we wanted to be, but because we were shunned into it."

They altered the course of rock music by blending rock, the avant garde, and dark and brutal lyrics portraying life on the other side—the daily existence of junkies, drag queens, and the lost. Their appearance was a supreme example of poor timing. The Beatles were singing "All You Need Is Love," flower power was in fashion, and hippies were passing the peace pipe and searching for bliss. The Velvets were way too bleak and brooding and too much of a bummer to be embraced by a mass audience.

The initial version of the band was formed in 1964 during the sweet innocence of the British Invasion. Classically trained avant-gardist John Cale (viola)—who had performed with La Monte Young—teamed with songsmith and recording studio jockey Lou Reed (guitar, vocals), Sterling Morrison (guitar), and Angus MacLise (drums) first as the Primitives, the Warlocks, and the Falling Spikes, then taking their name from a pornographic novel: Michael Leigh's *The Velvet Underground*.

In late 1965 they were performing regularly at the Cafe Bizarre in New York's Greenwich Village. They caught the attention of Andy Warhol, who was looking for a band to accompany his precursor to performance art, the Exploding Plastic Inevitable. Before Warhol's interest waned, he connected them with Federico Fellini actress Nico (née Christa Paffgen, vocals), created their famed banana cover artwork for album one, and saw the act signed to Verve Records. MacLise dropped out, to be replaced by bedroom drummer and dreamer Maureen "Mo" Tucker.

Their debut album failed commercially, as did *White Light/White Heat* and their eponymously titled third album. Verve canceled their contract. Nico had been asked to leave after their first release. Cale, after numerous disagreements with Reed, left after their second. After *Loaded*, a one-off LP for Atlantic—issued without Reed's approval—Reed was gone; Morrison and Tucker were likewise, within months. Although the name remained alive for two years, with Doug Yule fronting various aggregations, no original members were present and all was over by late 1973.

In 1993, the surviving members got together to tour Europe. "Within three minutes, we were like, 'Wow, this sounds like it used to be,'" said Tucker to Kot. "So many of those songs sound like they were recorded yesterday."

Old tensions arose between Cale and Reed, and the reunited revolutionaries scattered again, never touring the States.

"Whatever night we were playing, there was a tension there," said Cale of what made the Velvets great and what keeps blowing them apart.

KEY RECORDINGS: *The Velvet Underground and Nico* (1967), *White Light/White Heat* (1967), *The Velvet Underground* (1969), *Loaded* (1970), *Live at Max's Kansas City* (1972); "Sunday Morning" (1966), "Heroin" (1967).

THE VENTURES

Like Harlow and Valentino, the Ventures are an American institution; though no longer spoken of much by the mainline media, they're cherished by a clutch of devotees, worldwide. The Ventures are no doubt the most prolific instrumental group on record (with eighty-plus releases in the U.S. and claims of double that in Japan and various regions in Europe)—and the most successful (with over three dozen albums and two dozen singles charted). Global sales stagger near 100 million copies.

Still performing an estimated 150 concerts a year, thirty-five years after their debut—though mostly overseas—the Ventures can boast of being one of the most indirectly imitated musical acts of the twentieth century. The idea was simple: guitars, two percussive guitars. Add some bass and drums. That's it. The lineup was not totally new. Buddy Holly's Crickets and other rockabillies had worked it before. But stripped of all else—notably vocals—it would make a generation of baby boomers and their offspring feel that they too could create rock and roll music.

"In 1959, I was washing cars in a used-car lot from nine to five in Tacoma, Washington," Don Wilson told *Goldmine*'s Robert J. Dalley. "After work, I would go home, wash up, and return as a salesman. That's how I met Bob Bogle. He came in looking for a car." Before the sale, the two talked and struck up a friendship.

"About two months later, Bob and I discovered we both knew a few chords on the guitar and had similar musical interests." With a few months' practice they were a duo, the Versatones—so called because Bob and Don would trade off playing lead and rhythm—working nights at parties and small dives. Because they had cheap equipment and lacked a bass and drummer they developed the strong rhythmic foundation that became their trademark. "I was using a Harmony guitar and Bob had a Kay; you know the kind, where the strings are six inches off the fretboard," said Wilson. "Playing on these guitars we developed a heavy bottom sound. I sounded like I almost had dead strings. I used to beat the hell out of them."

"Walk Don't Run," the tune that shook the pop world, was composed by jazzman Johnny Smith and found on a Chet Atkins album rendered in a faintly classical style. "We had to simplify it," Wilson added. "We really had a hard time with it. But we loved that melody." And so has most of the known world ever since.

Two singles' worth of tracks were cut in a dank basement on a two-track Ampex tape recorder. "Walk Don't Run," the second of these issued in lots of three hundred copies on their own label—managed by Wilson's mother, Josie—became the top-of-the-hour radio news break-away tune for KJR in Seattle. When the station's phones ceased to stop ringing, Dolton Records, with a distribution arrangement from the nationwide Liberty label, acquired the disc, and the Ventures were set for the adventure of their lifetime.

"We never woulda figured things turning out as they have," Wilson told *Guitar Player*. "We just thought it would be great if we never had to pick up anything heavier than a guitar."

After a few more major hits— "Perfidia" and "Ram Bunk Shush"—the Ventures turned their attentions to assembly-lining a constant flow of two or three chart-moving albums a year for the remainder of the sixties. Their sound proved so popular that they issued several albums in a Play Guitar with the Ventures series that an army of future rock stars studied. The pace slowed beginning in the mid-seventies, but the tours never stopped.

The Ventures were one of the first Western acts to break into the Japanese market, eventually honored with membership in the cloistered Conservatory of Music for selling over forty million recordings.

Guitar Player, in 1986, referred to Bogle and Wilson as "the quintessential '60s guitar band" and called their debut LP "the album that launched a thousand bands."

KEY RECORDINGS: *Walk Don't Run* (1960), *The Ventures* (1960), *Another Smash* (1961), *The Ventures Play Telstar and Lonely Bull* (1963), *Surfing* (1963), *The Ventures in Space* (1963), *The Fabulous Ventures* (1964), *The Ventures Knock Me Out* (1965), *The Ventures Christmas Album* (1965), *Wild Things* (1966); "Walk Don't Run" (1960), "Perfidia" (1960), "Bluer Than Blue" (1961), "The 20,000 Pound Bee Parts 1 & 2" (1962), "Hawaii Five-O" (1969).

GENE VINCENT

He was the real thing—wilder than Jerry Lee Lewis, sexier than Buddy Holly, more down 'n' dirty than Elvis. Gene Vincent was tough, greasy, hopped up, and freaked out; a dangerous embodiment of the defiant tension that gave birth to rock and roll. Dressed in black leather, dragging a crippled leg, roiling in yelps, screams, and menacing stage swagger, Vincent influenced untold scads of punks and future metalheads.

The image is intriguing, but dark and ultimately sad. Vincent was an alcoholic, a rebel without a cause, a rule-breaker on a death trip. Those who knew him too well got away as soon as possible. "He was crazier than a bedbug," author Randy McNutt was told by Bobby Rambo, a Vincent accompanist. "I mean, he used to get drunk and pull pistols out and fire them. We used to hide them because we were afraid he'd shoot us. He was *wild*."

Vincent Eugene Craddock, Jr. (b. February 11, 1935, Norfolk, Virginia) took an interest in country music, learning the guitar by the time he—though underage—enlisted in the Navy. He would sing for his shipmates, though his military career ended abruptly when he severely injured a leg in a mishap in Korea, variously attributed by Vincent to a gunshot wound, a land mine, or a motorcycle accident.

It was 1956, RCA Victor Records had acquired Elvis Presley, and Capitol—looking to advance its standing—set up a contest to find its own rock and roll idol. Vincent won the search with a tune research indicates he probably did not write. "Me and Don Graves were looking at this bloody comic book," he told a reporter. "It was called *Little Lulu* and I said, 'Hell, man, it's be-bop-a-lulu.' And he said, 'Yeah, man, swingin'.' And we wrote the song. Just like that. And some man came to hear it and he bought the song for twenty-five dollars. I recorded it and told all my friends that I was going to get a Cadillac, because all rock 'n' roll singers had Cadillacs."

Backed by the Blue Caps, so named for the blue golf caps worn by President Eisenhower, Vincent had a few more modest hits— "Lotta Lovin' " and "Dance to the Bop"—and recorded some treasured albums of rock, country, and pop before American radio wearied of rockabillies and their raw, echoey recordings.

In 1960, Vincent was in the taxi crash that took the life of fellow rockabilly Eddie Cochran. His injuries sidelined him for months; he moved to England, where he remained popular and was treated as a rock god for the duration of the sixties.

Broke and suffering a bleeding ulcer, Vincent returned to the States in 1971. He died in his mother's arms shortly after.

KEY RECORDINGS: *Bluejean Bop!* (1956), *Gene Vincent and His Blue Caps* (1957), *Gene Vincent Rocks! and the Blue Caps Roll* (1958), *Gene Vincent Record Date* (1958), *Sounds Like Gene Vincent* (1959), *Crazy Times* (1960); "Be-Bop-A-Lula" (1956), "Race with the Devil" (1956), "Blue Jean Bop" b/w "Who Slapped John?" (1956), "Crazy Legs" (1957), "B-I-Bickey-Bi, Bobo-Go" (1957), "Lotta Lovin'" (1957), "Dance to the Bop" (1957).

VIOLENT FEMMES

If the mind pictures leather-clad, lipstick-smeared banshees of indeterminate sex terrorizing club patrons with howling decibels of skull-cracking death metal—then the mind is mistaken. The Violent Femmes have long been but three identifiably male musicians, their music acoustic in volume, folk-punk in flavor, harmless in tone. They took the name as a joke, at a time when it seemed they wouldn't be around long enough to have to live with it.

The Milwaukee-based band came together in 1981 when singer-guitarist Gordon Gano began jamming with bassist Brian Ritchie, who was playing in an Irish folk duo, and drummer Victor DeLorenzo. They were first noticed by the Pretenders, one of whom heard them playing in the street and invited the trio to open their show that same night.

The Femmes subsequently signed with the independent Slash label and released their debut, an "acoustic rock album before any of this unplugged stuff," as Gano told writer Brian Newcomb. Its Gano-penned tales of teen torment clicked with the like-minded (it eventually went gold) and opened the gate for succeeding albums of increasing electroacoustic variety. The band remained intact until drummer Guy Hoffman replaced DeLorenzo in 1993.

Little about the Femmes fits standard pop molds. They've been called anarchic, off-center, a "weirdo band." Leader Gano, a short but conventional-looking guy, sings with an oddball quaver that unsettles and disturbs or induces nervous laughter. His songs can be sinister (one about following women in the dark—"nobody knows what's in my heart"), funny/scary ("Nightmares"—"thinking about getting together with you"), or suffused with a sincere gospel spirituality (Gano's the son of a Baptist minister). The band's sound varies from punkish energy assaults on one extreme to slow, aching laments on the other, held together by what many have come to see as their trademark: the rough-hewn interplay of Gano's strums with pattering percussion and Ritchie's acoustic bass guitar.

Mass recognition has remained elusive—even as other "alternative" bands have found themselves climbing the charts. Gano told writer Laurie Notaro, "We've never been allowed to do that. . . . We come up with these conspiracy theories. It just doesn't make sense."

KEY RECORDINGS: *Violent Femmes* (1983), *Hallowed Ground* (1984), *The Blind Leading the Naked* (1986), *3* (1988), *Why Do Birds Sing?* (1991), *Add It Up (1981–1993)* (1993), *New Times* (1994); "Blister in the Sun" (1983), "Country Death Song" (1984), "Jesus Walking on the Water" (1984), "Children of the Revolution" (1986), "Fool in the Full Moon" (1988).

TOM WAITS

With goatee and secondhand suit, his image is of a displaced hipster, or a liquor-laced, jivey-mouth bum. In part, the multilayered Tom Waits is a tortured, vulnerable beat poet caught in a decades-long confessional reverie. Not the reincarnation of Howlin' Wolf, or merely a yarn-stringing bluesman, Waits—at least in part—is a rip-throated cross-genre vocalist with a Kerouac charisma and personal tales of the streets and the underbelly, homeless bums in the rain, hookers from Minneapolis, tattooed barmaids, and a mutant dwarf community caught in a steam tunnel.

Born December 7, 1949, in the backseat of a taxi in Pomona and growing up in La Verne, California, Waits never gave thought to being a performing artist. Dropping out of high school, he drove a delivery truck, attempted to sell vacuum cleaners, and worked as a doorman at a dive in San Diego. "I saw a variety of acts—string bands, country-and-western, comedians," Waits told author Irwin Stambler. "I made eight bucks a night and lived next door. I liked it."

With little forethought, Waits pecked away at an accordion and piano in his ma's garage. Soon he was doing Elvis impersonations, folk fluff, and originals. While performing on the amateur shows, called Hoot Nights, at the Troubadour in Los Angeles, Waits was approached by Herb Cohen. Cohen became his manager and remained so for years.

Following the release of his critically received *Closing Time* in 1973, stories started surfacing about Waits's liquor and the girls and all-night rambles, skid-row hotels, cross-country hitchhikes.

The offbeat nature of much of Waits's material gave critics the notion that he was some kind of anachronistic beatnik. "I'm not nostalgic. I wouldn't want to live in the fifties," said Waits. "I'm not a throwback. I don't live in a vault. I try to stay abreast of current affairs."

Waits's theatrical performances caught Hollywood's attention. A movie career started with a spot in Sylvester Stallone's *Paradise Alley* in 1978. Waits has appeared in Ralph Waite's *On the Nickel*, Jim Jarmusch's *Down by Law*, Hector Babenco's *Ironweed*, and Francis Ford Coppola's *The Cotton Club*, *The Outsiders,* and *Rumble Fish*. Waits also wrote the score to Coppola's *One from the Heart*, winning an Oscar nomination.

"It's not just young people that listen to me," said Waits, with pleasure, of his off-mainstream audience. "I get letters from waitresses, truck drivers, fry cooks."

Waits insists his gravestone epitaph will read: "I told you I was sick."

KEY RECORDINGS: *Closing Time* (1973), *The Heart of Saturday Night* (1974), *Nighthawks at the Diner* (1975), *Small Change* (1976), *Foreign Affairs* (1977), *Blue Valentine* (1978), *Heartattack and Vine* (1980), *Bounced Checks* (1981), *Swordfishtrombones* (1983), *Rain Dogs* (1985), *Franks Wild Year* (1987), *Big Time* (1988).

BRIAN WILSON

Surf-rock kings the Beach Boys made history as one of America's main answers to the Beatles-led British Invasion in the early sixties. Brothers Brian, Dennis, and Carl Wilson, cousin Mike Love, and buddy Al Jardine rode the airwaves regularly during those endless summers of yore, sending many a hit single down the radio pipeline from 1962 to '89. Rock Hall of Famers, the Beach Boys were—still are—the stuff of legend and mass acclaim.

But the larger Beach Boys story contains another, less widely known tale. It is that of Brian Wilson—composer, producer, arranger, singer, pianist, bass player—revered by insiders as the "amazing" creative force behind the Beach Boys, but also lamented as "a troubled soul," his talent squandered in drug-hazed psychoses, his intended masterpiece—the legendary album *Smile*—heard by the public mostly in unfinished snippets.

"When it comes to music, he *is* a genius," said Lenny Waronker, Warner Bros. president, to *Rolling Stone*'s Michael Goldberg. The songs of Brian Wilson have been embraced as part of the cultural fabric of the sixties. "I Get Around," "Little Deuce Coupe," "Fun, Fun, Fun" remain classic anthems of sun worship, surfing, cars—all those symbols of the California Dream, teen-party version.

Wilson not only etched the themes, he brainstormed the intricate wall-of-sound vocal arrangements that made the Boys' music instantly identifiable. And, even without the Beach Boys, he could commit them to tape. "What bowled me over also was how fast Brian was in the studio," said producer Russ Titleman in a *New York Times* interview. "He plays and sings virtually every part . . . For tracks like [1988's solo] 'Love and Mercy' and 'There's So Many,' which have complex overdubbed harmony vocals, Brian would rush out to the microphone, put on his headphones, and shout, 'I need eight tracks!' He laid down all these interlocking vocal parts in fifteen minutes." Wilson, intuitively, was rock's master contrapuntalist.

But there was the "other" Brian Wilson—the disturbed child-man who lived a decades-long beach bummer of fear, introversion, and all-around nuttiness. The seed, some say, was planted early. "I've always believed that I was dropped shortly after birth," he wrote in his autobiography *Wouldn't It Be Nice,* "since almost everything that's happened to me afterward has been painful."

Born Brian Douglas Wilson on June 20, 1942, he grew up the eldest of three brothers in a Hawthorne, California, household. "It was the damned boondocks," he told Timothy White. "I walked around paranoid that somebody was going to pound the hell out of me every second." Tales abound of his father, Murry, doing just that. Murry, a machine-shop owner and aspiring songsmith, was hard on the budding Brian, complementing occasional slap-arounds with intentionally disgusting displays of his glass eye and the empty socket from which he'd removed it.

Brian, though deaf in one ear, showed an early aptitude for music—a sweet, high voice; church choir solos; songwriting. A childhood fan of the voice-heavy Four Freshmen, Wilson would arrange his brothers' and parents' vocals during family sing-alongs. When he was given a tape recorder at age sixteen, he experimented with recording voices and then singing harmony with the playback—an early stab at overdubbing.

The ultrasensitive Brian spent hours a day tuning out the world, banging on the piano, and tuning in to music—all in the safety zone that would one day be the subject of his ballad "In My Room."

When he and the brothers went pro—first as the Pendletones, then as the Beach Boys on a single, "Surfin'," released in late 1961—Brian became the act's ongoing source of original songs. Their phenomenal and consistent success year after year meant pressure on him to keep the hits coming. Meanwhile, the band's first manager—Murry Wilson—remained ever critical. "[The other Beach Boys] left me with this feeling inside of 'You better get another album out or we'll kill ya!'" Brian told Tim White.

A series of psycho-implosions began in 1964—well into the Beach Boys' career. Right around the time Brian was penning "Fun, Fun, Fun" and other party paeans, he had a breakdown while aboard a commercial airplane. Then, initiating a rift with the Beach Boys that would later widen, he announced a retirement from the stage to concentrate on recording (he'd be replaced on tour first by Glen Campbell, then by Bruce Johnston). "As I lost touch with myself," he recalled, "I became even more distant from them."

A musical wake-up call from the Beatles—their *Rubber Soul* album was remaking rock while the Beach Boys were still in teen-stripe short sleeves—shocked Wilson in 1966. The not egoless Wilson was moved to match them, abandoning the Beach Boys hit-making formula and aiming for "a higher plateau"—"where a whole album becomes a *gas,*" as he told writer Steven Gaines. The result was the Wilson-written-produced-arranged *Pet Sounds* album—an introspective, "no blondes in bikinis, no beach" collection that irked the money men but intrigued the art-inclined. Ironically, its intricately melodic "God Only Knows" became a favorite of Paul McCartney, and the entire *Pet Sounds* album an inspiration for the Beatles' own masterful *Sergeant Pepper's Lonely Heart's Club Band.*

The later single "Good Vibrations"—complete with eerie sci-fi sounds from a thing called a theremin—was another intended musical "summation." "Al didn't like it, Carl . . . thought it was bizarre, and Mike called it more avant-garde crap," claimed Brian. The rest of the world consumed it in large quantity.

To top *Pet Sounds,* Wilson embarked on what was to be his "teenage symphony to God," which he initially titled *Dumb Angel.* Working with lyricist Van Dyke Parks, he sketched out ideas, recorded work tapes, and sonically experimented. The word on the grapevine was that a masterpiece was in preparation. An expectancy built up around it. But the record never happened. Deadlines were missed. The other Beach Boys didn't like what they heard. The record label officially shelved it, and what had come to be known as *Smile* entered the vaults of rock music arcana, its remnants turning up only on bootlegs and in revamped versions on later commercial albums, to the unending interest of studious Wilson aficionados.

Wilson's world grew weird. Around the "Good Vibrations" period he turned his home into a "drug-addled, supercharged fun house." A giant sandbox was built around the piano, for "inspiration." A tent was set up, filled with fabric, cushions, and hookahs. "I went in once or twice," said TV producer David Oppenheim, "but never understood what it was about. Brian was looking at the TV set with the volume off and just the color, detuned, and lots of vegetables around."

In a noted *Smile* recording session—for a piece called "Mrs. O'Leary's Cow," a.k.a. "Fire"—Brian had the many gathered musicians wear fire helmets, ordered a fire set in a bucket, and afterward saw significance in reports that Los Angeles had an unusual number of conflagrations that night. "I began to lose it," Wilson recalled.

In 1975 Brian's wife hired Dr. Eugene Landy, flamboyant "shrink to the stars," to handle the growing problem. The idiosyncratic Landy worked with Brian for about a year, then was dismissed.

Six years later, a drug-riddled, food-inflated 340-pounder ("I

was too concerned with getting drugs to write songs," he told
Rolling Stone), Brian was entrusted again to the care of Landy.

Their relationship later became a point of contention. Few
disputed Landy's success: In 1987, after a lengthy spell of inten-
sive therapy, a physically fit Wilson was seen embarking on a
solo career that eventually yielded a solo album, *Brian Wilson,* and
in the mid-nineties spawned a collaboration with producer Don
Was. (A 1990 album, *Sweet Insanity,* never saw release.) Many,
though, took issue with Landy's growing involvement in Brian's
musical career. The two formed a business partnership, Brains
and Genius. Landy was the executive producer of the *Brian Wilson* album. For years, Brian was reported to make nary a decision
without a Landy approval. Some feel that Brian's autobiography
was strongly influenced, in part, by Landy. "I believe Brian has
been brainwashed," Mike Love told *People's* Peter Castro.

Since the last full-bore Wilson–Beach Boys disc—1977's *The
Beach Boys Love You*—the band has continued recording and
performing. Brian has occasionally appeared with them. His
loyalists remain ever alert for signs of revitalization and new
creative activity.

KEY RECORDINGS: Beach Boys—*Surfer Girl* (1963), *Summer Days (And Summer Nights!!)* (1965), *Pet Sounds* (1966), *Smiley Smile* (1967), *Wild Honey* (1967), *Sunflower* (1970), *15 Big
Ones* (1976), *The Beach Boys Love You* (1977); "Surfin'" (1961),
"In My Room" (1963), "I Get Around" (1964), "Help Me,
Rhonda" (1965), "God Only Knows" (1966), "Good Vibrations"
(1966), "Surf's Up" (1967); **Brian Wilson**—*Brian Wilson*
(1988). Songs salvaged from the unreleased *Smile* album turned
up on later discs as follows: "Heroes and Villains," "Vegetables,"
"Wonderful," and "Wind Chimes" on 1967's *Smiley Smile;* "Cab-
inessence" and "Our Prayer" on 1969's *20/20;* "Cool Cool
Water" on 1970's *Sunflower;* "Surf's Up" (a reworked version) on
1971's *Surf's Up;* bootlegs of original *Smile* tracks became available in the early 1980s.

WIRE

The cult musician's cult band, Wire is little known to residents of the surface world though legendary and influential in the shadowy recesses of the rock and post-punk underground.

First active in the mid-seventies, British singer-guitarist Colin Newman, bassist-singer Graham Lewis, and guitarist Bruce Gilbert—all former art-school students—joined with drummer Robert Gotobed to fashion *Pink Flag*, an album now viewed by many as a model of punk-infused anarchy, minimalism, and cool irony. Years later, Newman described it to *Creem's* Richard Grabel as "basically a trashed-up history of rock music, using everything that had happened but perverting it. Stripping it, as the Ramones had done with a certain style of music." That musical "perversion"—carried further via the albums *Chairs Missing* and *154*—inspired legions of others to follow a similarly iconoclastic path. "Rock died then," said Newman. "The corpse keeps crawling out and making lots of money, but there's nothing new in it." Wire disbanded in 1980, and members pursued separate projects.

They reconvened five years later, launching a new phase of Wire activity first with the EP *Snakedrill* and then with an album, *The Ideal Copy*, the latter suggesting the sonic equivalent of David Lynch's or Fritz Lang's cinematic nightmares: dark, eerie, mechanistic, with dance-oriented technopop (and an oddly cheery hook on "Madman's Honey") refracted through a warped subjective lens. Lyrics are fragmented, their meanings obscure and surreal. The music, often metallic and harsh, employs minimalist harmonies, blasts of processed electronic sound, and machinelike interlocking instrumental patterns over which vocals are understated and detached—or completely over the top, as on the ranting "Feed Me." Tense as a tightly stretched wire, the band's sound suggests creeping dehumanization—a pervasive dementia roiling beneath the surface of a technologically driven world.

Though less influential than the band's late-seventies output, new discs continued to spin forth into the 1990s, delving notably into musical atmospherics and synth textures. Following fourth member Gotobed's departure, the band continued as the three-lettered Wir starting in 1991. Members have recorded various non-Wire oddities over the years, including Colin Newman's solo work and the Lewis–Gilbert collaboration Dome.

KEY RECORDINGS: *Pink Flag* (1977), *Chairs Missing* (1978), *154* (1979), *Snakedrill* (EP, 1986), *The Ideal Copy* (1987), *Ahead* (EP, 1987), *A Bell Is a Cup Until It Is Struck* (1988), *It's Beginning to and Back Again* (1989), *Manscape* (1990), *The Drill* (1991), *The First Letter* (as Wir, 1991); "Mannequin" (1977), "Mercy" (1978), "I Am the Fly" (1978), "Ambitious" (1987), "Ahead" (1987), "Kidney Bingos" (1988).

LINK WRAY

"This is the king," said Pete Townshend, kneeling with head bowed. "If it hadn't been for Link Wray and 'Rumble,' I never would have picked up a guitar."

Wray is a legend—King of the Power Chord—among punks, metal-heads, and grunge guitarists. Every kid who has strapped on a guitar since one 45, "Rumble," with its extreme echo and menacing distortion, has—knowingly or not—been heavily affected.

Lincoln Wray was born May 2, 1930, in the Appalachian Mountain region of North Carolina. Grandmother was a full-blooded Shawnee Indian. Mom encouraged, and with the help of Hambone, an itinerant bluesman, Wray learned to fiddle with his four-dollar guitar. By the mid-forties, Link, brothers

Vernon (guitar, vocals) and Doug (drums), and Shorty Horton (bass) were working the juke joints and whorehouses.

Wray served in the Korean War, contracted tuberculosis, was hospitalized for a year-and-a-half, and lost a lung. As Lucky Wray and the Palomino Ranch Gang the brothers first recorded in 1956.

In early '58, while playing a record hop for deejay Milt Grant in Fredericksburg, Virginia, the brothers were asked to make up some music. "Milt says, 'Link. Play the stroll.' The Diamonds, who had the number-one hit, were going to dance the stroll while I tried to play live. I told him, 'I don't know the fuckin' stroll!' My brother Doug said, 'I know the stroll beat. Just start playing something.' So, God zapped it. 'Blowm, blowm, blowm.' I just started playing it.

"When we went into the studio to record 'Rumble,' I didn't get that live sound. It was too clean." To dirty it up, Wray got an idea that would change the course of rock and roll and the incentive for numerous distortion gadgets. "I had a Premier amplifier with a big speaker on the bottom and two tweeters on each amp," he told Chris Gill of *Guitar Player*. "With a pen I started punching holes in the tweeters. I got that distorted sound, plus a tremolo. We got the song in three takes, on one track, for fifty-seven bucks. Isn't God wonderful?"

"Rumble" sold a million and a half copies. "Rawhide" earned a similar status. Problems quickly arose: Wray wanted to record "honest music." Not being the sort to conform to the wishes of any money-minded record people, Wray was often without a label. Sporadically—often incognito as the Moon Men, Spiders, and Fender Benders—Wray put out dirty black-blues rock and roll; sales were near nil.

Beginning early in the seventies, Wray experienced a revival of interest, recording three acclaimed albums for Polydor. In 1977 Wray linked up with retro-rockabilly Robert Gordon for a couple of successful LPs and European tours.

Wray settled down in Denmark. Vernon, Doug, and Shorty **✗**
have all passed away.

Link Wray told *Guitar Player*: "My ten-year-old son says,
'Daddy, does God love rock 'n' roll?'" Wray replied, "I know
that some churches say rock 'n' roll is evil. But, honey, He
pulled me out of the death house and gave me 'Rumble.' I
recorded it three months after I had my lung taken out. Yeah, I
think God loves rock 'n' roll."

KEY RECORDINGS: *Link Wray and the Wraymen* (1960),
Jack the Ripper (1963), *Bullshot* (1979); "Rumble" (1958),
"Rawhide" (1959), "Run, Chicken, Run" (1963).

X

With a name that conjured images of anonymity, X was born in
the explosive late-seventies L.A. music scene. Never with a national hit, X to the knowledgeable were the nation's most critically approved purveyors of punk rock—a form they worked
but didn't fully embrace. While influenced by the power and
speed, X exuded lyrics inordinately sophisticated for the genre.
They were distinct from their punk peers in New York and London in their affinity for rockabilly and old-time country music.

X happened when John Doe and Billy Zoom met in 1977
through a classified ad in *Recycler*, a local underground rag.
Doe's family had been perpetually on the move, from Decatur
to Knoxville to Madison . . . "In Baltimore, I started playing
bass in a bunch of bands," Doe told author Irwin Stambler.
"There was no place to go, musically speaking, in Baltimore, so
I came to L.A. on Halloween night, 1976." Zoom, who had
backed Bobby Day and Etta James and played sax and guitar
with rockabilly primal Gene Vincent, had the love of music in-
stilled while a baby. His dad, who had played with jazz guitar

great Django Reinhardt, "started teaching me before I could walk," Stambler was told. "My mother played all kinds of different music while I was growing up. After high school I played with black R&B bands." As front man for the Billy Zoom Band, Zoom recorded some sides for revivalist preserver Rockin' Ronny Weisner.

Exene (née Christine Cervenka) was raised in rurality. "It was a little town," she told Stambler, "no movie theater." For her late teens she lived in Florida. "I was living in Tallahassee writing poetry when a friend said he was going to California, did I want a ride." There she continued to write.

Exene met Doe at a poetry reading in the Venice section of L.A. "She was wearing dark lipstick and read this poem about Lois Lane," said Doe. "We went out that night, got drunk, and became a couple."

After listening to the music made by Doe and Zoom, Exene reworked her poem "I'm Coming Home" into a song; soon she

was their distinctive and often drunk—screeching, pitch-free,
leapfrogging—lead vocalist. With Don "D. J." Bonebrake—then
a member of the Eyes, a resident act at the Masque, a short-
lived premier Hollywood punk palace located in a naked-bulb
basement under a porno theater—X began building a local
following.

X worked the new-wave turf; a close examination revealed
lyrics—largely autobiographical—that oozed kinship with
avant-garde poetry.

Slash Records took an interest, as did ex-Doors keyboardist
Ray Manzarek, who produced their debut album, *Los Angeles*.
The package sold well for a release by an independent label, as
did their pundit-popular follow-up, *Wild Gift*, a nominee by
many critics for album of the year.

Elektra signed the poetic punksters in 1982 for an eight-
album haul that would not see completion. With the issuance
of *Ain't Love Grand* (1985), Zoom left the group and Doe and
Exene ended their marriage. Lone Justice's guitarist Tony
Gilkyson was added, and for *See How We Are*, their last studio
album, the Blasters' Dave Alvin was included in the X fold.
"Confused, exhausted and directionless," wrote a critic of the
latter effort. After a live LP, X ceased to exist.

After passed-over solo efforts, Exene and John Doe announced the reformation of X in 1990. *Hey Zeus* was released in
1993.

KEY RECORDINGS: *Los Angeles* (1980), *Wild Gift* (1981),
Under the Big Black Sun (1982), *More Fun in the New World*
(1983), *Ain't Love Grand* (1985); "We're Desperate" (1981),
"Wild Thing" (1984).

XTC

Songs that "painted great brain pictures" were what attracted Andy Partridge when he first started paying attention to such things. There were the "Strawberry Fields"–era Beatles, lush Beach Boys vocals, the mind-altering sonic substances of Pink Floyd. "I did love psychedelic singles," Partridge told *Musician*'s Scott Isler, "singles that had a high magic content."

As singer-songwriter for the British trio XTC, Partridge went on to cast a few spells of his own to rival the ear-candy creations of his idols. With bassist-vocalist Colin Moulding adding ditties and Dave Gregory providing unique guitar parts, XTC's blend of clever words, curling melodies, and trippy sound textures earned them a place of distinction in post-new-wave rock and roll.

Their style peaked, some contend, on the multiflavored 1989 album *Oranges & Lemons* (complete with florid Peter Max-like cover art) and especially on its splashy sunburst opener. Written by Partridge for his toddler kids as a kind of welcome to the wonders of life, "Garden of Earthly Delights" explodes with exotica: throbbing Eastern percussion, Latin-tinged bass, *Arabian Nights* allure, and a snake-charm twister of a fuzz-guitar line, all ensuring that, like the lyrics say, "you won't die of boredom."

Boredom has rarely infected the hardcore hordes long hooked to XTC's intoxicants. But seekers of nonmusical thrills have had to look elsewhere. For years, XTC hasn't toured. They prefer not to make videos. Their activities are notoriously low-key and glam-resistant. "Our band doesn't have any rock and roll lifestyles," Partridge admitted to *Rolling Stone*'s Steve Pond. "We're horribly mundane, aggressively mundane individuals. We're the ninjas of the mundane, you might say."

Since the early eighties they've been refugees from fame, living quiet, slowed-down lives in their southern England hometown of Swinton. Occasionally the three mutate back into rock-band form for the sole purpose of recording and releasing fresh product. But it is done without much fanfare. "I like people to buy the records," said Partridge, "but I'd be quite happy if we were faceless musicians and it was just the name XTC that they bought, like a steak sauce."

It was when the name meant least that they performed the most. In the late sixties, Partridge played as a teen amid surrounding Swinton. He later served as a part of Star Park, an entity that included Moulding and drummer Terry Chambers. They morphed into XTC in 1976 (the name suggesting "short, sharp, shocking" music) and, with keyboardist Barry Andrews, barged into the big-time music business.

Virgin Records, perhaps thinking them part of the trendy new wave, signed the band in 1977. Discs of quirky-jerky, slightly addled, and somewhat cranky music were issued. An album registered in the top forty of the British pop charts. XTC did its duty and took to the road.

Dave Gregory came on board to replace Andrews—without damage—and the ninjas marched on, moving ever further in sound and style from the beaten path.

Then came the turning point. It was in 1982 while readying for a Hollywood concert that Partridge collapsed in panic—struck by an attack of stage fright so severe he couldn't go on. "I was forced by the manager to feign physical illness," he told *Rolling Stone*, "so promoters wouldn't have my legs broken." "Andy was in tears back at the hotel," said Moulding. "It was all pretty squalid." Partridge retreated to Swinton and, acknowledging a phobia, swore off touring altogether. "I thought I couldn't handle this rock and roll nonsense," he said. He spent a year trying to "get over the shock." Meanwhile the drummer quit, and the live XTC of yore was no more.

But the albums—critically acclaimed ones—kept coming. Pop mastermind Todd Rundgren came in as a producer to help them score a commercial hit. The 1986 result—a Rundgren-conceived "suite" of such savory songs as Moulding's "Grass" and Partridge's "Ballet for a Rainy Day"—emerged as the XTC breakthrough, *Skylarking*. Along with some controversy generated at the time by a separate single, the religion-challenging "Dear God," the album made XTC a recognized entity in the U.S.—some ten years after their debut.

They recorded the follow-up knowing that substantial numbers were finally going to pay attention.

Oranges & Lemons, showered with praise, became their most successful release.

But all is relative. Whether because the lyrics are too sophisticated, the "classic" roots are of too little current interest, or the exotic flavors are too rich for the abrasion-tuned ears of youth, the exquisitely rendered music of XTC remains, to this day, a specialty taste.

"I've got an awful feeling," Partridge told Dag Juhlin of the *Illinois Entertainer*, "that we're one of those bands that we either have to die off . . . or we'll have to split up, and they'll say, 'What a shame; they were really brilliant!' "

KEY RECORDINGS: *White Music* (1978), *Go 2* (1978), *Drums and Wires* (1979), *Black Sea* (1980), *English Settlement* (1982), *Skylarking* (1986), *Oranges & Lemons* (1989), *Nonsuch* (1992); "Making Plans for Nigel" (1979), "Senses Working Overtime" (1982), "Dear God" (1986), "Grass" (1986), "The Garden of Earthly Delights" (1989), "The Mayor of Simpleton" (1989).

FRANK ZAPPA

He started as a little-known producer of doo-wop tracks out of a small facility in Cucamonga called Studio Z. Yet Frank Vincent Zappa went on to become the father—make that the Mother—of all cult rockers.

As leader of the legendary sixties band the Mothers of Inven-

tion, and as a solo entity, Zappa had "no commercial potential," some charged. But heavy underground support ensured more than a quarter century of thriving action nonetheless, way out on the commercial fringe.

His first disc to come within mainstream earshot—the Mothers' 1966 double-LP *Freak Out!*—brought outside agitation to the placid pop world and made him its resident Yippie. A studio-expert West Coast answer to East Coast weirdos the Fugs, the Mothers skewered the greasy "Duke of Earl" sound, experimented with dissonant "contemporary classical" music, and ridiculed the prevailing social establishment—all on two pieces of anarchy-inciting vinyl.

Its songs announced a rising tide of "freaks"—the "left-behinds of the Great Society . . . who aren't afraid to say what's on their minds." The liner notes called on listeners "to join us . . . become a member of the United Mutations . . . *freak out!*" Many a long-haired "freak" could soon be heard decrying the "plastic" values and shallow lives of the uptight authorities.

A song called "Plastic People" on the second album even found receptive ears among the day's dissident Czechoslovakians, spawning a group called the Plastic People and a cult of followers.

Long after the Plastic People, the freaks, and the United Mutations disappeared and the hubbub faded, Zappa's sounds were circulating among the general populace. By the time he died, on December 4, 1993, he'd risen to rock-icon status and earned praise as a composer of serious music. Along the way, he'd played some burning guitar, led a few state-of-the-art bands, and built a noted business empire that included Barking Pumpkin Records, Honker Home Videos, the Joe's Garage recording facility, and the Barfco-Swill merchandising unit.

Zappa spent plenty of time in his last years hunkered down in his home studio, the Utility Muffin Research Kitchen, editing vast quantities of recorded matter for eventual public consumption. That would add to the fifty-odd albums of mixed pop, rock, doo-wop, jazz, experimental, and classical tracks already on the market.

Among them are "The Dog Breath Variations." *Freak Out!*'s noisy "The Return of the Son of Monster Magnet." The jazz-tinged "Invocation and Ritual Dance of the Young Pumpkin." His classic "The Duke of Prunes." The rarely heard "Son of Prelude to the Afternoon of a Sexually Aroused Gas Mask." The more frequently heard "Don't Eat the Yellow Snow." Zappaphiles, in short, have had more than adequate supplies of vital circular and celluloid matter.

Zappa (b. December 21, 1940) began with a taste for R&B and Edgard Varèse and "an affinity to creeps." As a teen, he bashed drum skins in the Antelope Valley High marching band in Lancaster, California. With school friend Don Van Vliet, later known as Captain Beefheart, he formed the short-lived Blackouts ("the only R&B group in the entire Mojave Desert"). He later played in bar bands, scored a couple of B movies, and amassed enough money to fund his own Studio Z, where he wrote songs, played guitar, and did production.

The Studio Z recordings, involving a number of obscure

artists (the Rotations, Baby Ray and the Ferns), included a 1963 ditty called "Memories of El Monte," cowritten with singer Ray Collins, waxed by the famed Penguins, and given more than a few spins by those in doo-wop circles. Its royalties were reportedly used to pay bail for a female participant in a "sex tape" that Frank had made, and for which he had spent ten days behind bars.

In those pre-Beatlemania days, Frank played in the Soul Giants, a band that included Collins (vocals), Jimmy Carl Black (drums), Elliott Ingber (guitar), and Roy Estrada (bass). It was this unit that, in 1964 Los Angeles, became first the Mothers and then, at the insistence of a concerned Verve Records, the Mothers of Invention. The time was right, they felt the itch, and Zappa had a vinyl *Freak Out!,* mating his doo-wop and avant-garde tendencies to yield such songs as "Help, I'm a Rock"—a "suite in three movements" employing Middle Eastern–style chant, babbling nonsense, a greasy fifties basso, some sonic eruptions, and way-out, Cecil Taylor–style jazz piano.

With a direction thus set, the Mothers held on for a wild ride—highlighted by 1967's *Absolutely Free* (Zappa's "masterpiece," said *Time*) and the hippie-lampooning parody *We're Only in It for the Money*—until Zappa disbanded them in 1969. One year later he bore new offspring, gathering a fresh batch of Mothers that included star drummer Aynsley Dunbar, keyboardist (and future fusion ace) George Duke, and the Phlorescent Leech and Eddie (former Turtles Mark Volman and Howard Kaylan). Among their key artifacts was the film and album *200 Motels,* described by critic Leonard Maltin as a "visual, aural assault disguised as movie; completely berserk."

Zappa waxed a steady flow of solo discs both during the Mothers years and long afterward (the last Mothers album was *One Size Fits All* in 1975). They leaned at times toward the brain-blowing sounds of progressive rock and electronic jazz-fusion, as on *Hot Rats* of 1969 (the same year Zappa produced Captain Beefheart's masterful *Trout Mask Replica*), while generally offering his usual ambitious mixture of parody and audio adventure. Written, arranged, and produced by Zappa (and released on his own Bizarre, DiscReet, and later Barking Pumpkin labels), the difficult creations demanded assemblages of idiosyncratic instrumental experts.

Many of the latter passed through the revolving door of the Zappa band, and many went on to further notice as soloists or band collaborators. Lowell George (on board for three albums) formed Little Feat. Aynsley Dunbar later joined Journey and Starship. Guitarist Adrian Belew achieved solo fame and played with David Bowie, Talking Heads, and King Crimson. Drummer Terry Bozzio launched Missing Persons. Drummer Vinnie Colaiuta wound up with Sting. Violinist Jean-Luc Ponty became a fusion star.

Even Zappa's offspring have taken Frank-fueled flights: guitarist Dweezil Zappa has issued a couple of solo albums and one under the band name Z with singing brother Ahmet Rodan Zappa. Their sister, Moon Unit, is heard on the single "Valley Girl," her dad's lone entry on the top-forty charts.

Impressively topping the untoppable, by the 1990s Zappa had broken into the classical-music mainstream, attracting prestigious commissions and placing his serious works in concert programs at Lincoln Center and elsewhere. "I never had any intention of writing rock music," Zappa told Dan Ouellette. "I always wanted to compose more serious music and have it be performed in concert halls, but I knew no one would play it."

It seemed the United Mutations/freak influence had spread a mite further than expected. "I get requests for scores all the time," Zappa said in 1993. "The most recent was from the President's own U.S. Marine Corps Band in Fairfax, Virginia. They want to play 'Dog Breath Variations.'"

KEY RECORDINGS: Mothers of Invention—*Freak Out!* (1966), *Absolutely Free* (1967), *We're Only in It for the Money* (1967), *Uncle Meat* (1969), *Burnt Weeny Sandwich* (1970),

Weasels Ripped My Flesh (1970), *200 Motels* (1971); "Hungry Freaks, Daddy" (1966), "Who Are the Brain Police?" (1966), "Help, I'm a Rock" (1966); **Frank Zappa**—*Lumpy Gravy* (1967), *Hot Rats* (1969), *Chunga's Revenge* (1970), *Waka Jawaka* (1972), *The Grand Wazoo* (1972), *Apostrophe* (1974), *Sheik Yerbouti* (1979), *Joe's Garage Acts I, II, & III* (1979), *Shut Up 'n Play Yer Guitar* (1981), *London Symphony Orchestra Vols. I & II* (1983, 1987), *The Perfect Stranger* (with Pierre Boulez, 1984), *You Can't Do That on Stage Anymore Vols. I–VI* (live, 1988–92), *The Yellow Shark* (1993).

THE ZOMBIES

Three decades after the Zombies' all-too-brief career, *Rolling Stone's Album Guide* continues to proclaim them "the most musically intriguing of the British Invasion bands."

How did they lose out on what in a just world would have been colossal and long-enduring stardom? Their timing could not have been better. They appeared in 1964 amid a stateside hysteria for the Beatles and anything British. The Zombies had the all-important credentials: They were British, youthful, and musically adept, with a pile of great material and a breathy, choirboy vocalist. Their sound was catchy; haunting and sophisticated, though top-forty simple. They had big hits in the States, quite soon—"She's Not There," "Tell Her No," "Time of the Season"—but their existence as a working group is totaled in months. A scant two albums were issued, and now, hundreds of months later, their legend and hardcore following remain solid.

In 1962 Rodney Argent (keyboards, born June 14, 1945), Paul Atkinson (guitar, born March 19, 1946), and Hugh Grundy (drums, born March 6, 1945) formed a musical trio while attending St. Alban's School in their hometown of Hertfordshire, north of London. Months later, the Sundowners had added Colin Blunstone (vocals, born June 24, 1945) and Paul Arnold, soon to be replaced by Chris White (bass, born March 7, 1943).

The Zombies, as Arnold incongruously labeled them, were not your Stones, Animals, or scruffy R&B fans. The boys were well-healed, bashful, and bright—honor students. From the beginning, music was a shared interest but merely a fleeting dalliance—a hobby, a part-time play—to be shelved for life's real work after graduation. Argent and Atkinson had been accepted at a university. White was ready to attend a teacher's college. Blunstone had started working as an insurance broker; Grundy was a bank employee. The *London Evening News* announced the Hert's Beat Competition, a rock-band contest, and as a last offering, a rite of passage to the world of real work, the Zombies attended.

They won first place. A contract was offered by British Decca, Parrot in the U.S. "She's Not There," cut in one take with no overdubs, was their first recording. The tune was moody, jazzy, with offbeat drumming, a delicate guitar break, and Blunstone's pained-angel voice. "She's Not There" scored top ten, as did the similarly styled "Tell Her No," but only in the U.S. Despite numerous efforts, the Zombies were never to make it big in their homeland, and only after the group had separated did the classic "Time of the Season," cut in the Abbey Road Studios, top the American charts.

Atkinson reminisced to *Goldmine*'s Kathy Kassabaum that it all happened "too easy": "[We never were forced to] pay our dues; we didn't work or starve or sleep in a van . . . we just made a record . . . and by Christmas it was number one."

KEY RECORDINGS: *The Zombies* (1965), *Odyssey and Oracle* (1968); "She's Not There" (1964), "Tell Her No" (1964), "I Love You" (1965), "Is This the Dream" (1966), "Time of the Season" (1968).

PHOTO CREDITS

page 21, Syd Barrett
Courtesy of Blackhill Entertainment and Harvest Records

page 23, Alex Chilton

page 29, Blue Öyster Cult
Courtesy of Bolle Gregmar and the Blue Öyster Cult Fan Club

page 33, Roy Buchanan
Courtesy of Alligator Records

page 37, Jimmy Buffett
Elizabeth Zeschin/Courtesy of Margaritaville Records

page 40, Kate Bush
Anthony Crickmay/Courtesy of Columbia Records

page 45, Buzzcocks
Ron Delany

page 54, The Clash's Joe Strummer
Roberta Bayley

page 57, George Clinton
Scott Morgan/Courtesy of Warner Bros. (Paisley Park)

page 68, Julian Cope
Ed Sirrs © K.A.K. Ltd. 1994 C.E./Courtesy of American Recordings

page 71, Elvis Costello
Roberta Bayley

page 81, Dick Dale
Courtesy of Hightone Records

page 85, Stiv Bators (center) with a revamped Dead Boys lineup
Chuck Pulin/Courtesy of Bomp Records

page 88, Dead Kennedys' Jello Biafra
Alison Braun/Courtesy of Alternative Tentacles Records

page 91, Devo
Courtesy of Rykodisc

page 94, The Dictators
Roberta Bayley

page 100, Dr. John
Joseph A. Rosen/Courtesy of Rhino Records

page 105, Joe Ely
Alan Messer/Courtesy of MCA Nashville

page 108, Brian Eno
Roberta Bayley

page 115, The Fall
Courtesy of Matador Records

page 119, The Flamin' Groovies
Peter Hujar/Courtesy of Buddah Records

page 123, Robert Fripp
Jeff Bender/Courtesy of Virgin Records Ltd.

page 128, The Fugs
Courtesy of Fantasy Records and the Fugs

page 130, Grateful Dead
Ron Delany

page 139, Richard Hell and the Voidoids
Roberta Bayley

page 142, John Hiatt
Courtesy of MCA Records

page 145, Hüsker Dü's Bob Mould
Ron Delany

page 149, Joe Jackson
Ron Delany

page 160, New Order
Donald Christie/Courtesy of Qwest Records (Warner Bros.)

page 163, King Crimson, 1972–73 *Lark's Tongue in Aspic* lineup
Courtesy of Robert Fripp

page 177, Nick Lowe
Ron Delany

page 193, Moby Grape
Jim Marshall/Courtesy of Columbia Records

page 201, The Neville Brothers
Jeffrey Newberry/Courtesy of A&M Records and Bill Graham Management

page 207, NRBQ
Brian Smith/Courtesy of Rhino Records and Forward Publicity

page 215, Pere Ubu's David Thomas
Ron Delany

page 221, Iggy Pop
Ron Delany

page 230, The Ramones
Roberta Bayley

page 235, The Replacements
Greg Helgeson/Courtesy of Sire Records

page 245, Todd Rundgren
Alen MacWeeney/Courtesy of Bearsville Records

page 250, Mitch Ryder
Beverly Parker/Courtesy of Dot Records

page 254, Sam the Sham
Bill and Joy Webb/ Courtesy of MGM Records

page 260, Johnny Rotten
Roberta Bayley

page 271, Morrissey of the Smiths
Ron Delany

page 279, Spirit
Courtesy of Tap/Ko Entertainment Associates

page 291, Talking Heads
Roberta Bayley